CHURCHILL'S BRITAIN

ABOUT THE AUTHOR

Peter Clark is a writer and translator with degrees from Keele and Leicester universities. He worked in the overseas career service of the British Council for thirty-one years and has published many books, including *Dickens's London*. Clark has also published nine books as a translator from Arabic.

CHURCHILL'S BRITAIN

From the Antrim Coast to the Isle of Wight

PETER CLARK

First published in 2020 by
Haus Publishing Ltd
4 Cinnamon Row
London SW11 3TW

This paperback edition published in 2023

Cartography produced by ML Design

Maps contain Ordnance Survey data © Crown copyright and database right 2011

A CIP catalogue for this book is available from the British Library

ISBN 978-1-914982-05-7
eISBN 978-1-909961-75-3

Typeset in Garamond by MacGuru Ltd
Printed in the United Kingdom by Clays Ltd (Elcograf S.p.A.)

www.hauspublishing.com
@HausPublishing

For Stella and John

CONTENTS

INTRODUCTION

Winston Churchill needs no introduction. No British historical figure has been so abundantly documented. The authorised biography comes to eight volumes – over 8,000 pages of text – and sits alongside many more companion volumes of relevant papers. Churchill himself wrote six volumes of memoir/history about each of the two world wars. Many volumes of his journalism and speeches have also been published. It is reckoned that a thousand biographies have been penned. Many of his political and military colleagues, his domestic staff and his family have written about him. Every year a significant work of scholarship appears on some aspect of his life, personality or career.

So why add another volume? All my life, I have been interested in places associated with people and events. Specialists and scholars can analyse documents and old newspapers. Anyone can visit a location and allow their imagination to recreate what it was like in the past. Churchill was a great traveller and had fought wars in three continents before he was twenty-five. He was frequently on the move and left records, sometimes even paintings, of the places he visited. My aim in this book is to consider the places in Britain – including Ireland before its independence in 1921 – that have associations with Churchill. Some are well known, such as Blenheim Palace where he was born and Chartwell which he made his home over his last forty years. The Cabinet Rooms in Whitehall are full of the spirit of Churchill during the years of the Second World War: the only thing missing is the smell of his cigars. I have noted the homes he lived in, his places of study, the offices he occupied and locations where he delivered significant speeches. I have tried to examine the relationship he had with each of the four constituencies he represented in the House of Commons between 1900 and 1964. But there are also many lesser-known locations that tell stories that shed light on Churchill's personality or politics.

The book is in the form of a gazetteer, divided into geographical regions. (I have retained the names of counties as they were in Churchill's time.) Many of the locations are private homes or working institutions and not open to the public. Privacy must be respected.

The book is restricted to Britain. From childhood to old age, however, Churchill was a frequent visitor to France, which he loved. He travelled extensively, in war and in peace, to the United States and Canada. His travels never took him to China and the Far East, to South America or to Australia and New Zealand, but there are many sites abroad – from the North-West Frontier to Cuba, from South Africa to Carthage in Tunisia, from Yalta to Normandy, from Marrakesh to Tehran – that could provide material for other books.

Peter Clark
Frome, Somerset, 2020

1

LONDON

SW 1

"London was like some huge prehistoric animal, capable of enduring terrible injuries, mangled and bleeding from many wounds, and yet preserving its life and movement."[1]

In 1954, Queen Elizabeth II and Prince Philip, Duke of Edinburgh, were returning from a Commonwealth tour on the Royal Yacht *Britannia*. Winston Churchill, in his eightieth year, was prime minister and joined the yacht when it was in British territorial waters and together they sailed to London. The queen saw the Thames as a dirty commercial river, but, as she said, Churchill "was describing it as the silver thread which runs through the history of Britain".[2]

Churchill had more to do with London than with any other city. He went to secondary school on the outskirts of the capital but, from the beginning of the century, he always had a home in London. Over a third of the locations celebrated in this book are found in London, so I have divided the city into two. First we have the postal area of SW1, which covers the City of Westminster – the centre of Britain's political life – and the socially elite area to the north.

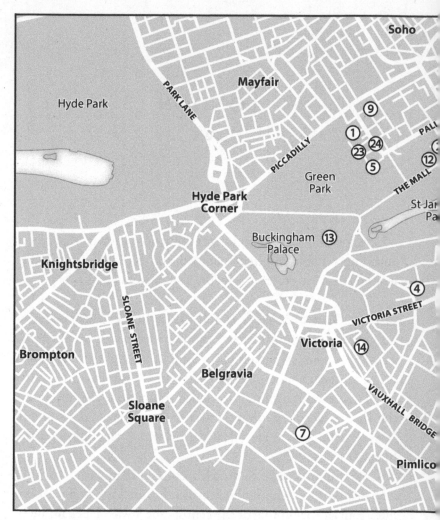

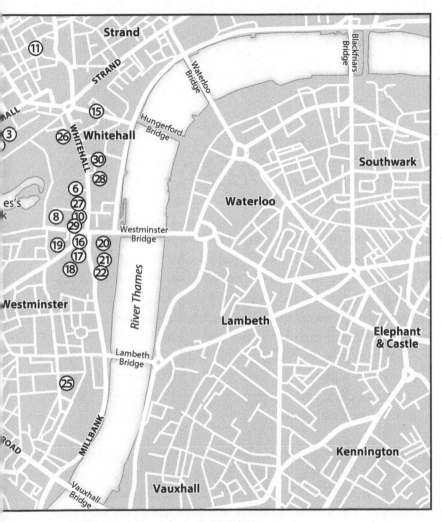

Arlington Street
21 Arlington Street

USEFUL ARISTOCRATIC CONNECTIONS

Arlington Street was part of the early development of the fashionable St James's quarter of London. It was originally built in the late seventeenth century.

Although there is no plaque, the street featured the London home of the third Marquess of Salisbury, prime minister when Winston Churchill first became a Member of Parliament in 1900. Lord Salisbury was an intellectual, a dabbler in amateur chemistry and, in his earlier days, an essayist dealing with political history. He had just about pushed Churchill's father, Lord Randolph, out of the cabinet in 1886, and there was a brittle relationship between the older man and the young Churchill. But Salisbury was generous and took a paternal interest in him. Salisbury's son, Lord Hugh Cecil, became a close friend of his, and was best man at his wedding in 1908. While Churchill was still a Conservative – until 1904, that is – he used to spend time with Lord Hugh Cecil and others who formed an awkward squad known as 'the Hughligans'.

Not far away is Number 21, a house with a forecourt. Formerly known as Wimborne House, it was the principal London home of the family of Viscount Wimborne, Churchill's cousin (Wimborne's mother was a sister of Lord Randolph Churchill). Wimborne's son, Ivor Guest – successively a Conservative and Liberal MP – made Wimborne House available to Churchill and his family after he ceased to be First Lord of the Admiralty in 1915.

Carlton Gardens
4 Carlton Gardens

CHURCHILL AND DE GAULLE

Carlton Gardens and Carlton House Terrace were built in the 1820s, designed by John Nash to replace Carlton House, the residence of the Prince Regent, later King George IV. Both streets became the homes of the 'new rich' – the 'old rich' already had their houses to the northwest, in Mayfair and Belgravia.

Next to the gardens is a statue of General Charles de Gaulle, uniformed and with one hand outstretched. A junior minister when France capitulated in June 1940, de Gaulle slipped out and came to Britain. Here, he became the leader of the Free French, directing a consistent resistance to Nazi-occupied France. This address, as a plaque indicates, was the headquarters of *France Libre*.

Winston Churchill welcomed de Gaulle and gave him resources and moral support. But over the years they had a prickly relationship. Both men saw themselves as personifying the ideals and the history of their countries.

Carlton House Terrace
German Embassy

APPROACHED BY HITLER'S MAN IN LONDON

The German Embassy lies alongside the Waterloo Steps, which descend to the Mall, the long, majestic road leading from Trafalgar Square to Buckingham Palace. In 1937, Winston Churchill was invited to a meeting with the ambassador there, Joachim von Ribbentrop. Ribbentrop was a familiar personality in

London's upper-class social circles, and Churchill had met him several times before. Churchill was received in a large room on an upper floor, and their conversation lasted for over two hours. Ribbentrop argued that Germany sought only friendship with Britain and its empire, but that it must have *Lebensraum* – living space – to the east for its expanding population. Churchill, who was not a government representative at the time, argued that Britain could not give Germany a free hand in Eastern Europe, even though Britain detested Soviet Communism as much as Hitler did.

Ribbentrop later became German foreign minister and negotiated the Nazi–Soviet Pact of 1939 with his Soviet counterpart, Molotov. After the war, he was found guilty at the Nuremberg trials and sentenced to death.

Caxton Street

10 Caxton Street, Caxton Hall

A CELEBRITY BY-ELECTION

Found at the heart of Westminster, the red-brick Caxton Hall has witnessed many important political events. In March 1924, the results of a by-election were declared here: Winston Churchill lost.

Before the reform of the parliamentary electoral system in 1832, the Westminster parliamentary constituency was the most democratic of English constituencies: almost all of its adult male constituents had the vote. What is more, because of its central metropolitan location, it always attracted attention. In 1780, Westminster had 12,000 voters who, after a riotous election, returned Charles James Fox as Member of Parliament. The following century, the philosopher and early advocate of women's rights John Stuart Mill was MP for Westminster.

In 1924, Winston Churchill was edging away from the Liberal Party and towards his first allegiance, the Conservative Party. He stood in the by-election as an independent, anti-socialist Constitutionalist. He had been a Liberal MP (and minister) until 1922, and he had fought and lost an election at Leicester in 1923. He had campaigned ferociously against the 1917 Bolshevik Revolution and saw no great difference between Soviet Communism and the gentle English socialism of the Labour Party which, in January 1924, had formed the first Labour government under Ramsay MacDonald. In this by-election, Churchill was not endorsed by the Conservative Party, who put up their own candidate, but he was supported by individual Conservatives. In effect, he was splitting the right-wing vote. This displeased the 'Conservative machine' and contributed to the deep distrust that many Conservatives had for Churchill over the next twenty years.

The Westminster constituency was called the Abbey division, and it included Westminster Abbey, Victoria station, Pall Mall, Drury Lane and Covent Garden. It was reckoned that, in 1924, over one hundred Members of Parliament lived within the constituency, as well as "dukes, jockeys, prize-fighters, courtiers, actors and businessmen".[3] Among these distinguished constituents was the playwright George Bernard Shaw, who got on well personally with Churchill. Shaw thought Churchill had been right about the disastrous Gallipoli campaign but, as a socialist, he voted for the Independent Labour Party candidate, Fenner Brockway. Another constituent was the former prime minister and leader of the Conservative Party, Arthur Balfour, who issued a letter backing Churchill. But Westminster was not home to wealth alone: there was a working-class element around

Horseferry Road. As well as Otho Nicholson, the official Conservative candidate, a Liberal stood.

The by-election became an entertainment. Churchill had the enthusiastic and resourceful support of a new friend, a twenty-three-year-old red-headed Irishman with a flair for promoting himself and Churchill. His name was Brendan Bracken. He organised a coach and four horses to take his candidate around the constituency. Chorus girls came to address envelopes for circulars for constituents and deliver election addresses.

The glamour did not win against the machine. Nicholson was returned with a majority of forty-three over Churchill. Brockway came a reasonable third, and the Liberal at the bottom of the poll. At the count, Brockway recalled, the first indications were that Churchill had won. But when his defeat was confirmed, his spirits slumped. His hopes of returning to the House of Commons were dashed. He shared his disappointment with the Labour candidate: "You know, Brockway, you and I have no chance. We represent ideas – Nicholson represents the machine".[4]

Later that year, Churchill managed to get a constituency and the backing of the Conservative Party: Epping, a constituency he held for the rest of his parliamentary life.

Cleveland Row

Stornoway House

MAX BEAVERBROOK, HIS OLDEST FRIEND

Tucked away to the west of St James's Street is an eighteenth-century mansion, Stornoway House. On one side, it overlooks Green Park, giving it an almost rural air; on the other, it overlooks St James's Palace. The house was built in the 1790s for the first Lord Grenville, a future prime minister. Today, it accommodates the offices of a financial house.

From the early 1920s, Stornoway House was the London home of Lord Beaverbrook, a friend of Winston Churchill from before the First World War until the 1960s, and Churchill was an occasional guest here before the Second World War. Beaverbrook and Churchill were both allies of King Edward VIII at the time of his abdication, and Churchill dined here on 2 December 1936, during the abdication crisis, to discuss the king's situation.

The political and personal lives of Churchill and Beaverbrook interacted over the decades. Beaverbrook, born Max Aitken in 1879, was a Canadian, the son of a Scottish Presbyterian minister. He came to London before he was thirty years old, by which time he was already a multi-millionaire, riding on the crest of Canadian development and his native country's early-twentieth-century prosperity. He made his money in steel and cement, in the development of the West Indies, and in finance. After he arrived in London, Aitken had an extraordinary career. He became an ally of the Unionist (Conservative) Member of Parliament Andrew Bonar Law – also born in Canada – who became the leader of the Conservative Party in 1911. Promotion and honours were showered on him: Aitken effortlessly became the Conservative MP for Ashton-under-Lyne in Lancashire, was knighted, made a baronet and then became a peer, taking his name from a stream in New Brunswick – Beaver Brook. He became at the centre of British public affairs, an ally of senior politicians and instrumental in the accession of prime ministers Lloyd George in 1916 and Bonar Law in 1922. Lloyd George made Beaverbrook minister of information in 1917, and so he became a privy counsellor before he was even forty years old. At the end of the First World War, he bought the *Daily Express* newspaper, and it is as a newspaper proprietor – though he preferred to see himself as "principal share-holder" – that he is best known. He founded the *Sunday Express* and was a regular contributor to his own newspapers; indeed, he described himself on his passport as a journalist.

Beaverbrook and Churchill held each other in mutual regard. Churchill's closest friends were mavericks and, like Beaverbrook, not from the same upper-class background – Brendan Bracken and Professor Lindemann were similar outsiders. Beaverbrook and Churchill both had a sense of fun, even mischief. Both enjoyed their alcohol, and both had strong interests outside politics. Both had close friendships across the political spectrum. Both were serious historians. Beaverbrook always had access to Churchill. As Franklin D. Roosevelt's confidant, Harry Hopkins, said, Beaverbrook was a man "who saw Churchill after midnight".[5] Clementine Churchill was, however, no fan of Beaverbrook, whom she referred to as "Bottle Imp".

They did not always see eye to eye. Beaverbrook was critical of Churchill's desire to snuff out the Bolshevik Revolution after 1917 and of his role as chancellor of the exchequer between 1924 and 1929; nor did he join in Churchill's campaign for rearmament in the 1930s. But with the outbreak of the Second World War, the old friendship bloomed. Churchill wanted Neville Chamberlain to make Beaverbrook minister of food and, when Churchill became prime minister on 10 May 1940, he looked to Beaverbrook for comfort and support. They lunched together – just the two of them – on 11 May and again the next day. And, on the evening he finally moved from Admiralty House to 10 Downing Street in June 1940, he even spent the night at Stornoway House. He brought Beaverbrook in as minister of aircraft production. But Churchill also seemed to depend on Beaverbrook for emotional support. When he made his fourth visit to

France in the five weeks after he became prime minister – a visit that saw the collapse of morale of the French leaders – he took Beaverbrook with him.

Beaverbrook was an unorthodox minister in 1940. Stornoway House became the first offices of the Ministry of Aircraft Production, and Beaverbrook recruited businessmen and staff from his newspapers, who were unpaid. Beaverbrook's drive and dynamism built up the country's arsenal of shells and guns as well as fighter aircraft, which were a key factor in the Battle of Britain later in 1940. At this time, the two men were very close. One evening during the Blitz in 1940, Churchill and Beaverbrook gazed out of Stornoway House's large windows overlooking Green Park. They watched flashes of guns and the glare of an exploding bomb. Even Churchill thought they were taking needless risks, and they moved across central London to the ICI building on the South Bank, from which there was also a good view.

In time, the ministry moved to more conventional quarters, before Stornoway House suffered bomb damage in 1941. Beaverbrook was minister for twenty-one months, but he was regularly consulted by Churchill during the rest of the war. He was sent as a personal envoy to see President Franklin D. Roosevelt and to Moscow to break the ice and initiate talks with Stalin. Beaverbrook was loyal to Churchill, even though the former argued strongly against Churchill in favour of a 'Second Front' to distract German forces from their concentration on Soviet Russia.

Beaverbrook tried to remain detached from party politics. He supported many journalists in their careers, regardless of their politics, and was very close to left-wing politicians such as Michael Foot (whom Beaverbrook appointed as editor of the *Evening Standard* at the age of twenty-nine). More conventional

Conservatives were wary of Beaverbrook, who was a reluctant adviser of the party during the General Election of 1945.

In their later years, both Churchill and Beaverbrook were absorbed in their own writing of twentieth-century history: Churchill with his war memoirs and Beaverbrook with a series of volumes – he called them "chronicles" – of the years between 1914 and 1924. As Churchill became frailer in his last decade, Beaverbrook did what he could. His villa in the south of France was made available to him, and he would call on Churchill in the last months of his friend's life – though Churchill hardly knew who he was.

Beaverbrook's body also became frailer, but his mind was as sharp as ever. Though four and a half years younger, Beaverbrook died in June 1964, seven months before Churchill.

In his final year, he gave an interview and spoke of Churchill as "a man without rancour".[6] Churchill, he said, could get emotional and be strongly critical of someone, but he then had the habit of touching you, "of putting his hand on your hand – like that – as if to say that his real feelings for you were not changed".[7]

Downing Street
10 Downing Street

THE BEATING HEART OF BRITISH POLITICAL POWER

Since the 1980s, access to Downing Street has become restricted. There is a heavy police presence, and one has only a distant view of buildings 10 and 11. Number 10 of this rather ordinary terrace has been the official residence of the prime minister since the time of Sir Robert Walpole in 1735. It was Churchill's official home between May 1940 and July 1945, and again between

October 1951 and April 1955. During the war years, although he used Number 10 as an office, he had a flat at "the Annexe" in Storey's Gate, two hundred yards away, and he used the Cabinet War Rooms close by as his operational headquarters.

At the beginning of 1938, the then prime minister Neville Chamberlain hosted a farewell luncheon for Joachim von Ribbentrop, the outgoing German ambassador. Clementine and Winston Churchill were among about fourteen guests. During the meal, a foreign office messenger brought a letter for the prime minister announcing that Hitler had invaded Austria and that German troops were heading for Vienna. The prime minister and Mrs Chamberlain were restless, anxious for the guests to go; Ribbentrop seemed totally unconcerned, even unaware. Churchill was conscious that something was up. He turned to Frau von Ribbentrop.

"I hope England and Germany will preserve their friendship," he said.

"Be careful you don't spoil it," she answered.[8]

Churchill never saw Ribbentrop again. He was hanged at Nuremberg after the war.

On Thursday 9 May 1940, the prime minister Neville Chamberlain summoned Churchill, then First Lord of the Admiralty, to 10 Downing Street. The previous day, there had been a debate in the House of Commons on the disastrous campaign to prevent a German takeover of Norway. The government had won a vote, but some Conservatives had voted against the government or abstained. It had been a moral defeat for Chamberlain. His time was up. Chamberlain was ready to consider a coalition government with the Labour Party.

Churchill arrived to find the Lord Privy Seal, Sir Kingsley Wood, and the foreign secretary, Lord Halifax, with Chamberlain. They were joined by Clement Attlee, the leader of the opposition and leader of the Labour Party, and Arthur Greenwood, his deputy. Chamberlain said there was a need for a national government to include the Labour Party. Attlee was non-committal; the Labour Party was at that moment in conference at Bournemouth and must be consulted. The meeting was adjourned.

The following day, Wood came to see Churchill at the Admiralty and brought a further summons from Chamberlain to come to a meeting. Wood, Halifax and the Conservative chief whip, David Margesson, were present. The Labour Party had agreed to a national government – but not under Neville Chamberlain. Chamberlain himself recognised that he had to step down. Whom should he advise King George VI to invite to form a government in his place? There was a long silence. Even Churchill, normally verbose, kept mum. Halifax, whom Chamberlain preferred, said his membership of the House of Lords would debar him from being an effective prime minister. Churchill was the only choice. Chamberlain resigned, and Churchill was called to Buckingham Palace later that day and agreed to form the new government.

After being appointed prime minister in May 1940, Churchill was slow to move into Number 10 and instead continued to use Admiralty House, his official residence as First Lord of the Admiralty. He loved this building; it was grander than 10 Downing Street. He finally moved in on 14 June 1940, but he used it as his regular base for just three months. In September he was advised, for security reasons, to move to what became known as "the

Annexe", a specially prepared flat above the Cabinet War Rooms in nearby Horse Guards Road. 10 Downing Street was used as a place of work during the day.

King George VI visited 10 Downing Street regularly during the Second World War, fourteen times in all. On two occasions he was there during an air raid; Churchill had to escort him to the air-raid shelter.

Churchill was present at Downing Street during one raid in February 1944 when a bomb fell yards away on Horse Guards Parade, breaking windows in Downing Street. Churchill, whose physical courage might well be seen as recklessness, would make only a gesture of self-protection by donning a heavy overcoat and wearing a tin hat.

On 14 October 1940, Churchill was dining in the garden room with three colleagues when there was an air raid. He had an instinct to tell the kitchen staff, who were preparing the meal, to go down to the underground shelter. They all did so, and minutes later a bomb fell on the Treasury building 200 yards away. The blast shattered the Number 10 kitchen's large plate-glass window, creating havoc in the room. Had they not withdrawn, the staff would have been killed or seriously injured. The underground Treasury shelter suffered a direct hit, killing three civil servants working late.

A permanent resident at Number 10 during the first part of the war was a black cat called Nelson. Like all cats, he was terrified of the air raids. Churchill, a great cat lover, chided him for not living up to his name. "Try to remember," he said to the cat, "what those boys in the RAF are doing."[9] In consideration for Nelson's nerves, the cat was taken forty miles away to Chequers, the Prime Minister's country residence in Buckinghamshire.

One of Number 10's visitors in January 1941 was President Roose-velt's special representative, Harry Hopkins. Physically frail but determined, Hopkins was an intimate of Roosevelt. He arrived at 10 Downing Street after an air raid that had broken the windows. He and Churchill immediately hit it off. Churchill had a strong faith in the virtues of the English-speaking peoples. His four-volume history, which uses those words in the title, was a joint history of the two countries of his parents. Churchill was des-perate for United States involvement in the war, but Roosevelt had just won his third election as president and was extremely cautious about becoming embroiled in a European conflict. He and Churchill corresponded regularly, and Roosevelt expressed great sympathy for the cause; in late 1940 and 1941, he even pro-vided material support. During 1941, Britain and the United States shared an interest in protecting Atlantic traffic – but Japan's bombing of Pearl Harbor at the end of the year spurred the United States to join the Allies officially the following day. Hitler also declared war on the United States and, to Churchill's relief, the United States became a full belligerent.

The alliance was close at many levels. Hopkins was followed by another envoy from the president, Averell Harriman, who later married Pamela Digby after her divorce from Churchill's son, Randolph.

In the spring of 1942, Number 10 hosted the Soviet foreign minister, Vyacheslav Molotov, who was breaking his journey from the United States to Moscow. Churchill described this old Bolshevik as being "of outstanding ability and cold-blooded ruthlessness".[10] There was a rare moment of intimacy between the statesmen when Churchill grabbed Molotov's arm and they looked each other in the eye. "Silently we wrung each other's hands."[11] Human feelings and a shared sense of danger seemed to erase all Churchill's earlier rhetoric against the Soviet Union.

On 8 May 1945, after announcing to the nation from here at 3 p.m. that the war was over, Churchill got in his car to go to the House of Commons. He was pushed by cheering crowds all the way.

Churchill's methods of work could be somewhat disconcerting for a visitor. In May 1945, after the dissolution of the Grand Coalition, he set out to reconstruct the Conservative caretaker government. The Conservative chief whip, James Stuart, was summoned to discuss the formation of the new government. Churchill – who did most of his business from his bed – ate off a tray, and the chief whip was invited to eat from a table nearby. They made the appointments by telephone and Churchill observed, "Well, that's it and all done by telephone from my bed. Think of poor old Mr Gladstone with all those letters he had to write."[12]

Two months later, the Conservatives lost the general election. On 27 July, a final cabinet meeting was held: "a grim affair", the foreign secretary, Anthony Eden, noted.[13] In his final remarks to the cabinet, Churchill indulged – uncharacteristically – in some self-pity: "Thirty years of my life have been passed in this room," he said. "I shall never sit in it again. You will, but I shall not."[14] He was wrong; he was back six years later.

A notable feature of his second premiership, Churchill's relationship with trade unionists was curious. In September 1953, one of Churchill's visitors at Number 10 was Tom O'Brien, Labour MP, president of the Trades Union Congress and general secretary of the National Association of Theatrical and Kine Employees; they got on famously. O'Brien's war service would likely have impressed Churchill. In the First World War, he had lied about his age in order to enlist and had served in the Dardanelles (as had Clement Attlee). "He is a sensible man," wrote Churchill to his wife. "I gave him a good dose of Tory Democracy – quite as good a brand as your Liberalism."[15] By then, the Conservative Party needed Churchill more than he needed them and, in his last decades, was somewhat detached from the party, referring to it as 'them' rather than 'us'. At the end of his life, he seemed sometimes to be nostalgic about his earlier radical phases. He saw his own Liberal spell as a manifestation of 'Tory Democracy' – a fairly woolly concept that suggested a union of the upper classes and the working class, with a programme to improve the conditions of the latter.

Churchill's last days in Downing Street were sad and painful. He announced to Queen Elizabeth II and to close colleagues that he would resign on 5 April 1955. On 1 April, he threw a party here for Clementine Churchill's seventieth birthday. Among the guests were the leader of the opposition, Clement Attlee, and his wife. Lady Churchill, to the surprise of Churchill's doctor, gave Mrs Attlee a kiss as they left.

Three days later, the Churchills hosted a farewell dinner at Number 10. The principal guest was Queen Elizabeth II, who was accompanied by Prince Philip. As well as political and former military colleagues, other guests included the Attlees and Herbert Morrison from the Labour Party. (Churchill's other great Labour colleague of the war years, Ernest Bevin, had died in 1951.) Neville Chamberlain's widow, Anne, was also graciously invited.

Among those in Downing Street to see the queen off was Martin Gilbert, who was between school and national service at the time. He was later to become Churchill's main biographer and the author of dozens of volumes on aspects of his life.

The following morning, Churchill chaired his last cabinet meeting and signed off final papers. At noon, he got into a waiting car. He gave an unsmiling V-sign to the small crowd that had gathered in Downing Street. To one boy in the crowd (me) who joined in a half-hearted cheer, the V for Victory sign seemed inappropriate. The old man was driven off to Buckingham Palace to hand in his formal and final resignation.

11 Downing Street

HOME OF THE PERSON WHO HOLDS THE NATIONAL
PURSESTRINGS

Since 1828, 11 Downing Street has been the official residence of the chancellor of the exchequer. The chancellorship has since become the second most important political office, and the relationship between the chancellor and the prime minister – living next door at Number 10 – has been key to the stability and success of any government. Unlike the prime minister, who lives 'over the shop', the chancellor's office is at the Treasury, two hundred yards away on the corner of Whitehall and Parliament Square. There are interconnecting doors between Number 10 and Number 11.

Number 11 was the home of Winston Churchill from November 1924, when Stanley Baldwin appointed him as chancellor, until June 1929. The two years before his appointment had, for Churchill, been a period of complete political and personal turmoil. In 1922 and 1923, he had stood for election unsuccessfully as a Liberal candidate. He had been horrified at the Bolshevik Revolution in Russia and, in his mind, conflated Communism and Socialism. He was appalled at the arrival of a Labour government – though this did not prevent him sending a letter of congratulation to Ramsay MacDonald on his appointment in January 1924 as the first Labour prime minister. During 1924, he stood at a by-election but not on a party ticket – seeking, unsuccessfully, support from Conservatives. Later that year, Churchill was adopted as candidate for Epping with the support of the local Conservative Party and won at the general election of autumn 1924. He was delighted – and surprised – to be invited to be chancellor of the exchequer, for at the time of his appointment he was not even a member of the Conservative Party. The Conservative prime minister, Stanley Baldwin, saw himself as capturing and taming a big Liberal beast. He was happy to see his chancellor implementing policies that were a continuation of the great Liberal reforms of the 1908–1911 years. Churchill's move helped to make the Liberal Party, already split between the followers of Lloyd George and of Asquith, superfluous and even irrelevant. Two other factors may have influenced Baldwin. He is reported as having said that he wanted to form a government of which his – and Churchill's – old school, Harrow, would be proud. And he may have appointed him on the Lyndon Johnson principle that it was better to have him inside the tent pissing out, than outside the tent pissing in. Churchill accepted the invitation, hardly believing his luck at bouncing back to the top rank of politics. Initially, he had to face resentment from many Conservatives who had been the butt of his eloquent hostility for the previous twenty years. But, in contrast to the years when he was in the cabinets of Asquith and Lloyd George, he turned out to be a loyal and fairly good team player.

Although Churchill had made his name in military matters and foreign affairs, he had wanted to be chancellor of the exchequer in early 1921 when the post became vacant – but he was in Cairo at the time reshaping the Middle East. It was the post that his father had, briefly, held. The chancellor robes worn by Lord Randolph Churchill had been kept and the son was sentimentally happy to get them out and wear them on formal occasions.

Churchill's main contribution to domestic politics so far had been as a social reformer in Asquith's government. As chancellor, he was keen to enact continuity in his political life and, in his first budget, he brought down the age when people were to receive old age pensions from seventy to sixty-five. (Some in the Labour Party had pointed out that most working-class people never reached the age of seventy.) He also brought in widows' pensions. More controversially, Churchill restored the country to the gold standard. This move affected exports – most notably raising the price of exported coal, which reduced the profits of coal mine owners, who then imposed pay cuts on their workers. This led, in part, to a prolonged miners' strike in 1926 and a briefer general strike in May of that year.

The position Churchill took in the general strike was nuanced. He was critical of the mine owners but, when the general strike started, his bellicose instincts got the better of him. Many newspapers were affected by the strike so, for the duration, the government produced its own – the *British Gazette* – which was edited by Churchill. It was fiercely partisan against the strikers. The paper was produced on the printing machines of the Conservative newspaper, the *Morning Post,* in Fleet Street.

Churchill's budget speeches were entertaining, good-humoured events. Budget Day would start with a beaming Winston Churchill walking with his wife, some of his children and his parliamentary private secretary, Robert Boothby, from 11 Downing Street along Whitehall to the Houses of Parliament. They looked as if they were all setting out for a family picnic, as they smiled to the cameras of press photographers and were followed by well-wishers.

His relationship with Stanley Baldwin during these years was good. Churchill would often pop through the interconnecting door into Number 10 on his way to the Treasury building.

The prime minister enjoyed his holidays and leisure and did not interfere; Churchill, on the other hand, was no great respecter of departmental boundaries. He lectured his colleagues on how to run their departments and had an extended disagreement with the minister of health, Neville Chamberlain, about local government rating. Churchill wanted to reduce rates to promote local enterprise; Chamberlain saw the reduction as a threat to the finances of local government for which his ministry was responsible. Churchill appreciated that Baldwin had recharged his career and helped to redefine his politics. He was loyal to the prime minister and, in some ways, the years at the Treasury were among the most relaxed and happiest of his political life. He still had time to paint, to develop an interest in bricklaying, to write two (of six) volumes of *The World Crisis* and to start writing *My Early Life*.

Eccleston Square

33 Eccleston Square

HOME OF THE NEWLY WEDS

Eccleston Square was designed by the architect William Cubitt and built in 1835. Grand, uniformly white classical houses faced gardens in the middle of the square. Number 33 was the home of the newly married Clementine and Winston Churchill between 1909 and 1913, when Churchill was successively president of the Board of Trade, home secretary and First Lord of the Admiralty. Churchill initially took the house on an eighteen-year lease, paying a rent of £195 a year. A plaque commemorates their years of residence here.

Number 33 was on the fashionable side of the square, which had been created to provide London homes for the upper classes. The land was owned by the Duke of Westminster, and the square itself was named after a village in the duke's Cheshire estates. But it was only just fashionable. "For heaven's sake, my dear," said a character in *The Small House at Allington*, the 1864 novel by Anthony Trollope, "don't let him take you anywhere beyond Eccleston Square."

It was twenty minutes' walk from the House of Commons and not far from Belgravia and the cut and thrust of political London. Set over five floors, 33 Eccleston Square was a good place to entertain and to bring up children. The Churchills' two elder children, Diana and Randolph, were both born here. In 1911, Churchill became First Lord of the Admiralty. The job came with a fine residence, and the Eccleston Square house was rented out to the foreign secretary, Sir Edward Grey.

When Churchill finally sold the lease of the house in 1918, the buyer was the Labour Party, to which Churchill also sold the carpets for £50.

Horse Guards Road
Cabinet War Rooms

WHERE THE WAR WAS PLANNED

No place reveals the atmosphere of London during the Second World War and Churchill's place at the helm in such a comprehensive way as the Cabinet War Rooms. Today they are an excellent museum, managed by the Imperial War Museum and visited by 400,000 people a year. Visitors are able to see an audio-visual display of Churchill's life, and also wander past the rooms that played such an essential part during the war.

After he became prime minister, Churchill continued to work at his official residence at 10 Downing Street. But in July, August and September 1940, London became the target of German bombing. Churchill was seemingly reckless about his personal safety, but he was persuaded that Number 10 was a target and that there should be an alternative base for the prime minister and his principal advisers.

The issue had been anticipated before the war. The idea of a secure base went back to 1938, when the site was selected. Should the government base, in the event of war, be in the suburbs of London? Or should it be away from the Home Counties altogether, say in the west of England? Seven million people had no choice but to live in the capital. It was not thought good for morale if the country's leaders were to abandon the city. The chosen location – the so-called 'New Government Buildings' – had been erected earlier in the twentieth century between King Charles Street and Great George Street, and the basement of these buildings would become the government headquarters during the war. The lofty building, it was argued, would protect the lower floors. Extensive work was carried out. The man in charge of the arrangements was General Hastings Ismay, secretary of the Imperial General Staff. There were offices for work and rooms for residence; partitions, telephone lines and broadcasting facilities were installed. Extra security measures included safeguards against gas attacks and flooding. Employees would be able to stay overnight, if necessary; there were bedrooms for the senior staff and dormitories for the rest, equipped with kitchens and bathrooms. All this was completed in the months immediately before war broke out. In the autumn of 1940, during the period of prolonged and repeated air raids – the Blitz – the rooms were reinforced by the insertion of a slab of concrete above the ceiling and empty spaces were filled with cement.

The first months of the war seemed to be tranquil. They were called 'the Phoney War'; in April 1940, the prime minister Neville Chamberlain even declared, infelicitously, that Hitler had "missed the bus". But events moved rapidly in the next few months. Chamberlain was replaced by Churchill in May, France fell to the Nazis in June, the bombing of London started in July, the Battle of Britain – in which the British Royal Air Force outgunned the German Luftwaffe – took place in July to September. Throughout that summer there was fear of invasion.

The War Cabinet first used to meet at 10 Downing Street, but from July 1940 they met in these rooms. Churchill was punctilious in keeping the cabinet informed of his decisions and referring matters to them. He was conscientious in observing constitutional proprieties but, as he wrote in his war memoirs, "All I wanted was compliance with my wishes after reasonable discussion".[16]

Churchill's main working base was the Map Room. Controlled by Captain Pim, a large map of the world was kept up to date with the movement of ships, aircraft and armies. For all strategic decisions, Churchill was reliant on his maps, and a mobile 'map room' went with him wherever he travelled, even to the White House.

In his work, Churchill was dynamic, overbearing and inspirational. He had an extraordinary capacity for absorbing information, thinking intensively and drawing conclusions for courses of action. He combined a clear idea of the overall global strategy with details as it might affect individuals. His working pattern was idiosyncratic: waking at seven or so, he spent an hour flipping through all the newspapers, including the Communist *Daily Worker*. He soaked himself in a bath, then dressed and came from his living quarters to the Map Room. He would be followed by a small army of secretaries (men) and typists (women). He believed everything should be documented and, although he used the telephone, he preferred instructions to be written down. After lunch – which would be a working lunch – he would go to bed and sleep for an hour or so. Sleep, he said, "was the healer of all".[17] He reckoned that by breaking up the day in this way he could turn one day into two. He might have another bath when he woke up and would then work through the evening, broken by dinner, and on into the early hours of the morning – two, three or sometimes four o'clock. His staff had to adapt to this pattern. A corps of secretaries and typists would work in relays round the clock. His personality and cigar smoke were pervasive. In the critical days after the fall of France in June 1940, he was so sarcastic and bullying towards those working with him that Clementine Churchill was moved to tell him to be kinder to his staff. No one else was able to restrain him. Those who stayed the course – surviving long hours, moods and tantrums – were utterly devoted to him, and he reciprocated that loyalty.

Churchill imposed his personal quirks on everyone. He devised a sticker reading "Action This Day" to be attached to written instructions, which often started politely, "Pray..."[18] He demanded the summary of an issue to be submitted to him on one side of a sheet of paper: a constraint, however, that he was unable to apply to his own documentation. He hated the noise of typewriters and special silent machines were designed and installed. He could not stand people whistling and disliked noises such as hammering. He also did not like paperclips and staplers, preferring documents to be held together with tags.

In the War Rooms, his principal lines of communication with the military and civil sides of the government machine were through General Hastings Ismay and Sir Edward Bridges, respectively. Ismay, known as 'Pug', was a calming influence, able to cope with Churchill's working methods and personality and to reassure staff who might have been upset at a Churchill outburst. Bridges was similarly calm, genial and discreet, the son of former poet laureate Robert Bridges and the head of the civil service. An Old Etonian, he had won the Military Cross in the First World War and was a fellow of All Souls College, Oxford. The other key figures were the professional heads of the services: the army, navy and air force. The political heads of the services were politicians from each of the three political parties in the coalition. Anthony Eden, former and future foreign secretary, was the Conservative secretary of state for war and responsible for the army; A. V. Alexander was a Labour man and replaced Churchill when he became prime minister as First Lord of the Admiralty; and Archie Sinclair, a Liberal and old personal friend of Churchill – they had served together in France in the First World War – was air minister. Churchill was prime minister and minister of defence, though at that time there was no ministry of defence building.

We see Ismay's bedroom. Like much of the War Rooms, it is spartan – it holds only a desk, lamp and a single bed – but its decorative carpet is a sign of status (Churchill's bedroom was the only one to be completely carpeted). Though a general, he had had limited combat experience himself. He was originally in the Indian Army and had seen some military action on the North-West Frontier. In the First World War, he was in charge of a camel corps in British Somaliland, but his main experience was as a military administrator in the War Office and in the Committee for Imperial Defence. He was with Churchill throughout the war, and was always close to him. Though he was not a politician, in 1951 he was brought into Churchill's government as secretary of state for commonwealth relations and served reluctantly for a year before being appointed to the post of secretary general of the North Atlantic Treaty Organisation (NATO). In spite of physical frailty, he was a pallbearer at Churchill's funeral in 1965 and later that year, after Clementine Churchill was made Baroness Spencer-Churchill of Chartwell, Ismay was one of her two sponsors when she took her seat in the House of Lords. He died in December 1965.

Below these senior figures were other regulars in the War Rooms. Brendan Bracken, quixotic Irishman, had been devoted to Churchill from the early 1920s. He understood the prime minister's demands and could make him smile. He was able to say things bluntly to Churchill that no one else dared to. He was minister of information during the war and had his own room here. Another with privileged access was 'the Prof', Professor Lindemann, who had the capacity of explaining in simple and comprehensible English complex scientific and technological issues, from weaponry to radar to nuclear physics. He had a formal post as head of the statistical office.

And there was a small army of younger people, service officers and women who were ready to type at speed and interpret Churchill's English. All had their assigned roles and work stations.

In December 1940, Churchill, his family and his private staff moved into the building above the War Rooms. This was regarded as safer than 10 Downing Street. Clementine Churchill brought some personal items to give a homely feel to the quarters.

Today, the Cabinet Room has been reconstructed as if ready for a meeting: places prepared, ashtrays provided and a map of the world behind Churchill's chair. Below this was another floor, with a low ceiling and uncomfortably low doors. This area was turned into two dormitories, one for men and one for women. When London was being targeted by bombs – 1940, 1941 and towards the end of the war, 1944–1945 – staff were able to stay overnight. It was not comfortable. The air-supply system did not reduce the heat and humidity, and the place would have been thick with cigarette smoke. Recesses with chemical toilets were provided.

Off one corridor there appears to be a toilet. The appearance is misleading. It was not a toilet for the exclusive use of the prime minister, but rather a telephone booth where Churchill could conduct confidential conversations with the US president, Franklin D. Roosevelt. Another small room has a basic kitchen where meals were prepared.

Churchill's own bedroom is on display. This was rarely used – he preferred the flat in the Annexe above – though he stayed here a few nights when the city was a target. He also had the habit, when there was an air raid, of going up to the roof and watching what he called "the fireworks".[19] His bodyguards were worried by the recklessness of Churchill's instinct and sometimes had to manhandle him away from exposed and vulnerable points.

On 14 October 1940, Winston Churchill had been dining at 10 Downing Street when bombs struck the Treasury building. The raid continued through the night and with one of his guests, Archie Sinclair, Churchill came to the New Buildings roof, from where they had an extensive view of the city. Most of Pall Mall was ablaze. Five fires were burning in Piccadilly and St James's Street. They stayed watching until the raid died down and they heard the 'all clear' signal.

Five months later, Churchill took other guests – including President Roosevelt's envoy, Averell Harriman – up to the roof to see a heavy air raid. It involved a climb up a ladder and through a manhole on to the roof. Churchill quoted lines of Tennyson's *Locksley Hall* to his guests, prophesying aerial bombing:

> *Heard the heavens fill with shouting,*
>   *and there rain'd a ghastly dew*
> *From the nations' airy navies*
>   *grappling in the central blue.*

It was in the Annexe that Churchill heard the result of the 1945 general election.

The election had been held on 5 July, but the results were not announced until three weeks later: there were hundreds of thousands of soldiers still serving overseas and their votes had to be collected and counted. Churchill was shocked to learn that he was being ousted from the job he had gloriously filled for five years.

When victory over Germany was secured in May, the Labour Party and Liberal Party withdrew from the Coalition, and

Churchill became the leader of an exclusively Conservative government.

After the casting of votes, Churchill had gone to Potsdam in Germany for a summit conference with Stalin (which Churchill pronounced "Starleen") and the new US president, Harry S. Truman, who had succeeded Roosevelt after the latter's death in April. Churchill had, chivalrously, taken the leader of the opposition, Clement Attlee, with him to emphasise the national character of the British delegation and as his possible successor if – as he thought unlikely – Labour were to win the general election. He and Attlee arranged to leave for two days to be in Britain for the results.

The night before the announcement, Churchill had had a strange dream. Just before dawn, he recorded in his war memoirs, "I woke suddenly with a sharp stab of almost physical pain. A hitherto subconscious conviction that we were beaten broke forth and dominated my mind."[20]

The first results came through at ten in the morning of Thursday 26 July. Churchill was in the bath at the time, and Captain Pim, who had set up an electoral map of the constituencies in the Map Room, came to see him. Pim gave him a towel and a few minutes later Churchill donned his blue siren suit, lit a cigar and went to his chair in the Map Room, where he stayed for the rest of the day. His daughter, Mary, and his brother, Jack, were with him as the results poured in. Labour victory after Labour victory. Lord Beaverbrook and Brendan Bracken joined the sad group.

The number of Conservative MPs fell from nearly 600 to 213. Churchill had been confidently expecting a win with a majority of thirty, fifty or a hundred seats. Instead there was a Labour majority of 146 over all other parties. Churchill's son, Randolph, and son-in-law, Duncan Sandys, both lost their seats.

Churchill himself won in Epping comfortably. Both the Labour Party and the Liberal Party had decided not to put up a candidate, and he faced only an independent, who nonetheless polled over 10,000 votes.

"We lunched in Stygian gloom," said Mary later.[21] Clementine Churchill tried to cheer up her husband.

"It may well be a blessing in disguise," she said.

"At the moment," said Churchill, "it seems quite effectively disguised."[22]

In the evening, he had dinner in the Annexe with his family and a few close friends, including Anthony Eden. "Dinner was a somewhat muted affair," recalled Mary, with everyone trying to say the right thing.[23]

Churchill was emotionally resilient, acknowledged reality and accepted his fate. He submitted his resignation to the king at Buckingham Palace and did not return to Potsdam – that was left to Clement Attlee and the new Labour foreign secretary, Ernest Bevin. He dealt with the immediate aftermath and then took a painting holiday in Italy.

Many people at the time – and since – were surprised at this reversal of fortunes. Churchill had dominated British public life for five years, but the affection and respect in which he was held was personal; it did not extend to the Conservative Party. Three of the leading figures in the new government, Attlee, Bevin and Herbert Morrison, had been prominent in the Coalition government, which had introduced successful, necessary and beneficial measures – such as rationing and the state control of utilities – that fitted in more with Labour than with Conservative values. Collectivism, not competitive capitalism, was in the air. Churchill had been detached from the Conservative ministers of the depression and the 1930s. He himself had virulently criticised Stanley Baldwin and Chamberlain. His role as leader during the war seemed a vindication of his rejection of pre-war Conservatism.

Jermyn Street

71–72 Jermyn Street

WHERE THE SIREN SUITS WERE MADE

The shop Turnbull & Asser, a bespoke shirtmaker, has provided shirts and ties to those who could afford them for a hundred years and more. Winston Churchill ordered his shirts from this shop, and it has not changed much since – many of its original features have been kept. Situated on a premium corner location, the shop's large window displays are framed in dark wood, an aesthetic that continues inside.

Churchill also had his iconic 'siren suit' made here. This was a practical, comfortable but informal overall, rather like a boiler suit. He wore it when working and not on public duty. Churchill even designed some for himself, and he gave King George VI a siren suit as a Christmas present in 1940. In the basement of the shop, in what is called the Churchill Room, an original green velvet siren suit is on display in a glass cabinet. The shop used to provide him with what one of the staff described as a "smart boiler suit", in either velvet or wool. It was once possible to purchase your own siren suit here, but no longer.

Facing the shop, at 16 Bury Street, is the fashionable Quaglino's restaurant. Churchill came here in November 1961, four weeks before his eighty-seventh birthday, to attend the coming-out dance of his granddaughter, Celia Sandys.

King Charles Street

Winston Churchill, normally tolerant and even good-natured, disliked hearing people whistle – an aversion he shared, oddly enough, with Adolf Hitler.

During the Second World War, accompanied by his bodyguard who told the story, Churchill was walking from the Cabinet War Rooms to Downing Street along King Charles Street, a short street off Whitehall. Coming towards him was a young teenager, hands in his pockets, whistling loudly. As he came up to them, Churchill said sharply, "Stop that whistling."

"Why should I?" the lad said, coolly.

"Because I don't like it and it's a horrible noise."

"Well, you can shut your ears, can't you?"[24]

Churchill was taken aback by this insolence and for a few seconds was furious. He then began to smile and muttered the boy's words and chuckled to himself.

Leicester Square
Empire Theatre

CHURCHILL'S FIRST CAMPAIGN FOR FREEDOM

Winston Churchill always enjoyed the music hall. His father took him to the Empire Theatre in his youth, and he remembered songs he had first heard in the 1890s for the rest of his life. The Empire Theatre was the most celebrated music hall in late Victorian London. It was first built in the 1880s and was issued a licence by the local government authority, the London County Council (the LCC). The licence was periodically renewed. The

Empire was famous for its promenade on the balcony where high-class prostitutes touted for custom. Saturday evenings were particularly lively.

In 1894, the licence was up for renewal, but a Puritan faction in the LCC insisted that there be a screen erected on the balcony to conceal whatever was going on. Churchill, then a cadet at Sandhurst, was roused by the issue and became involved in the defence of the traditional arrangements. He was in touch with some organisation called the Entertainments Protection League, and his first publication was a letter in defence of his cause that appeared in the *Westminster Gazette*.

On 3 November that year, four weeks before his twentieth birthday and the first Saturday after the screen had been erected, Churchill led a mob of two hundred people and tore the screen down. He climbed on top of the debris and addressed the crowd with a speech he had prepared. It was his first public speech. In it, he urged people, just as they had brought down the screen, to bring down the councillors who had been responsible for it at the forthcoming municipal elections.

The old theatre was demolished in 1927 to be replaced by the present Empire Cinema and Theatre. It is now the venue for important film premieres with the red carpet stretched out to the middle of the pedestrianised square. In the square is a statue of Charlie Chaplin, who became a friend of Churchill on the latter's visit to the United States in 1931. Chaplin was invited to Chartwell, where he amused Churchill's children.

The Mall

Royal statues

CHURCHILL AND THE MONARCHY

Overlooking the Mall from the north, halfway between Admiralty Arch and Buckingham Palace, are statues of King George VI and of his consort, Queen Elizabeth, known and loved as the Queen Mother for her fifty years of widowhood. King George was on the throne for Winston Churchill's first spell as Prime Minister, and the latter had a romantic deference to the institution of the monarchy.

After his death in January 1936, King George V was succeeded by his eldest son, who became King Edward VIII. A playboy prince, Edward was indiscreet in his relationships and politics. He fell madly in love with an American, Wallis Simpson, whose politics were very right-wing and sympathetic to Nazism. The ageing prime minister, Stanley Baldwin, saw the dangers and acted with unaccustomed vigour in telling the king he had to choose between Wallis and abdication or the throne. Churchill had known King Edward VIII since he was a teenager and liked his personality, if not his politics, and he gave him moral support. But by December, the king had abdicated and went to live overseas for the rest of his life.

The second son, Albert, became king, choosing the name George VI. He was a shy, retiring man who assumed the role of monarch reluctantly. In the first years of his reign, he and Queen Elizabeth were deeply suspicious of Churchill, who had championed the departed king. (Churchill was not supported by his wife, Clementine, in this; she was more in tune with popular opinion.) Unlike Churchill, the new king and queen also backed Chamberlain's appeasement of Hitler at Munich, and they were not initially keen on Churchill becoming prime minister in May 1940. But this soon changed. King George became a generous and supportive confidant of his prime minister.

Churchill was prime minister again when King George VI died in February 1952, to be succeeded by Queen Elizabeth II. The king's widow, Queen Elizabeth, lived on until 2002, when she died at the age of 101.

The statue of the king was designed by William McMillan and unveiled by Queen Elizabeth II in 1955; the statue of Queen Elizabeth was designed by Philip Jackson and also unveiled by Queen Elizabeth II in 2009.

Buckingham Palace

CHURCHILL AND THE ROYALS

On Friday 10 May 1940, Churchill was summoned to the palace after the resignation of the then prime minister, Neville Chamberlain. He was ushered in to see King George VI.

"I suppose you don't know why I have sent for you?" joked the king.

"Sir," replied Churchill in the same vein, "I simply could not imagine why."[25]

The king laughed and then asked him to form a government.

Churchill, who behaved like a courtier with a romantic devotion to the institution of monarchy, steadily overcame the king's suspicions and, within months of his premiership, the king was his strongest ally. During the war, the prime minister and monarch had lunch together every Tuesday when they were both in the country, often at Buckingham Palace. It was a buffet lunch. Servants were dismissed and the two men helped themselves to their food. Churchill shared all his problems and concerns with the king who became a kind of 'Father Confessor'.

On VE Day, 8 May 1945, Churchill joined the nuclear royal family – King George VI, Queen Elizabeth, Princess Elizabeth (later Queen Elizabeth II) and Princess Margaret – on the balcony of the palace to wave to the triumphant and joyful crowds that had gathered to celebrate the end of the war.

In February 1955, Churchill, then prime minister, attended a dinner hosted by Queen Elizabeth II for commonwealth prime ministers at Buckingham Palace. The leader of the Labour Party, Clement Attlee, came up to Churchill and... collapsed in his arms. With Mrs Attlee's help, Churchill got Attlee to a nearby couch. "Poor Attlee," commented Churchill later, "he is getting old; he is seventy-two."[26] Churchill was then eighty.

In January 1957, Churchill was again at Buckingham Palace. His successor as prime minister, Anthony Eden, had resigned. Until the 1960s, there was no democratic process for choosing a new Conservative leader. The selection of the prime minister was seen as part of the royal prerogative, and there was no obvious successor to Eden. R. A. Butler and Harold Macmillan were both possibilities. Churchill was invited, along with the Marquess of Salisbury, to give advice to Queen Elizabeth II (who was then only thirty). In 1938, Salisbury, as Lord Cranborne, had resigned with Eden from Neville Chamberlain's government in opposition to appeasement. He was replaced as under-secretary of state for foreign affairs by Butler, who became one of the architects of the Munich Agreement. Macmillan, on the other hand, had been a supporter of Churchill during the 1930s in opposition to the Chamberlain government's foreign policy. So it is perhaps no surprise that Salisbury and Churchill recommended Macmillan as prime minister. Queen Elizabeth II followed their advice, and Macmillan was invited to form a government.

Morpeth Terrace
Morpeth Mansions

HIS LONDON HOME DURING THE 'WILDERNESS YEARS' OF THE 1930S

In the early nineteenth century, the area between Westminster Abbey and Victoria Station was a slum. Between 1847 and 1851, a road – named after the queen, Victoria – was built through it and the slums gradually gave way to offices and shops. A new feature for London at the time was the construction of mansion blocks based on the Scottish or European model. Among the smart residential apartments that were being built at the same time was Morpeth Terrace. It stands in the shadow of Westminster Roman Catholic Cathedral, which was built in the 1890s in a neo-Byzantine style. It is the base for the Archbishop of Westminster, the head of the Roman Catholic Church in England.

A plaque on the red-bricked Morpeth Mansions, in the middle of the terrace, indicates that Winston Churchill had a home here between 1931 and 1939. His spacious flat occupied the top two of six floors and overlooked a school, itself overlooked by Westminster Cathedral, and he arranged for a large study on the top floor. The 1930s were the most critical years in Churchill's life. He had alienated himself from the Conservative Party by vocally opposing their plans for granting dominion status to India, effectively advancing Indian self-government. His quixotic support for King Edward VIII during the abdication was not well-received, and he was even booed in the House of Commons. His unpopularity among the leaders of his own party did not help his campaign warning about the dangers of Nazi Germany and the need to build up more robust defences.

Churchill's home at Morpeth Terrace became an alternative focus of politics. In the years after 1936, he built up contacts and support from other parties. In July 1936, he hosted a luncheon party that included people from the Labour Party, such as the trade union leader Sir Walter Citrine and Sir Norman Angell, former MP and winner of the Nobel Peace Prize. Other guests were Asquith's daughter and one of Churchill's closest woman friends, Lady Violet Bonham Carter, as well as the former editor of *The Times*, Wickham Steed. (The then editor of the paper, Geoffrey Dawson, was a strong supporter of Stanley Baldwin and Neville Chamberlain's policy of appeasement.) Other regular visitors to the Mansions in the following years were the writer and National Labour MP Harold Nicolson and the Conservative MPs Brendan Bracken, Duff Cooper, Robert Boothby, Duncan Sandys (who was at the time married to Churchill's daughter, Diana), Harold Macmillan and Anthony Eden (future prime minister and future husband of Churchill's niece, Clarissa).

Churchill also received European visitors as part of his programme of creating an extraordinary personal intelligence network. In May 1938, one such guest was Konrad Henlein, the leader of the Sudeten Germans in Czechoslovakia. The presence of the German minority was the pretext for Hitler's invasion and annexation of Czechoslovakia. The other guests at that meeting were Archibald Sinclair, the Liberal leader and an old friend of Churchill, and Professor Lindemann.

In January, he entertained his new son-in-law, Vic Oliver, the Austrian-born entertainer and band leader. Churchill's daughter

Sarah had married him in the United States. He had met Vic the previous year, before they were married, and had not been impressed: "Common as dirt ... twice divorced, 36 or so he says."[27] He had hired a private detective to check on Oliver's divorces. But by now he graciously, if with gritted teeth, welcomed him.

In May 1939, Neville Chamberlain's government brought in a White Paper with the policy of restricting Jewish immigration into Palestine. This was strongly opposed by Zionists, who backed the project of a Jewish national home. Churchill had long been a supporter of Zionism. Before he gave a speech attacking the White Paper in the House of Commons, he had lunch with Chaim Weizmann, the Zionist leader and later first president of Israel, at Morpeth Mansions. Weizmann had come to brief his host. Churchill's son, Randolph, and Professor Lindemann were also present. Beforehand, Weizmann had seen his colleagues of the Zionist Executive, who had told him, "Don't forget this thought; don't forget that thought."[28] Weizmann, who had known Churchill for over thirty years, knew that a parliamentarian of Churchill's experience would not need such briefing. And sure enough, Churchill was well prepared. He had a collection of cards on which he had written points.

Churchill received no briefing from any Palestinian. He was of the belief that Palestine was the obvious national home for persecuted Jews; their historic connection with the land was paramount. Three years earlier, he had given evidence to the Peel Commission, which was trying to find a solution to the problem after the (Palestinian) Arab Rebellion against Jewish immigration into their country. He argued that the Palestinians had forfeited any claim to their land because, he asserted, they had sided with the Ottomans in the First World War. Churchill never had any Arab friends, and he had no sympathy for the Palestinians, saying in 1936 that the dog in the manger does not have "the final right to the manger".[29] But he later qualified this in October 1938 by actually anticipating the policy of the White Paper, suggesting "there should be an agreement to which Arab and Jew should be invited to subscribe, that the annual quota of Jewish immigration should not exceed a certain figure for at least ten years".[30]

Churchill's commitment to the Zionist project was consistent, though nuanced. At the suggestion of Lady Violet Bonham Carter, he even met the revisionist far-right Zionist leader Vladimir Jabotinsky. His support wavered only when Jewish terrorists assassinated Lord Moyne, the British minister of state in the Middle East, and when British soldiers were killed in 1946. But he became a supportive friend of the State of Israel, and in retirement received the first prime minister of Israel, David Ben-Gurion, giving him a copy of an essay he had written on Moses.

Before Zionism became a political issue, Churchill had long been friendly with Jews. He inherited his father's friendship with the Rothschilds and Sir Ernest Cassel. His closest American friend for over thirty years was Bernard Baruch, who was not enthusiastic about the Zionist cause, leading Weizmann to refer to him as "the wrong type of Jew".[31]

On 3 September 1939, Neville Chamberlain's policy of appeasement had failed to avert war and he broadcast the announcement that Britain was at war with Germany. Churchill heard the radio broadcast at his flat on Morpeth Terrace. Immediately afterwards, there was an air-raid warning – but this was premature. With the announcement of war, the system was switched on and "bluebottles or something" had got into the works.[32] Churchill went up to the roof "to see what was going on" and saw thirty or forty barrage balloons above the city.[33] Aware that he was setting a bad example, he moved to the air-raid shelter a hundred yards away. It was an open basement, not yet sandbagged, that was assigned for the residents of the flats. "Everyone was cheerful and jocular," he noted.[34]

Within days, Churchill was reappointed First Lord of the Admiralty, and he was able to move back to Admiralty House, the residence that went with the post.

Northumberland Avenue
Hotel Métropole, Hotel Victoria and the National Liberal Club

TRADE UNIONISTS AND A POET: WAR AND PREPARATION
FOR WAR

Many new roads were built in London during the nineteenth century, often cutting through slum areas, like Victoria Street. Northumberland Avenue, however, constructed in the 1870s, was built over the former town house and gardens belonging to the Dukes of Northumberland. It became a broad street, lined with smart hotels. There is a dull, imposing uniformity of the neoclassical architecture, the buildings all dating to within a decade of each other.

One of the smartest of the hotels was the Hotel Métropole – note that classy acute accent on the first e. It was built in the triangle between Northumberland Avenue and Whitehall Place. The hotel had over 550 bedrooms and was a fashionable rendez-vous. King Edward VII, when Prince of Wales, liked to entertain here. After the outbreak of the First World War in 1914, the hotel was requisitioned by the government and the following year became the headquarters of the newly founded ministry of munitions, set up to coordinate the production and distribution of ammunition and arms for the war effort.

Winston Churchill, after two years without a frontline job, was appointed minister of munitions in July 1917 by the new prime minister, David Lloyd George. He brought to his office a bust of Napoleon. His home was then in Cromwell Road, but, workaholic as he was, he often slept at the ministry. His office can be spotted from Northumberland Avenue, behind the bow window on the first floor above the entrance.

Two visitors to Churchill at the ministry illustrate aspects of his personality.

As minister of munitions, Churchill inherited an acute labour dispute, which his three predecessors had failed to resolve. Munition factory workers in Glasgow had been organised by militant Clydeside trade unionists to come out on strike. The factory owner, Sir William Beardmore, would not concede to any of their demands. Some of the militants were deported from Glasgow by the authorities. Churchill invited their leader, David Kirkwood, to call on him at the ministry. Kirkwood had expected to meet an arrogant, swashbuckling militarist, but Churchill was all smiles and affability. He ordered tea and cake, and the two men sat down and stated their positions.

Kirkwood wanted to be reinstated as an engineer at Beardmore's. If he was not, he would advocate a down-tools policy for the men.

"You must not mention that here, Kirkwood. I will not tolerate it. Remember you are in the Ministry of Munitions."

Kirkwood persisted. There was a long pause, ended by Churchill roaring with laughter.

"By Jove, and I believe you would! But there's no good getting heated about it. You feel wronged, and only one thing can change that feeling."[35]

In the next few days, Churchill persuaded Beardmore to take Kirkwood back as a manager of a shell factory.

Kirkwood later became a left-wing Labour Member of Parliament, but he and Churchill always entertained a personal respect for each other. When Kirkwood wrote his memoirs, it included a foreword written by Churchill.

Churchill was a great admirer of the poetry of Siegfried Sassoon, author of *Memoirs of a Fox-Hunting Man* and considered an anti-war poet. He knew some of Sassoon's poetry by heart. Churchill's secretary, Edward Marsh, was acquainted with the poets of the day – he was the first biographer of Rupert Brooke – and he arranged for Sassoon to call on Churchill at the ministry. Sassoon was apprehensive, but found his host "leisurely, informal and friendly".[36] The only other fox-hunting poet he knew, Churchill explained, was Wilfrid Scawen Blunt, a campaigner against imperialism in Ireland and Egypt and a breeder of Arab horses; but he profoundly disagreed with Blunt's politics. The conversation, Sassoon recalled, "developed into a monologue".[37] Churchill paced the room, a cigar in the corner of his mouth, and asserted that "war is the normal occupation of man".[38] Sassoon was a little troubled by this and his host added, with perhaps a touch of self-mockery, "War – and gardening".[39] Sassoon was offered a job in the ministry, but he declined.

One person who did work for the ministry was the young Stafford Cripps. A chemistry graduate before he became a lawyer and politician, Cripps managed a chemical factory producing armaments. Cripps later became a Labour MP, very left-wing, but during the Second World War Churchill brought him into the government and, when Churchill sought more wartime cooperation with the Soviet Union, he sent him to Moscow as an ambassador, with the idea that Left could speak to Left.

Churchill remained minister of munitions until January 1919, two months after the end of the war. He was at the ministry when, at 11 o'clock on the morning of 11 November 1918, the armistice came into force. As the church bells struck the hour, Churchill watched hundreds, thousands of people rushing into the streets, shouting and screaming with joy. Trafalgar Square was swarming. In the ministry itself, "disorder had broken out. Doors banged. Feet clattered down corridors. Everyone rose from the desk and cast aside pen and paper. All bounds were broken. The tumult grew. It grew like a gale, but from all sides simultaneously. The street was now a seething mass of humanity. Flags appeared as if by magic. Streams of men and women flowed from the Embankment. They mingled with torrents pouring down from the Strand on their way to acclaim the King. Almost before the last stroke of the clock had died away, the strict, war-straitened, regulated streets of London had become a triumphant pandemonium."[40]

After the war, the hotel continued to be a government building, mostly dealing with defence and security. In recent years, it has been converted back into a hotel, the Corinthia, which is owned by a consortium that includes investment from Libya and the United Arab Emirates.

Between the Hotel Métropole and Trafalgar Square was another hotel built in 1887: the Hotel Victoria. In its heyday, it was lavish in its public rooms and had five hundred bedrooms – but only four bathrooms.

In the 1930s, Churchill was not a tribal Conservative politician. He had opposed the party's policy on India and was
constantly criticising the Conservative-dominated government
for not rearming sufficiently to confront German rearmament.
From 1936, he was building up informal personal contacts with
members of the opposition. On 15 May 1936, he hosted a lunch
(which he always called "luncheon") at the Hotel Victoria for
members of the left-dominated Anti-Nazi Council. The other
lunchers were: Sir Walter Citrine, general secretary of the
Trades Union Congress; Margaret Bondfield, who had been
the first woman cabinet minister, having served as minister of
labour in Ramsay MacDonald's 1929 government; Sir Norman
Angell, a former Labour MP; and Hugh Dalton, a Labour MP
and former minister.

Dalton was appointed minister of economic warfare in
Churchill's wartime coalition in 1940. This was a cover for the
Special Operations Executive (SOE), whose headquarters were
in this hotel. The task of SOE was to undertake non-military
activities to undermine the Nazi occupation of Europe. These
operations were to "set Europe ablaze", and the hotel was used to
recruit agents.[41] Dalton was later president of the Board of Trade.
Churchill's urbanity enabled him to get along with most people
– political allies and opponents alike – but with Dalton, it was
an effort. Dalton was an Old Etonian, brought up in the shadow
of the royal court, but had – to Churchill's incomprehension –
become a socialist politician. Nonetheless Churchill respected
his commitment and administrative competence.

Churchill's courting of Labour politicians like Dalton was
a curious pre-echo of the wartime coalition; it was as if he
was already preparing the ground. But his behaviour did not
go down well with more tribal Conservatives. In spite of – or

perhaps as a result of – his hostility to the Trades Union Congress during the 1926 General Strike, he built up friendships later in his life with trade unionists including Walter Citrine. But above all, he had a great respect and affection for Ernest Bevin, whom he described as "a good old thing, with the right stuff in him and no defeatist tendencies".[42] Churchill, as a socially self-assured aristocrat, was devoid of snobbery and had no problems in being 'mates' with Bevin, the working-class champion who had had hardly any formal education. They worked supremely well together in the war. It was as if, in contrast to the First World War, Bevin was ensuring that the organised working classes were loyal to the war effort. Churchill had much less affection for the charismatic Welsh Labour politician Aneurin Bevan. To avoid confusion, he always referred to the latter as "Mr BevAN".[43] (Ernest Bevin did not think much of Aneurin Bevan either.)

In 1941, Churchill attended a lunch given by the Trades Union Congress in honour of the United States ambassador, John Gilbert Winant. Churchill gave an impromptu speech and, as they drove away, his secretary observed that he seemed to get "on better with the Trades Union people than with the Tories".[44] Churchill agreed and said he thought trade unionists were basically Conservative, and that they had "a certain native virility", with not much of "the pale intellectual about them".[45]

In his 1951 government, Churchill was seen by more ideological Conservatives as surrendering too easily to trade union demands. He maintained friendships with Labour-supporting trade union leaders, even inviting them to parties at 10 Downing Street. Eyebrows were raised by some Conservative guests. When the leader of the Transport and General Workers Union, Arthur Deakin, fell seriously ill in 1952, Churchill asked his doctor, Lord Moran, what could be done for him. Lord Moran observed that when trade unionists "dine with him at No 10, that it will do them no good in the Party. But they cannot help liking him. He doesn't seem at all like other Tories."[46]

To the east of the Hotel Métropole, across Whitehall Place, is the National Liberal Club. This was – and still is – the venue for clubbable Liberals. The architect was Alfred Waterhouse, and the foundation stone was laid by William Gladstone in 1882. In January 1908, Churchill was guest of honour at the Club after his tour of Africa as under-secretary of state for the colonies.

At the beginning of the First World War, when Churchill was First Lord of the Admiralty, Ernest Townsend was commissioned by the Club to paint a portrait of him. Wartime commitments made it impossible for him to be available to unveil it. By the time he did become available, he was a Conservative cabinet minister and therefore no longer acceptable to the members of the Club. The portrait was put into store in the cellar. Nearly thirty years after it was painted, Churchill's defection to the Conservatives was forgiven and overlooked in light of his wartime premiership. He walked here from 10 Downing Street to unveil the portrait in July 1943, surrounded by supporting crowds. The portrait of the quondam Liberal is still on display in the lobby.

There is an apocryphal story about the Club and Churchill's great friend F. E. Smith, lawyer, wit and Conservative politician. He regularly used to walk from the law courts to the Houses of Parliament and drop in simply to use the lavatory. When he was challenged about this by a member of staff asking whether he was in fact a member of the Club, he is alleged to have said, "Is this a Club? I thought it was a public convenience."

Parliament Square
The Square

THE CENTRE OF POLITICAL BRITAIN

In medieval times, the Palace of Westminster was the site of the monarch's palace, and the governance of the kingdom has since grown out of the royal household. The Palace of Westminster refers to parliament – the House of Commons and House of Lords – and Westminster Abbey was the parish church of the nation, once the scene of royal weddings and funerals. All the sites below are within sight of Parliament Square.

On VE (Victory in Europe) Day, 8 May 1945, Winston Churchill spoke to the nation from the Annexe of the Cabinet War Rooms. The broadcast was relayed to thousands who had gathered in Parliament Square and Whitehall. His voice almost broke with emotion when he concluded with the words, "Advance, Britannia! Long live the cause of freedom! God save the King!"[47] In the square, the crowds broke into spontaneous cheering and clapping.

To the northeast of the square is the statue of Churchill. With no false modesty or illusions about his place in British history, Churchill had himself chosen the spot where a statue of himself in London should be sited. The statue was sculpted by Ivor Roberts-Jones and unveiled by Clementine Churchill in 1973, eight years after Churchill's death, in the presence of Queen Elizabeth II and four former prime ministers and the current one. It depicts him as an old man, leaning on a stick, head hunched forward.

The statue became a target of demonstrations in June 2020, when the anti-racism movement raised awareness about historic figures with connections to Britain's colonial past and the slave trade. Churchill believed unapologetically in the British Empire and white superiority. Such views were held widely at the time, though even then he clashed with the Conservatives on Indian self-determination. Shortly after, the decision was taken to board up the statue.

Nearby is the statue of Jan C. Smuts (1870–1950), the South African prime minister who had been Churchill's stalwart friend from before the First World War. Smuts had brought South Africa into the conflict on Britain's side. Churchill was due to unveil the statue in November 1956, but the Speaker took his place. This was at the height of the Suez crisis, which led to the resignation of Churchill's successor, Anthony Eden.

St Margaret's Church

WHERE CHURCHILL WAS MARRIED

Between Westminster Abbey and Parliament Square is St Margaret's Church, which has the appearance of an English country parish church. Though it has a history going back a millennium, the present church was built in the sixteenth century and its tower two centuries later. It is the parish church of the Houses of Parliament.

Members of Parliament are able to celebrate Christian rites of passage at St Margaret's, and Winston Churchill married Clementine Hozier here on 12 September 1908. Churchill had just joined the Privy Council on his appointment as president of the Board of Trade in Asquith's Liberal government and, though he was about to enter his most radical phase, his best man was a High Tory: Lord Hugh Cecil, son of the former Conservative prime minister the third Marquess of Salisbury. Churchill's former headmaster at Harrow – Dr Welldon, a canon of Westminster and former Bishop of Calcutta – gave the address. The blessing was given by the Reverend Edgar Sheppard, canon of Windsor, whose son was to achieve notoriety (in Churchill's eyes) as Dick Sheppard, an outspoken pacifist preacher who came to prominence in the 1930s.

The bridegroom was two months short of his thirty-fourth birthday; the bride was twenty-three. When they married, they were both Liberals and, unlike her husband, Clementine remained a Liberal for the rest of her life. She loyally supported her husband in his political changes and canvassed with him when he was a Conservative candidate, though she was often wary about the Conservative Party as an establishment. Nonetheless, theirs became one of the most successful political marriages of the twentieth century. But it was an unusual marriage. Neither partner had money behind them. Clementine's parents had long since split up. Her father, Sir Henry Hozier – but was he in fact her father? – was an army officer and author of a multi-volume history of the Russo-Turkish War of 1877–1878. Clementine had been living with her mother, Lady Blanche Hozier – so-called because she was the daughter of the Earl of Airlie, a Scottish peer. But so poor had Lady Blanche and her children been that they could not always afford to live in Britain and were often resident on the north coast of France. Clementine's youthful experience of relative poverty – and also perhaps her Scottish blood – always made her cautious about money. She was apprehensive about many of her husband's financial risks, most of all his reckless gambling.

The couple often lived almost separate lives. They rarely took holidays together and were sometimes apart for weeks, even months on end. The advantage of this to historians is that they wrote copious affectionate and revealing letters to each other. Even when they were home together, Churchill and Clementine had separate bedrooms and always had their breakfast apart. Indeed, it is hard to imagine how they managed to produce five children. But there is no convincing evidence that they were anything but faithful to each other.

Two other women played a great role in Churchill's life and might have been possible brides. One was Violet, the daughter of prime minister Asquith. The other was Pamela Plowden, whom Churchill had known in India in 1897 where they travelled around Hyderabad on the top of an elephant. Plowden later married the Earl of Lytton. Both women survived Churchill, and Churchill had the fondest feelings for them for his whole life.

The marriage at St Margaret's Church was made to last.

The political elite attended the wedding. King Edward VII sent as a present a gold-headed malacca cane. The prime minister, H. H. Asquith (whose fifty-sixth birthday it was), did not attend but sent a ten-volume set of the collected works of Jane Austen. The Jewish businessman Sir Ernest Cassel, friend of Lord Randolph Churchill and King Edward VII, gave the more useful gift of £500.

Nearly forty years later, in the bitterly cold winter of 1947, St Margaret's was the scene of another Churchill wedding: that of his youngest daughter, Mary, to Christopher Soames. The Labour prime minister at the time, Clement Attlee, was a guest at the church and, to the distress of the Churchill family, was booed by some of the 'toffs' as he arrived. In spite of political differences, Churchill always had a high personal regard for Attlee, who had been his loyal deputy for five years during the Second World War.

When a visitor to Chartwell referred to the statesman as "silly old Attlee", Churchill snapped back, "Mr Attlee is Prime Minister of England. Mr Attlee was Deputy Prime Minister during the War, and played a great part in winning the War. Mr Attlee is a great patriot. Don't you dare call him 'silly old Attlee' at Chartwell or you won't be invited again."

Westminster Abbey

PARISH CHURCH OF THE NATION

The scene of royal rites of passage from the early Middle Ages, Westminster Abbey symbolises the continuity of English history. Winston Churchill was not a conventional religious believer. He frequently invoked God but rarely Jesus and declined being seen as a pillar of the church, suggesting he was rather "a buttress". To Churchill, the Church of England was part of the fabric of an inherited orderly nation. He attended funerals here as well as other major services.

A fortnight after Churchill became prime minister in May 1940, during the most critical days of the war, a short service of Intercession was held at the Abbey. Churchill attended and, from his seat in the choir, he sensed "the pent-up, passionate emotion, and also the fear of the congregation, not of death or wounds or material loss, but of defeat and the final ruin of Britain."[48]

Six months later, Churchill was a pallbearer here for the funeral of Neville Chamberlain. Bomb blasts had shattered some of the Abbey's windows. Chamberlain's ashes were buried in the Abbey, next to those of Andrew Bonar Law.

In April 1945, Churchill attended a memorial service for David Lloyd George.

To mark the twenty-fifth anniversary of the Battle of Britain, in September 1965, Queen Elizabeth II unveiled a memorial stone for Churchill just inside the west door by the Tomb of the Unknown Warrior. It says simply, "Remember Winston Churchill". Clementine Churchill used to leave flowers at this memorial on the anniversaries of her husband's birth and death. Near the stone is another tablet to the memory of Churchill's great American ally President Franklin D. Roosevelt, unveiled by the then prime minister Clement Attlee in 1948 in the presence of Winston Churchill and Roosevelt's widow, Eleanor.

Methodist Central Hall

CHURCHILL AS LEADER OF THE OPPOSITION

In September 1945, the Conservative Party held its annual conference in this hall. Winston Churchill gave a speech on the last day. He had been leader of the opposition since July after losing the general election. Of course, he was an infallible and revered figure, and his years as leader of the opposition were inevitably an anticlimax. During the summer, Churchill had gone for a much-needed rest in northern Italy, and in the years ahead he spent many months holidaying and painting in the south of France. He was also preoccupied with his writing of the *History of the Second World War*, his monumental account of his wartime stewardship. Party management was left to his acknowledged deputy and ultimate successor, Anthony Eden, and to the 'background boys' in the Conservative Central

Office who were to adjust Conservative policies to the post-war world.

Big Ben

THE SILENCING OF THE CHIMES

Though generally used to refer to the clock tower itself, 'Big Ben' is actually the name of one of the bells in the clock tower of the Houses of Parliament. In spite of its prominence alongside the River Thames, Big Ben escaped bomb damage during the Second World War. Its chimes were silenced on the day of Winston Churchill's funeral on 30 January 1965 as a mark of respect.

House of Commons

SCENE OF CHURCHILL'S GREATEST PERFORMANCES

The House of Commons was the focus of Winston Churchill's public life. He loved it: "The House of Commons is a jealous mistress; you must give her the cream of your thoughts."[49] The buildings of the Palace of Westminster, which refers to the whole complex, were rebuilt in the 1830s following a fire. The architect was Charles Barry and the internal design was the work of Augustus Pugin. The style is quintessentially Victorian Gothic Revival.

It is possible to enter the House of Commons, talking one's way past the heavy security, passing Westminster Hall on the left. Then, head up some stairs and follow the corridor to the Central Lobby. The public are able to go to the Strangers' Gallery of the House of Commons chamber. Usually this can be arranged by a

Member of Parliament but, if there are spare places in the gallery, visitors can stroll in. Helpful police officers will guide the visitor and politely explain what they can and cannot do. It is then possible to look down on the House at work. There is an elaborate etiquette of behaviour, steeped in centuries of practice, to which MPs must become accustomed. The Speaker or one of their deputies presides, and all MPs' speeches are in theory addressed to them. Rows of green benches face each other like choir stalls in a church, which was the original model. The government and its supporters are on your left (from the Strangers' Gallery) and the opposition on your right. This arrangement emphasises the confrontational nature of British politics. Certainly, Churchill thought this binary form made the defection from one side to the other, 'crossing the floor', a significant act not to be undertaken lightly – not that this restrained him. He started as a Conservative, switched to the Liberals in 1904, and returned to the Conservatives for good in 1924.

Always conscious of his father's career as a Member, Churchill felt a family connection with the House of Commons. His only son was christened in the House of Commons chapel in October 1911 with the given names Randolph (after Churchill's father), Frederick (after Churchill's closest friend, the Conservative MP F. E. Smith) and Edward (after the Liberal foreign secretary, Sir Edward Grey). Clementine Churchill, it seems, made no contribution.

The chamber of the House of Commons was bombed in 1941. Churchill inspected the ruins, murmuring, "I shall never live to sit in the Commons chamber again".[50] He was wrong. MPs moved first to Church House for their sessions and then to the House of Lords, with its red rather than green benches, under the same roof. When the House of Commons was rebuilt,

Churchill insisted on there being no changes, despite the fact that there were (and are) more MPs than can fit on to the benches. Although some seats were informally reserved – for leading government and principal opposition figures, as well as some senior members – Churchill argued that, on important occasions when the House was full, the crowded nature of the chamber added to the sense of occasion and excitement. The apparent overcrowding of the chamber encouraged an intimacy and a "conversational style".[51] Churchill laid the foundation stone of the new chamber in May 1948; it was rebuilt over the next two or three years, and Members met in the new chamber for the first time in October 1950.

Though his father was an MP when Churchill was a child, Churchill never heard him speak in the House of Commons. In April 1893, at the age of eighteen and recovering from a serious fall while on holiday in Bournemouth, Churchill squeezed into the Distinguished Strangers' Gallery to watch the prime minister, William Gladstone, wind up the debate on the second reading of the Home Rule Bill. This was Gladstone's second Home Rule Bill, which was intended to give political autonomy to Ireland. Like its 1886 predecessor, the 1893 bill was doomed to failure because it would ultimately be rejected by the House of Lords. But it was no less a dramatic occasion to witness the oratory of the eighty-three-year-old statesman who could look back on sixty years of parliamentary life. "The Grand Old Man," recalled Churchill, "looked like a great white eagle, at once fierce and splendid. His sentences rolled forth majestically, and everyone hung upon his lips and gestures, eager to cheer or deride."[52] At the time, Churchill's family loyalties would have placed him among the deriders, but nineteen years later he was a member of the cabinet that brought in a more successful – though no less controversial – Home Rule Bill.

Churchill first became an MP, elected as a Conservative in the general election of 1900, when he was twenty-five, and he was a member of all but two parliaments elected between 1900 and 1959. It is reckoned that he delivered five hundred major speeches here during that time. The next paragraphs trace significant events in Churchill's parliamentary life, in chronological order, dealing with each new parliament after a general election.

In Churchill's first parliament, the prime minister was the third Marquess of Salisbury, the last prime minister to lead a government from the House of Lords. He was replaced in 1902 by his nephew, Arthur Balfour. When Churchill took his seat in the Commons, he sat in the seat his father had sat in. This was only five years after Lord Randolph Churchill's death, and many MPs would have remembered him.

In April 1904, Churchill was making a speech – and dried up. This was strange, as he had an excellent memory for facts, poetry and songs. He was also quick at repartee when responding to interruptions and hecklers. But older MPs remembered how his father, Lord Randolph Churchill, had dried up in a similar situation. (The father had then been seriously, irrecoverably ill. His brain was affected, and at the time it was thought he was suffering from syphilis.) The son, still in his twenties, had antagonised members of the Conservative Party with his bumptiousness and self-assurance; some now smiled with malicious satisfaction. After this embarrassing incident, Churchill always prepared his speeches carefully, relying not on memory but on comprehensive notes, just like the eponymous hero of the novel *Savrola* that Churchill had written seven years earlier. "His speech, – he had many and knew that nothing good can be obtained without effort. These impromptu feats of oratory existed only in the minds of the listeners; the flowers of rhetoric were hothouse plants."[53]

The following month, Churchill left the Conservatives, crossing the floor to join the Liberal opposition. He made a point of sitting next to David Lloyd George, the radical young Welsh lawyer. The seat Churchill took had also been the seat occupied by his father when in opposition and from where he waved his handkerchief in delight when Gladstone resigned in 1885.

In 1906, Churchill was no longer able to stand for his former constituency, Oldham, and he moved to North West Manchester as a Liberal. After the Liberals' landslide victory, Churchill was given a junior post in the government of Sir Henry Campbell-Bannerman who, two years later, was replaced as prime minister by H. H. Asquith.

Until 1918, whenever an MP was appointed to a cabinet post, they had to be re-elected in a by-election to be able to continue to sit in the Commons. Churchill stood again for his Manchester constituency and was defeated, but the Liberals in Dundee immediately offered him a seat and he was duly elected a Liberal MP. He thought he would have this constituency for life, and indeed did represent Dundee until he was defeated in the general election of 1922.

Churchill was at his most radical during this parliament, coming out with very left-wing sentiments. When the House of Lords rejected the 1906 Licensing Bill that had passed through the House of Commons, Churchill – then president of the Board of Trade and a member of the cabinet – said menacingly, "They have started the class war; they had better be careful."[54]

In 1909, Churchill sat next to Lloyd George on the front bench. Clementine Churchill had just given birth to their first child, Diana.

"Is she a pretty child?" asked Lloyd George.

"The prettiest child ever seen," said Churchill, with a big smile.

"Like her mother, I suppose."

"No, she is exactly like me."[55]

The year 1910 saw two general elections, both weakening the Liberal government's majority. The (second) 1910 parliament lasted, exceptionally, for eight years as a result of the outbreak of the First World War, during which Asquith was replaced by Lloyd George.

In the early years of the parliament, Churchill continued with such inflammatory language that the new monarch, King George V, complained to the prime minister about Churchill's "socialistic" speeches. Churchill became First Lord of the Admiralty during this parliament and the king resisted Churchill's proposal to name a warship after the regicide Oliver Cromwell.

In November 1911, the Irish Home Rule Bill was debated. This was a divisive issue between the Liberal government and the Conservative opposition. Churchill was a combative supporter of the measure, provided consideration was given to Ulster separatism. One day, he mockingly waved his handkerchief at the opposition as he left the chamber. This enraged Ronald McNeill (who had attended Churchill's school, Harrow, but a decade earlier), who snatched the Speaker's copy of the Standing Orders and threw it at Churchill, drawing blood. The following day, McNeill apologised. Churchill hardly bore resentments for long and, when he returned to the Conservative fold and became chancellor of the exchequer, McNeill became one of his junior ministers.

The general election of 1918 was the first in which women (over the age of thirty) were permitted to vote.

After Churchill's defeat in the general election of 1922, he was not an MP for two short parliaments. This was a period of rapid political change. Lloyd George was defeated in the 1922 general election, followed in quick succession as prime minister by Bonar Law, Stanley Baldwin and then the first Labour prime minister, Ramsay MacDonald. Churchill eventually returned to the Commons at the end of 1924 as MP for Epping – a constituency he held for the rest of his parliamentary life, until he retired in 1964. To the surprise of many Conservatives, the prime minister Stanley Baldwin appointed Churchill as chancellor of the exchequer.

Churchill was able to make public finance amusing, and his budget speeches became joyous occasions. In 1928, the Prince of Wales (the future King Edward VIII) listened, with his brother, the Duke of Gloucester, to the budget speech from the Peers' Gallery.

The House of Commons had many so-called 'special interest' dining clubs; such special interests transcended party allegiances. In the 1924 parliament, one exclusive group was made up of MPs who had defeated Winston Churchill in elections. Among them were men from all three main parties, some of whom reached high office. They included Walter Runciman (Oldham, 1899, Liberal), Sir William Joynson-Hicks (North West Manchester, 1908, Conservative) and F. W. Pethick-Lawrence (Leicester, 1923, Labour). All three ended up in the House of Lords, and Joynson-Hicks was Churchill's cabinet colleague in Stanley Baldwin's 1924 government.

Ramsay MacDonald formed a second Labour government after the general election of 1929. During this parliament, Churchill fell out with his Conservative colleagues and became a backbencher – for the first time since 1905 – for the next ten years. His constituency returned him to parliament in 1931, after which MacDonald led a National government. He was replaced by Stanley Baldwin just before the general election of 1935. No further general elections were held for ten years because of the war, and during this parliament Baldwin was replaced in 1937 by Neville Chamberlain who was in turn replaced by Churchill in May 1940.

After 1931, when Churchill was no longer a frontbencher, he took a seat below the gangway (a position conventionally occupied by supporters of the government who might have either retired from office or were in some dispute with government policy). As a frontbencher, he had been able to rest his notes on the despatch box in front of him "and pretend with more or less success to be making it up as you go along".[56] He now had to hold his notes in his hand.

During the abdication crisis – when King Edward VIII was obliged to choose between marrying the twice-divorced Wallis Simpson and staying on as king – Churchill championed the king, whom he had known since the latter was a teenager. He spoke up for the king in the House in December 1936, incurring hostility from Members. "Twister," cried out one. Others laughed and heckled him. Churchill got angry. "You won't be satisfied until you have broken him, will you?"[57] The support Churchill gave the doomed king contributed to many MPs deeply distrusting his judgment. One of the MPs present, the diarist Harold Nicolson, noted that Churchill had in a few minutes destroyed a reputation that he had built up over the previous two years. This did not help Churchill in his campaign warning against the rise of Hitler and the need for rearmament.

After Churchill became prime minister in May 1940, most Conservatives were still wary of the man who had been so disloyal to Mr Chamberlain and who had shown, in their view, such poor judgment by resisting moves towards greater devolution in India and supporting King Edward VIII in the abdication crisis. When he addressed the House of Commons for the first time as prime minister on 10 May, he noted that the "warmest welcome" came from the Labour benches. Conservatives were reserved, instead giving Neville Chamberlain enthusiastic cheers on his entry. In his war memoirs, Churchill noted that, in the early weeks, it "was from the Labour benches that I was mainly greeted".[58]

He also received encouragement from ordinary people. In the first week of his premiership, Churchill walked from his residence at Admiralty House along Whitehall, passing Downing Street – at whose entrance Bren guns had been set up – and on to the House of Commons. People greeted him with "Good luck, Winnie, God bless you."[59] But on entering the building, according to Lord Ismay, he dissolved into tears. "Poor people," he said, "poor people. They trust me, and I can give them nothing but disaster for quite a long time."[60]

This coolness from the Conservatives only changed in July 1940 after the fall of France. Churchill ordered the destruction of the French fleet at Oran in North Africa as a precaution against French ships and equipment falling into German hands. When this was announced in the House of Commons, Conservative MPs joined with Labour to give him a warm welcome.

Churchill was meticulous in reporting to the House of Commons. It symbolised the democratic process, and democracy was the ideology for which Britain was fighting. Some of his greatest and most moving speeches were first given in the House of Commons. On 4 June 1940, he gave his famous rallying speech: "We shall fight on the beaches, we shall fight on the landing grounds, we shall fight in the fields and in the streets, we shall fight in the hills; we shall never surrender."[61] The impact on those who heard these words uttered was immediate and intense. "Eloquent and magnificent," wrote Henry Channon, a Churchill sceptic, in his diary.[62] Some Labour MPs were moved to tears. The speech was carefully crafted. The language was simple – all the words with few exceptions are monosyllabic – Anglo-Saxon and simple. House of Commons debates were not then recorded, but even the reported words had a profound impact when they were repeated on the BBC News. Vita Sackville-West told her husband, Harold Nicolson, that the words, with their Elizabethan phrases, "sent shivers (not of fear) down my spine."[63]

In October 1940, Churchill's son, Randolph, became a Member of Parliament. He was returned without contest for Preston, Lancashire and was formally introduced by his proud father and the Conservative chief whip, David Margesson.

Churchill was so much at home in the House of Commons that he had a bed installed in his office there when he was wartime prime minister.

The Houses of Parliament, so distinctive from the air, were an obvious target for German bombing. The air raids were always at night so, during the first year of the war, it was decided to have parliamentary sessions only during the day, between eleven in the morning and four in the afternoon. If there were to have been a serious and direct strike when the House was sitting, "holding two or three hundred by-elections would," Churchill said, "be a quite needless complication of our affairs at this particular juncture."[64]

President Franklin D. Roosevelt died in April 1945. The House of Commons listened to tributes; giving his, Churchill was in tears, describing Roosevelt as "the greatest American friend we have ever known."[65]

On VE Day in May 1945, Churchill announced the end of the war in Europe. All Members of Parliament then went to St Margaret's Church, Westminster, to give thanks to God for the victory. As he walked across the Central Lobby, Harold Nicolson saw a small boy approach Churchill, asking for his autograph. Churchill paused, took out his glasses, polished them and, with an actor's timing, signed the boy's autograph book. (I wonder what happened to the boy and that autograph book?)

The wartime coalition was dissolved after the end of the war in Europe in May 1945. At the general election that followed, Labour won a landslide victory.

On 1 August 1945, Churchill made his first appearance in the House of Commons after the Conservatives' electoral defeat. He entered the chamber to enormous applause. The Conservative sang 'For he's a jolly good fellow' and Labour MPs responded by singing 'The Red Flag'.

Labour held on to power after a general election in early 1950.

In spite of his reverence for the traditions of the House of Commons, its history and rituals, Churchill was not beyond playing the buffoon. In February 1951, when he was on the opposition frontbench as leader of the opposition, he gave a speech that was followed by the future Labour leader Hugh Gaitskell.

Churchill was sitting and fidgeting with his waistcoat so much that Gaitskell was put off his stride and asked if anything was wrong. Churchill rose solemnly and said with a straight face, "I was only looking for a jujube."[66]

Two months later, the left-wing Aneurin Bevan resigned from the Labour government in protest against the introduction of charges for medical prescriptions. Bevan had been the minister in charge of introducing the National Health Service and felt strongly about a free medical service. In a debate in the House, Bevan arraigned the Labour government more fiercely than he would savage the Conservatives. Churchill sat on the opposition front bench, grinning at the Labour Party's discomfort and dangling his watch chain. As Henry Channon, a Conservative backbencher, noted in his diary, "He looked like a plump naughty little boy dressed as a grown up."[67]

In October 1951, a month before his seventy-seventh birthday, Churchill returned to power as prime minister. During the next three years or so, he was mainly concerned with foreign affairs, often sidelining the Conservatives' foreign secretary, Anthony Eden. Home affairs were left to R. A. Butler, with whom he had not always had a happy relationship. Butler had been a junior minister in the Foreign Office at the time of the Munich agreement and had been close to Neville Chamberlain. When Churchill became prime minister in 1940, Butler saw him as a great adventurer and "a half-breed American".[68] When Churchill finally retired from his premiership in April 1955, Eden replaced him.

Churchill had a good-humoured relationship with the Labour opposition. On one occasion in May 1953 as he left the chamber, Labour MPs called out, "Good night". He turned to them, bowed and blew kisses.

Churchill resigned as prime minister in April 1955, but he was re-elected as an MP at the general election that followed in May and regularly sat on the government benches. This was the same bench from where he had railed against the Baldwin and Chamberlain governments twenty years earlier. As Churchill came into the chamber for the first time after the election, the leader of the opposition, Clement Attlee, crossed the floor to hold him gently by the arm as he took the oath made by all the newly elected or re-elected MPs. There was general applause. The Labour MP Emanuel Shinwell called out, "Come and join us."[69]

Churchill was increasingly frail and did not speak in this parliament, but he was quite a regular attendee when he was in the country. He admitted that he might not listen to many of the debates, but he prided himself on voting nonetheless.

The parliament elected in 1959 was his last. He did speak in this one, acknowledging greetings offered to him on his eighty-fifth birthday in November 1959.

Churchill's last appearance in the House of Commons was on 27 July 1964, and he did not stand in the general election that October. He turned ninety in November and died on 24 January 1965.

In the Members' Lobby, not normally accessible to visitors, there is a statue of Churchill. It was sculpted by Oscar Nemon and unveiled in December 1969. The toes of the bronze statue are shiny, for it was long the custom of Conservative MPs to touch its feet before delivering a speech in the House. The statue stands within yards of statues of Churchill's old acquaintances Lloyd George, H. H. Asquith, Clement Attlee and Arthur Balfour, and a bust of Joseph Chamberlain.

Westminster Hall

THE SUTHERLAND PORTRAIT, AND LYING IN STATE

Dating back to the eleventh century, Westminster Hall is the oldest secular building in London that is still in use. It was part of the monarch's palace and was a centre of medieval administration. Parliaments have sat here and, until the nineteenth century, it was the scene of major trials. Sir Thomas More and Bishop Fisher were condemned in Westminster Hall in the sixteenth century, and Guy Fawkes in the seventeenth. Warren Hastings was tried here in the eighteenth century and it continued as a law court until 1882.

It was in Westminster Hall that Members of Parliament celebrated Churchill's eightieth birthday on 30 November 1954. An illuminated book signed by nearly every MP was presented to him. Members of the House of Commons and House of Lords had commissioned Graham Sutherland – for a fee of a thousand guineas – to paint his portrait. Churchill had seen the painting two weeks earlier and had taken an instant dislike to it. But, on this occasion, he was gracious. "The portrait," he said, "is a remarkable example of modern art. It certainly combines force with candour."[70] Pause, then gales of laughter. The portrait was taken to Chartwell and never seen again in public. It is believed that Clementine Churchill, who also hated it, had it destroyed.

In the last century or so, the bodies of many outstanding British people have lain in state to receive final tributes from citizens in Westminster Hall. Plaques in the floor celebrate those thus honoured – for it can take place only at the invitation of the sovereign. The first commoner to lie in state was William Gladstone, four times prime minister, in 1898; Churchill was the second.

After he died in January 1965, Churchill's body was brought to Westminster Hall and, over three days, more than 300,000 mourners filed past. At the four corners of the catafalque containing his body stood four soldiers, their heads bowed. The queues of those wishing to pay homage stretched out of the building and across Westminster Bridge, all the way to St Thomas's Hospital. The Hall was open for twenty-three hours a day. (It was closed for one hour for cleaning.)

The prime minister at the time, Harold Wilson, had the idea that for the last hour of Churchill's lying in state, the four soldiers would be replaced by the leaders of the three main political parties and the Speaker of the House of Commons.

On the day of the funeral, 30 January 1965, Big Ben struck a quarter to ten and, for the rest of the day, was silenced. At that hour, the coffin was taken to New Palace Yard in the Palace of Westminster and then began the slow procession to the funeral service at St Paul's Cathedral.

St James's Place
29 St James's Place

A CHILDHOOD HOME

The district of St James's is one of the most aristocratic areas in London. It was developed from the late seventeenth century, close to the royal palace of St James. Buckingham Palace only became the principal royal palace of London in the nineteenth century.

Winston Churchill's parents took number 29 St James's Place, off St James's Street, for three years from 1880. It was thus one of Churchill's childhood homes. This was the home he returned to after his brutal treatment at his first school at Ascot.

The house is spread over six levels and built of brick. A green plaque records the Churchills' residence. Sixty years earlier, the house next door had been the home of William Huskisson, an ill-fated politician who was the fatal victim of the first railway accident.

St James's Street
6 St James's Street

WHERE HE BOUGHT HIS HATS...

Lock & Co. Hatters are the oldest hat shop in the world. They have been in business continuously since 1676.

The silk top hat that Winston Churchill wore on his wedding day in September 1908 was bought here, and he regularly ordered from the hatters, including his familiar Homburg.

9 St James's Street

...AND POSSIBLY HIS BOOTS?

The bootmaker John Lobb, purveyor of footwear to royalty and the upper classes, dates back 1866.

In December 1941, Churchill had a mild heart attack while he was in the United States. The news was concealed from the public. Churchill spent time convalescing in Florida and used the pseudonym Mr Lobb.

19 St James's Street

BUT CERTAINLY HIS CIGARS

Winston Churchill and cigars are inseparable. He once said to the wartime chief whip, James Stuart, "I flatter myself that I have democratised cigars."[71] It is reckoned that he smoked ten a day – and so perhaps some quarter of a million during his lifetime. He rarely finished a cigar and did not inhale the smoke. Discarded stubs became collectors' items.

There are several cigar shops in and around St James's Street, which is close to gentlemen's clubland. Robert Lewis opened a shop at number 19 in 1787 and provided cigars to European royalty and the British aristocracy. Robert Lewis was taken over by James J. Fox, a Dublin cigar maker, in 1947. In the basement is a small but fascinating museum that, among other things, celebrates Churchill and cigars.

When, at the age of twenty, he was an army subaltern in India, Churchill had five months of leave a year. He was fascinated by war and keen to see action. What conflicts were going on in the world during his five months' leave in late 1895? For one, the Spanish government was suppressing a rebellion in Cuba. With a colleague, Churchill went off to the United States, met friends of his mother and travelled south to Cuba. His mother had put him in touch with the leaders of the Spanish army, and so Churchill spent his twenty-first birthday listening to the sound of gunfire in a real war situation. He also sent reports to the *Morning Post* (again, thanks to his mother's contacts) and so embarked on his successful – and lucrative – career as a military correspondent. It was also here that he acquired his habit of smoking cigars. (He had been a cigarette smoker at Sandhurst.) "Smoking cigars is like falling in love," Churchill wrote. "First you are attracted to its shape; you stay for its flavour, and you must always remember never, never to let the flame go out."[72] He did break this last rule, however.

Five years later, Churchill opened an account at Robert Lewis's shop. He had been introduced by his mother, who had been a customer here for twenty years. She had a taste for firm, handmade, gold-tipped Alexandra Balkan cigarettes. Churchill's first order – on display in the official ledger – on 9 August 1900 was for fifty Bock Giralda Havana cigars, costing £4. At the time, he was not an exclusive cigar smoker – he also bought a box of Balkan cigarettes, costing eleven shillings (55 pence).

Churchill continued to be a customer here for the rest of his life. He often called at the shop, and the chair in which he sat is on display. He was a valued and loyal customer – though he sometimes delayed the settlement of bills. Churchill's last order was sent on 23 December 1964, just thirty-two days before his death. He may not have had all his marbles, but he still loved his cigars.

The museum also celebrates Churchill's love of champagne, especially Pol Roger. "I could not live without champagne," he said. "In victory, I deserve it. In defeat, I need it."[73] He particularly loved the vintage of 1928. Churchill met the Pol Roger family in liberated Paris in 1944 and celebrated his love for the drink by naming one of his racehorses after it. That particular horse won a race at Kempton Park on 2 June 1953, the day of the coronation of Queen Elizabeth II.

69 St James's Street, The Carlton Club

THE CONSERVATIVES' CLUB

Founded in 1832, the Carlton Club is an elegant, members-only club with a long Conservative heritage. Winston Churchill was a member of the Carlton Club, which moved here after the Second World War, when he was a Conservative MP at the beginning of the twentieth century – membership was almost obligatory for male Conservative MPs. He had to resign when he abandoned the Conservatives in 1904, but rejoined in the 1920s once he was back in the Conservative fold.

The old Club received a direct hit during the Blitz in October 1940. The following morning, Churchill came to see the damage. The bomb seemed to have struck while members were having dinner: unfinished meals and decanters of wine were still on tables; pairs of slippers were on the floor in bedrooms. Churchill picked up a piece of fractured masonry. It had been part of a bust of William Pitt, Britain's prime minister during the Napoleonic Wars.

Westminster Gardens

A TEMPORARY HOME

Churchill's son-in-law, Duncan Sandys, had a flat here in 1945, and Churchill frequently stayed here before his new London home in Hyde Park Gate was ready. He was often greeted by cheering crowds on the street.

Whitehall
Admiralty House

HIS FAVOURITE LONDON RESIDENCE

As befits the senior service, the political head of the Royal Navy – the First Lord of the Admiralty – had his own residence "over the shop", as it were, in Admiralty House. This is an elegant brick villa built in the 1780s and designed by S. P. Cockerell. It can best be seen from Horse Guards Parade.

This was Churchill's home on the two occasions he was First Lord: from 1911 to 1915 and again from 1939 to 1940. There was no separate grand entrance, so access for Churchill, his family and household staff was through a wing of the building.

Apart from Chartwell, this was Churchill's favourite home. It enabled him to engage with British naval history, the spirit of which flowed through the office he was occupying. And both terms of his residency there were times of intense crisis, on which he thrived.

In his first period of occupancy, it was a happy family home. The Churchills' residential quarters occupied the top two floors. The only snag was the need to employ twelve servants, for which Churchill had to pay. Normally the post went to a wealthy aristocrat – or, as in the case of W. H. Smith in 1877, a very wealthy businessman – so this was not usually a problem. But at their house in Eccleston Square, the Churchills had managed perfectly well with only five. An arrangement was made whereby the grander rooms were mothballed and unused; this allowed the Churchills to cut the number of servants down to seven. Nonetheless, it was a good location for the family. Nannies would take the children for walks in St James's Park, extensive landscaped gardens that required no hassle of expense or management or the employment of gardeners. The Churchills' third child and second daughter, Sarah, was born here in October 1914.

Churchill was thirty-six when he was first appointed to the Admiralty. Whatever the role, he embraced his tasks with energy, commitment and dedication. But with the Admiralty Churchill was totally thrilled. He had many ideas and prepared the Royal Navy for the First World War.

As First Lord, he made two decisions before 1914 that had enduring consequences. First, he examined the issue of ships' fuel and decided that the navy should rely on oil rather than coal. Oil gave the ships greater speed and took up less space. Stokers were thus no longer needed, and ships could be refuelled at sea by tankers. The longer-term implications were that, because Britain produced no oil, the nation needed to control the sources of oil. This heralded Britain's 'moment' in the Middle East.

The second major decision was not popular with the navy. Churchill took the strategic decision to make the North Sea – rather than the Mediterranean – the principal defensive base for the British Isles. A posting in the sunny climes of Gibraltar, Malta or Cyprus had been attractive to sailors; Rosyth and Scapa Flow in the north of Scotland had less appeal.

It was also here that Churchill planned and directed the (unsuccessful) Gallipoli campaign of 1915–1916.

Churchill was reappointed First Lord of the Admiralty a quarter of a century later, when, on the outbreak of the Second World War, he joined the wartime government of Neville Chamberlain. The message went to all Royal Navy ships: "Winston is back."

Churchill loved maps. In 1939, the library overlooked Horse Guards Parade, and Churchill installed Captain Pim in this room to be in charge of his 'Map Room'. The walls were hung with maps and charts on which the ships of all nations were plotted. In the centre of the room was a conference table from where Churchill managed the war at sea. Even after he became prime minister in May 1940, this room was his headquarters for a few months until the move to the Cabinet War Rooms, 150 yards away.

In October 1939, Clementine and Winston Churchill entertained Neville Chamberlain and his wife. It was their first occasion of intimacy. Churchill's social world of raffish hard drinkers had little in common with the more bourgeois provincial values of Neville Chamberlain. But Churchill was a loyal cabinet minister before Chamberlain's resignation in May 1940. While he always deferred to the prime minister, he bombarded him – and other cabinet ministers – with minutes and ideas almost every day.

This dinner *à quatre* was a success. Neville Chamberlain unbent and spoke of the time when, as a young man, he lived in the West Indies and tried to develop a sisal crop for the family business. Churchill was both fascinated and impressed by this account of relative hardship, adventure and enterprise. Chamberlain was more than a weak man with the umbrella, privately mocked by Brendan Bracken as "the undertaker". Of course, no one else's young manhood matched his own, but Churchill often showed a lack of curiosity about the formative years of his colleagues – unless they had been in the armed forces. He had known Anthony Eden for over thirty years, for example, before he found out that he had studied Arabic and Persian at Oxford.

Churchill was living at Admiralty House when he became prime minister on Friday 10 May 1940. Within minutes of his appointment, he sent for the leader of the Labour Party, Clement Attlee, who came with his deputy, Arthur Greenwood. They discussed offices for the leading Labour politicians: Attlee, Greenwood,

Ernest Bevin, Herbert Morrison, A. V. Alexander and Hugh Dalton. Churchill had a cordial personal relationship with such men; for the previous eleven years, his political enemies had been members of his own Conservative party.

That evening, Churchill continued to work into the night, eventually going to bed at three o'clock in the morning. "I felt as if I were walking with destiny, and that all my past life had been but a preparation for this hour and for this trial."[74]

Churchill formed his ministry over the weekend. His central War Cabinet consisted of just five people: himself, Neville Chamberlain, Clement Attlee, Arthur Greenwood and Lord Halifax. Although Churchill was clearly in charge at all levels, the composition was instructive. All four had been political opponents; Chamberlain and Halifax had been the architects of appeasement. Chamberlain, however, would only live for six months. He died of bowel cancer in November. Churchill, a man without rancour, had an excellent relationship with Chamberlain in these last months. In some ways, he needed Chamberlain: he brought in the support of Conservative MPs who had been subjected to Churchill's scornful hostility in the last decade.

In that initial War Cabinet, only Halifax, as foreign secretary, had any departmental duties. The relationship between these two aristocrats was prickly. Halifax was a High Churchman, very tall with more than a touch of smug self-righteousness; he was known, a play on his name, as the Holy Fox. As Lord Irwin, Halifax had been viceroy in India, championing the government's India policies that Churchill had attacked so virulently in the early 1930s. When he came back to London and inherited the Halifax title, he had been, as foreign secretary, the champion of appeasement – even hunting in Germany with the Nazi leader Hermann Göring. In June 1940, Halifax was sympathetic to a reconciliation with

Germany and had the support of many Conservative MPs. It was with some relief, then, that Churchill took advantage of the sudden death of the British ambassador in Washington to despatch a reluctant Halifax to the United States as a replacement.

Bringing in the Labour leaders was an attempt to emphasise the national character of the government. In Churchill's absence, Attlee chaired meetings in his brisk, terse manner. The extended government also included two big beasts of the Labour Party: Herbert Morrison as minister of supply – he later became home secretary – and Ernest Bevin as minister of labour.

The political heads of the three fighting services – the army, the navy and the air force – were from each of the three main political parties. After Halifax's departure in December 1940, Anthony Eden once again became foreign secretary.

After becoming prime minister, Churchill treated Neville Chamberlain generously by not rushing him out of Number 10. Instead, the Churchills stayed on at Admiralty House. Three days after his appointment, early on Monday 13 May, Churchill summoned all the newly appointed ministers here and told them that he "had nothing to offer but blood, toil, tears and sweat".[75] These words were repeated later to MPs in the House of Commons.

Churchill recruited other staff from here in the first frenetic weeks of his premiership. His principal private secretary, John Martin, recalls how he was recruited: Churchill was genial and had an air of brisk confidence. Martin was asked to stand by the window. Churchill looked him up and down, and he was dismissed – but later taken on. His first day started at ten in the morning and ended at three o'clock the following morning. He struggled to find a taxi to take him home.

Another person to become part of what one might call Churchill's 'court' was Sir Charles Wilson, who later became Lord Moran. His friend Lord Beaverbrook and others were concerned about Churchill's health and physical resilience, so Wilson was called in to keep a regular eye on the prime minister. He first turned up at Admiralty House at noon. Churchill, as was his habit, was still in bed working on papers. Wilson waited while Churchill went through documents. The latter then looked up and said, "I don't know why they are making such a fuss. There's nothing wrong with me."[76]

Wilson stayed with Churchill as his personal doctor for the remaining quarter of a century until his death, by which time the now Lord Moran was in his eighties.

Foreign Office

CREATING THE MODERN MIDDLE EAST

The northeast corner of the Foreign Office, where Downing Street meets Whitehall, used to be the Colonial Office. After the dissolution of the Empire, most colonies became independent members of the Commonwealth and, in 1968, the Foreign Office was renamed the Foreign and Commonwealth Office.

Winston Churchill's first government post, in the 1905 Liberal government of the prime minister Sir Henry Campbell-Bannerman, was under-secretary of state at the Colonial Office. Churchill's immediate boss, the Earl of Elgin, was in the House of Lords. Once a viceroy of India, Elgin was now a retiring man and Churchill became the public face of the office, which he represented in the House of Commons. At that time, the British Empire covered a quarter of the surface of the globe, so Churchill was catapulted into a post of major responsibility at the age of just thirty-one.

In 1921, Churchill was appointed secretary of state for the colonies in Lloyd George's coalition government. He immediately convened a conference in Cairo to make settlements in the Middle East – a term that had not been much used before. Churchill's 'Middle East' was made up of modern-day Egypt, Israel, Jordan, Lebanon, Syria, Iraq and possibly Saudi Arabia, and the term became accepted from around this time, especially as Churchill created a Middle East department in the ministry. He selected as his adviser T. E. Lawrence, who agreed to serve for just one year. Churchill and Lawrence greatly admired each other. Lawrence's exploits in the Arab Revolt of 1916–1918 brought tales of glory and excitement to a public that had been used to stories of the awful conditions and deaths of the Western Front. The Lawrence of Arabia saga was sustained by public lectures around the country. It was very much like the story of Churchill in 1900: the Boer War in 1899 had been a chain of disasters. The story of Churchill's imprisonment in Pretoria and his daring escape was a similarly uplifting tale to offset the military defeats. This parallel probably added to the bond between the two men.

While Churchill was in Cairo, the post of chancellor of the exchequer – the second-highest job in the government – became vacant. Even though he had only just taken up an important and demanding post, Churchill was disappointed not to be chosen. The chancellorship went instead to an undistinguished Scot, Sir Robert Horne.

Without consulting Churchill, Lloyd George appointed a Conservative MP – the Honourable Edward Wood – as his under-secretary. Wood had not wanted the post, and Churchill had not wanted him. In his memoirs, Wood remembers calling at the Colonial Office and having to explain to the doorman who he was. They finally met on Churchill's return from Cairo, and it took some time for the two men to establish cordial relations. Within weeks of his appointment, Churchill sent Wood off on a four-month tour of the colonies in the West Indies. Wood was a very tall, hunting-obsessed High Churchman and landowner – a grandee among grandees. This was his first government post but, nineteen years later, as Viscount Halifax, he was the preferred candidate of both King George VI and Neville Chamberlain for prime minister in May 1940.

Home Office

A LIBERAL HOME SECRETARY

Winston Churchill's most radical period aligned with his time at the Board of Trade and the Home Office. He was home secretary from February 1910 to November 1911, during which time he worked closely with Charles Masterman, a radical Liberal MP and former journalist who wrote on the condition of the poor. He made some progressive observations to Churchill, who complained, "Oh, you are in one of your soup-kitchen moods."[77]

Masterman reported Churchill as arguing in favour of aristocratic government, observing in his diary that this revealed "the aboriginal and unchangeable Tory in him".[78]

Churchill was, however, both a Liberal *and* liberal home secretary. He was the first (and perhaps only) holder of the office to have actually served time in a prison himself – albeit in his case as a prisoner of war in South Africa. And in office he reduced the number of prisoners, especially young offenders. Churchill insisted on prisoners having diversions, either instruction or recreation. He was nonetheless prepared to be tough, and proved ready to send in troops to deal with strikes in South Wales. (The troops were stopped, however, at Swindon, after Churchill was assured that the local police were able to control the situation.)

His most difficult duty was to review all death sentences. He could offer a reprieve to some. A more gratifying task was to sign naturalisation papers. One that gave him personal satisfaction was to sign those of Chaim Weizmann, a lifelong friend whom he had met in Manchester in 1905 and who was to become the first president of Israel. Churchill thought Weizmann was "like an Old Testament prophet".[79]

The Treasury

MUSIC HALL ON THE TREASURY BALCONY

Winston Churchill was chancellor of the exchequer from 1924 to 1929 in Stanley Baldwin's Conservative government, and this building was his place of work.

On 8 May 1945, after the declaration of Victory in Europe, crowds gathered in and around Whitehall: in Birdcage Walk, Great George Street and Parliament Square. The War Cabinet appeared on the Treasury balcony overlooking the junction of Whitehall and Parliament Square. Then, Churchill appeared and 20,000 people shouted their affection and gratitude. He engaged in a kind of good-humoured music hall banter.

"God bless you all. This is your victory!"
"No," yelled the crowd. "It is yours!"

"I always said, London could take it."

Cheers.

"Were we downhearted?"

"NO!"[80]

Churchill then led the crowd in the singing of 'Land of Hope and Glory'.

Whitehall Court
The Old War Office

HAUNT OF THE BRASS HATS

The building fronting Whitehall Court and Horse Guards Avenue is the Old War Office. The vast building – which allegedly boasts two and a half miles of corridors – was designed in 1899 by the Glasgow architect William Young. Until 1964, the War Office was the ministry responsible for the British Army. In 2016, the building was sold to the Hinduja Brothers for a reported £350 million, for development as a luxury hotel.

Winston Churchill worked here as secretary of state for war and air from 1919 to 1921.

2

LONDON

OUTSIDE SW1

Living in London during the Second World War and experiencing the dangers of being bombed like everybody else, Winston Churchill became immensely popular with Londoners. When an area was bombed, he was often on the spot the following day to comfort and rally people in their losses.

After Churchill finally resigned as prime minister in April 1955, Queen Elizabeth offered him a dukedom; it would have been the first non-royal dukedom of the twentieth century. The title he would have taken was Duke of London. He respectfully declined the offer.

This second chapter dedicated to London includes all the postal districts outside the political and social centre of SW1. Some parts of Greater London featured in this book are beyond the London postal area, such as Enfield, Harrow on the Hill, Uxbridge and Woodford. The first three can be found in the Home Counties chapter, the last in Central Britain.

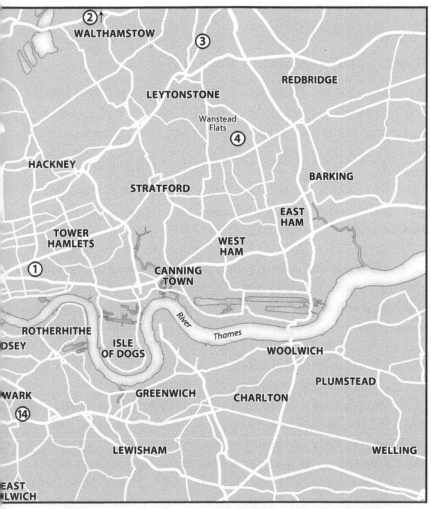

E1

100 Sidney Street

WHERE CHURCHILL DID NOT MEET ATTLEE

An abiding image of the younger Winston Churchill is of him, top-hatted, peering round the corner of a house and surrounded by London bobbies while he personally supervised a shoot-out in the East End of London. The 'siege of Sidney Street', as it became known, was also captured on cine film as an early Pathé News item. The Sidney Street 'siege' was a relatively minor episode in Churchill's life, but the image and story acquired an iconic significance.

From the 1890s, the East End became home to tens of thousands of immigrants, mostly Jewish, fleeing from persecution and pogroms in the Russian Empire. Some of these refugees were politicised and formed groups of socialists and anarchists. A vigorous press campaign playing on anti-Semitism led to the Aliens Act of 1905, which sought to control and limit immigration. Some anarchists were also criminals. A charismatic local leader, a Latvian, became known as "Peter the Painter".

In December 1910, an armed robbery of a jeweller's in Houndsditch led to a shoot-out between police and the thieves. Three policemen and one robber were killed. Some of those implicated were rounded up in the next fortnight. Caches of arms were discovered in suspects' homes, together with revolutionary literature. Evidence suggested that two remaining members of the gang were staying at a flat at 100 Sidney Street. The Metropolitan Police decided to move in and arrest them on 2 January 1911. They surrounded the house and evacuated the neighbouring buildings. Meanwhile, the two suspects were unaware of this activity. At sunrise on 3 January, the police politely knocked at the door, and one officer tossed pebbles at a first-floor window. One of the suspects appeared at the window and started shooting. The police were armed only with revolvers and shotguns, whereas the Latvians had more lethal high-velocity semi-automatic Mauser rifles. The policeman in charge phoned for reinforcements. The request went to the assistant commissioner of police and to the Home Office. Then home secretary, Winston Churchill was in the bath at his home in Eccleston Square at the time. He dressed, went to the Home Office and authorised a detachment of the Scots Guards stationed at the Tower of London to go to Sidney Street. Marksmen blocked off both ends of the street and took up positions in the house opposite.

Shortly before twelve noon, Churchill – unable to resist the lure of action – turned up, accompanied by his secretary, Edward Marsh. As they arrived, the pair were met by some anti-immigrant demonstrations, crying, "Who let 'em in?" In the hour after Churchill arrived, the shooting reached a peak. The house then caught fire. He pottered around the area in order, as he said to a later inquiry, to "satisfy myself that there was no chance of the criminals effecting their escape through the intricate area of walls and small houses at the back of No 100".[1] A second army detachment was summoned from the Tower. They brought a Maxim gun on the principle, in the words of Hilaire Belloc, that: "Whatever happens, we have got / The Maxim gun, and they have not."

One of the suspects, Sokoloff, appeared again at the window and was immediately shot dead. By now, the fire brigade had arrived. They wanted to enter the building, but the police refused access. The fire brigade appealed to Churchill, who upheld the decision of the police. Churchill left as the shooting died down, having been at the site for nearly three hours. The fire was left to burn itself out, after which the house was searched and the body of the second suspect found. One fireman died during the operation.

Churchill was much criticised for his presence at the scene. A home secretary should not, it was argued, be present at or be in charge of operational matters. Churchill denied taking command; he was there as an observer. Cinema-goers saw the newsreel clips of Churchill at the scene. He was by no means universally popular, and sometimes there were shouts in the audience of "Shoot him". Nevertheless, picture postcards depicting Churchill at Sidney Street were sold in their thousands.

The three-minute Pathé News clip can still be seen online. The streets are crowded, and there seems to be a carnival atmosphere – even though stray bullets are ricocheting around. All the men are wearing hats, which are a marker of class: from the cloth caps of the workers, the trilbys and homburgs of the middle-classes and Winston Churchill's top-hat to the professional policemen's helmets. Everyone gave up whatever they were doing to go and have a look. One of the spectators, not seen in the film, was a twenty-eight-year-old social worker, Clement Attlee, who would be Churchill's deputy prime minister in the wartime coalition government thirty years later. Attlee was accompanied by the headmaster of his old school Haileybury, Dr Wynne Willson, a future Bishop of Bath and Wells.

100 Sidney Street has been replaced by a housing estate, though the local population continues to be diverse. There is no plaque or any indication of those events of January 1911.

E4
Walthamstow, The Stadium

BOOED IN 1945

By the end of the Second World War, Winston Churchill was generally revered by the people of London. But not by everyone. He went canvassing in the 1945 general election in Walthamstow, the constituency next to his own, where the leader of the Labour Party, Clement Attlee, was standing.

Churchill was due to address 20,000 people at the stadium and was almost prevented from speaking because of the heckling and the booing. He commented sardonically (but mistakenly), "The winners cheer and the beaten boo."[2]

E11
142 Hermon Hill

AN UNEXPECTED GUEST AT A CHILDREN'S PARTY

Now home to the Ark fish restaurant, 142 Hermon Hill was once the site of the historic Fir Trees pub and hotel, founded in 1862. The Snaresbrook area was part of Winston Churchill's constituency of Woodford. Walthamstow notwithstanding, Churchill's general election campaign of 1945 was overall a triumphal tour, with cheering crowds greeting him wherever he went. Neither the Labour nor the Liberal Party put up a candidate against him. One afternoon in June 1945, a children's street party was held at a workman's canteen by the Fir Trees Hotel. Mothers and their children were surprised when Churchill arrived. He put on a small boy's coloured hat and made a pretty speech, "It is for the children that we have laid so many tyrants low."[3] The workman's canteen has not survived.

E12

City of London Cemetery in Manor Park

THE FIRST IMPORTANT WOMAN IN CHURCHILL'S LIFE

The City of London Cemetery in Manor Park was purchased by the Corporation of London from the second Duke of Wellington. It covers two hundred acres and opened in 1856.

The cemetery did not have the 'star appeal' of either Kensal Green or Highgate. The most celebrated people buried here are, perhaps, the actress Anna Neagle and the footballer Bobby Moore.

A few yards southeast of the striking neo-Gothic central funeral chapel lies the grave of Elizabeth Ann Everest, who was engaged as Winston Churchill's nanny in early 1875 when he was a few weeks old. His parents were occupied with a busy political and social life, and Mrs Everest provided the principal physical and emotional support for Winston and, later, his younger brother Jack. Mrs Everest was born in Chatham, Kent and praised the county of her birth. (Was this perhaps an influence on Churchill choosing his ultimate home, Chartwell, in Kent?) Mrs Everest was not married – "Mrs" was a common courtesy title for trusted servants; instead, she devoted herself to her charges. In his novel *Savrola*, Churchill described the relationship between the hero and his nanny. He compared the love of a mother for her child, the man for his wife, the lover for his sweetheart, even the dog for his master. For all these, he wrote, there is a rational explanation, but the love of a nanny for her charge is perhaps "the only disinterested affection in the world".[4] In his twenties, when Churchill was in India and undertaking an intensive course of self-education, he was particularly drawn to the work of politician and writer Edward Gibbon – probably because he, too, was eloquent about the role his nanny played in his childhood.

The young Churchill worshipped his parents, but from a distance. His letters were full of unrequited affection, and the letters he received in return were often tinged with reproof. For Churchill, Mrs Everest was 'Woom' or 'Woomany'; she was thus addressed in his letters to her. She bathed him, potted him, dressed him, told him stories, chided him and comforted him from his infancy. He never encountered such affectionate intimacy from either of his parents. At the age of eight, Churchill was sent into the care of the sadistic boy-beating headmaster of St George's School at Ascot. Mrs Everest would likely have seen the evidence of the ill-treatment he suffered and probably persuaded his parents to withdraw him. He was then placed at a more benign establishment, the Brighton School run by two Misses Thomson at Hove.

It was a nomadic childhood. Churchill's parents rented houses in London or Newmarket, lodged with ducal relations or stayed in the cool austerity of Blenheim Palace. They had no permanent home. Holidays from school were often spent at resorts or with Mrs Everest's relations in Ventnor in the Isle of Wight.

Churchill does not seem to have derived any religious guidance from either of his parents. The family had an instinctive acceptance of the Church of England and, at one stage, improbably, the young Churchill contemplated a career in the church. But there are hints that Mrs Everest imparted to her charges a Low Church bias, with a suspicion of Catholicism – both Roman and Anglo – and of ritualism.

The teenage Winston continued to correspond with "Dear Woomany" from Harrow and Sandhurst.[5]

In 1893, when Churchill was at Sandhurst, Lord and Lady Randolph Churchill found that they were unable to live within their ample means. Mrs Everest was to be dismissed. Churchill wrote to his mother protesting, "she is in my mind associated – more than anything else – with *home*."[6]

The gallant protest failed, and Mrs Everest withdrew to Ventnor, where her sister lived. Two years later, she fell seriously ill. When the news reached Churchill, he travelled to see her and arrived a few days before she died of peritonitis. She was sixty-two. He had wanted to hire a nurse for her. Churchill heard that her last words were about his brother, Jack, who was then fourteen. The elder brother made the necessary arrangements for her funeral.

The brothers attended the funeral on 6 July 1895 at Manor Park, meeting many of her relations. "I felt very despondent and sad – the third funeral I have been to within five months!"[7] (His father, Lord Randolph Churchill, and American grandmother had both died earlier in the year.)

Churchill paid for the headstone and for many years employed a local florist to maintain the grave, which lies a few hundred yards from the constituency that he was to represent in parliament for forty years.

Throughout his life, Churchill kept a photograph of Mrs Everest in his room.

EC2
Old Broad Street, Winchester House

AT ODDS WITH THE CONSERVATIVES ON INDIA

Winchester House is a sub-Art Deco building that houses Deutsche Bank's London office. Built in the 1990s, it replaced an 1885 building, described by Nikolaus Pevsner as a "gargantuan folly", that provided a venue for significant events and meetings in the career of Winston Churchill.

Churchill's constituency in the 1930s was Epping and Woodford. The constituency was scattered, covering the suburbs of Woodford, Epping Forest and several villages. But many of his constituency officials and backers, as well as officers of the West Essex Unionist (Conservative) Association, worked in the City of London. It was therefore more convenient to hold party meetings at a City venue. It was here, in September 1924, that the association adopted Churchill as their candidate for the forthcoming general election. This was perhaps surprising. Until two years earlier he had been a Liberal MP and minister, and at the time Churchill was not even a member of the Conservative and Unionist Party. His official label in the 1924 election was "Constitutionalist". Nevertheless, he won, rejoined the Conservative Party and held the seat for the rest of his parliamentary life, until 1964.

Churchill sometimes met Epping Conservatives here on special occasions. In February 1931, he was straining the commitment of his Conservative electorate by opposing the party's official line on India. The leadership, under Stanley Baldwin, was supporting the Labour Party's policy of giving more self-government to India as a stage to the dominion status enjoyed by Canada, Australia and New Zealand. This policy was also preferred by the then viceroy of India, the Conservative Lord Irwin (later Viscount Halifax, the foreign minister at the time of the Munich agreement of 1938 and Churchill's foreign secretary for the first seven months of his premiership in 1940). This rift began the decade of Churchill's alienation from the Conservative Party hierarchy.

The Epping constituency central committee even held a meeting at Winchester House to discuss the matter with their MP. The Indian nationalist leader Mahatma Gandhi had recently called on Lord Irwin in Delhi, and Churchill gave expression to the sense of outrage felt by imperially minded Conservatives. He made a speech at Winchester House in which he said it "was alarming and also nauseating to see Mr Gandhi, a seditious Middle Temple lawyer, now posing as a fakir of a type well-known in the East, striding half-naked up the steps of the viceregal palace while he is still organising and conducting a defiant campaign of civil disobedience, to parley on equal terms with the representative of the King-Emperor".[8] He went on to refer to Gandhi as "this malignant subversive fanatic".[9] These two contrasting icons of the twentieth century had little in common. However, in 1899, they had been physically close together at the Battle of Spion Kop in the Boer War – Churchill as the world's highest-paid war correspondent, Gandhi as a stretcher bearer.

Churchill's own intimate experience of India dated from the 1890s, and his outdated, racist rhetoric exacerbated his relations with the younger and more progressive Conservatives who had welcomed him, as a renegade Liberal, into the party six or seven years earlier. His Indian campaign contributed to the doubts of many Conservatives about his judgment and undermined another of his campaigns: warning against German rearmament in the 1930s.

Churchill's nostalgia for an India of white privilege was eventually combined with a pragmatic acceptance of reality. He never met Gandhi, but in February 1955, two months before he ceased to be prime minister, a Commonwealth Prime Ministers' Conference was held in London. There, he met Gandhi's political heir, Jawaharlal Nehru (another Old Harrovian), and got on very well with him, addressing him as "my dear Nehru".[10]

EC3
Tower Hill, Tower Millennium Pier

HIS FINAL JOURNEY

After Winston Churchill's funeral service, held at St Paul's Cathedral in January 1965, his coffin was brought down to the Pier – then just called the Tower Pier – and placed on a Port of London launch. It was transported upstream to Waterloo Station. The cranes that had been operating in the docklands dipped their extensions as if bowing in respect. This river passage would have stirred Churchill's sense of the past. "Liquid history" is how his 1908 cabinet colleague, John Burns, referred to the Thames.

EC4
Cannon Street, Southern House

IN ALLIANCE WITH COLONEL BLIMP

The spacious Southern House today accommodates shops and offices and forms an impressive façade to Cannon Street railway station. It replaces an 1867 construction erected as the Cannon Street Hotel. The hotel was never a success, and it closed in 1930. Some of the public rooms were rented out for meetings; others were converted into offices.

In its time, the old hotel had contrasting memories of British political history. In 1920, the Communist Party of Great Britain held its inaugural meeting here. Ten years later, the Indian Empire Society – with a very different agenda – held rallies here. In December 1930, Winston Churchill was their principal speaker. He spoke several times to the society, which was made up of senior British officials who had served in India. Its foundation in 1930 was a reaction against the dominion status proposed by the Ramsay MacDonald Labour government, which was also accepted by Stanley Baldwin's Conservative Party.

Churchill had spent happy and productive years in India in the 1890s, getting involved with combat on the North-West Frontier, playing a lot of competitive polo, and educating himself. He also had time to fall in love with Pamela Plowden in Hyderabad. It was a wonderful time to be a young British army officer, and Churchill always retained fond memories of those years. But he took no close interest in the development of Indian politics, the growth of the Indian National Congress Party and the significance of emerging political figures such as Mahatma Gandhi and the Nehrus – father and son, Motilal and Jawaharlal, the latter, like Churchill, an Old Harrovian.

Meanwhile, in response to these pressures, successive British governments were advancing measures for greater local involvement in the responsibilities of Indian governance. Looking back, we can see these as stages on the road to independence in 1947 – many of which Churchill himself had been involved in. Churchill was a member of the government that brought in the Indian Councils Act of 1909, known as the Morley-Minto reforms. Although Churchill had a high regard for John Morley, who was then secretary of state for India, he was himself preoccupied with social legislation and the 1909 'People's Budget'. Ten years later, the Government of India Act of 1919 introduced self-governing institutions, a further acknowledgement of Indian nationalism. Churchill was also a member of Lloyd George's coalition government responsible for this measure.

Churchill had joined the Baldwin government in 1924 – and rejoined the Conservative Party. He was deeply mistrusted by many Conservatives who remembered some of his harsh words about their party just fifteen years earlier. Churchill saw himself as bringing a liberal element into the government and hoped other Liberals would also switch their allegiance. (Some did, but more went to the Labour Party.) His budgets included elements that he saw as a continuance of the great Liberal social reforms of 1908–1910. His position on India did not fit in with his otherwise liberal conservatism.

Churchill opposed what he considered to be concessions made to Indian nationalism by Ramsay MacDonald's Labour government which were endorsed by Stanley Baldwin's Conservative shadow cabinet. He resigned from the latter and allied himself with people regarded as "die-hards" – British Empire enthusiasts who saw Britain as having a civilising mission in the East. There was more than an element of racial arrogance in their attitudes. Churchill *believed* in the British Empire. In India, he felt, it had brought peace and stability to a vast area for the first time. Public works, improvements in health and education were undeniable, and it was difficult for Churchill and his allies to see that things would improve if British control was relaxed. In his speeches, he argued that there would be great bloodshed if Britain withdrew – there was – and he distrusted the emerging articulate Indian political figures. They represented, he argued, nobody but themselves and would not serve the interests of Muslims, the vast rural poor or the Untouchables.

By allying himself with the imperial right wing of the Conservative Party, Churchill was alienated from younger, more progressive elements. His India campaigns also increased a suspicion of his political judgment in general.

There remain few memories of the resistance to the march of progress in India in the twentieth century. But Winchester House and Cannon Street Hotel once saw Churchill embracing the 'Colonel Blimps' in their resistance to those events.

St Paul's Cathedral

WHERE THE NATION – THE WORLD – MOURNS AND
CELEBRATES

This masterpiece of Christopher Wren – built during the lifetime
of Winston Churchill's illustrious forebear, the first Duke of
Marlborough – symbolises one aspect of Britishness. Against the
odds, St Paul's survived the bombing of London in the Second
World War. One memorable photograph depicts the cathedral emerging through the smoke of the bombed ruins around.
(Coventry Cathedral and some City churches were, sadly, not so
blessed.) St Paul's Cathedral was the architectural equivalent of
Churchill's own defiance in 1940.

The cathedral is the resting place of Britain's outstanding
military heroes such as Nelson and the Duke of Wellington.
Churchill, however, chose a modest country churchyard for his
final resting place, though he had toyed with the idea of being
buried at his country house at Chartwell in Kent.

St Paul's was the venue for other national commemorations,
both political and military. In April 1945, Churchill attended a
memorial service there for the recently deceased US president
Franklin D. Roosevelt, with whom he had an excellent personal
relationship. King George VI was also present. The foreign secretary, Anthony Eden, attended the president's funeral in the
United States. And one month later, Churchill visited St Paul's
for a service of thanksgiving for victory in Europe – effectively
the end of the war – with King George VI and Queen Elizabeth.
At this service, exceptionally, the second verse of the English
national anthem was sung, with the meaningful words referring
to foreign enemies:

Confound their politics,
Frustrate their knavish tricks.

After the war, Churchill came to St Paul's to commemorate other noted military and political leaders. In 1956, he unveiled a memorial to Lord Camrose, who owned the *Daily Telegraph*. The following year, he was present at the unveiling of a memorial to General Sir Ian Hamilton, who had been a personal friend of Churchill's from when he was a soldier in India in the 1890s. Hamilton had been the hapless general on the ground at the Dardanelles in 1915–1916. He later bought Churchill's farm at Lullenden at the end of the First World War.

Churchill took his time dying, and plans had long been afoot for the ceremonial funeral, which was organised by Earl Marshal, the Duke of Norfolk, under the instruction of the queen. His job was to manage state funerals and other great public events, such as the coronations of King George VI in 1937 and Queen Elizabeth II in 1953. (He also managed the English cricket team's tour to Australia in 1962–1963.) Meticulous preparations had been worked out as early as 1953, when Churchill suffered a major stroke. Before the event, his anticipated death was referred to as 'Hope Not'. Churchill died on Sunday 24 January 1965, and his funeral took place at St Paul's Cathedral just six days later, on Saturday 30.

Churchill's body lay in state in Westminster Hall and his coffin was brought here on the gun carriage that had borne the coffin of Queen Victoria. Clementine Churchill and her two surviving daughters followed in a coach lent to them by the queen. Randolph Churchill and his brother-in-law, Christopher Soames, followed the coffin on foot, walking from Westminster

Hall along the Strand and Fleet Street and up Ludgate Hill to the cathedral. Queen Elizabeth II and Prince Philip were already there when the coffin arrived. In attending, the queen was breaking a convention: she was not usually present at funerals.

Among the congregation of 3,500 were fifteen heads of state, including President Charles de Gaulle of France, with whom Churchill had often had a tricky relationship. Another soldier politician, the former US president Dwight D. Eisenhower, with whom there had been happier chemistry, attended, and three previous prime ministers – Clement Attlee, Anthony Eden and Harold Macmillan – were among the pallbearers.

The service itself included Churchill's favourite hymns, such as 'The Battle Hymn of the Republic', sung to the tune that he had first learnt at school at Harrow.

The prime minister of Australia, Sir Robert Menzies, gave an address, and after the service the coffin was taken to Tower Pier to start its journey by boat to Waterloo station and onwards by train to his final resting place at Bladon in Oxfordshire.

Walbrook, Mansion House

KEY SPEECHES MADE AT THE LORD MAYOR'S BANQUET

This magnificent eighteenth-century building was designed in the Palladian style by George Dance, with a huge portico and inner courtyard. It includes ceremonial areas, a banqueting hall and a ballroom and is the official residence of the Lord Mayor of London, head of the wealthy City of London Corporation (not to be confused with the Mayor of London, who has political authority covering the vast area of the Greater London Council). The City is the financial centre of the country. The Lord Mayor and Corporation host banquets for prime ministers and chancellors of the exchequer where they have the opportunity to make significant statements usually relating to foreign affairs.

As prime minister, Winston Churchill often gave important speeches during the Lord Mayor's Banquet, which is held each November. In November 1941, he said that if Japan attacked the United States, Britain would declare war against Japan "within the hour".[11] Japan attacked Pearl Harbor early the following month and war was indeed declared – not within the hour, but the following day.

In his Mansion House speech two years later, Churchill was cautiously optimistic. "It is not even the beginning of the end, but it is perhaps the end of the beginning."[12] He went on to say that he had not "become the King's First Minister in order to preside over the liquidation of the British Empire".[13]

N7
Caledonian Road, Pentonville Prison

A REFORMING PRISON MINISTER

This men's prison was completed in 1842 and has been in service ever since. It is based on a radial design with five spokes stretching out from a central block, enabling staff to keep an eye on things. Sir Roger Casement, the Irish nationalist, was executed here in 1916.

As home secretary between early 1910 and late 1911, Winston Churchill always showed an interest in prison conditions. In fact, in this Liberal government, he was a reformer.

In 1910, Churchill visited this prison accompanied by his ministerial colleague Charles Masterman and saw some of the young offenders. To Masterman, the boys had "nothing about them of the criminal type at all".[14] Fresh-faced and innocent-looking, they readily acknowledged their culpability with neither complaint nor resentment.

"What are you in for?" asked Churchill of one boy.

"Stealing, Sir."

"What did you steal?"

'£6.17.4d, Sir."

But he was unable to say why.

Churchill asked another boy why he was there.

"Assault, Sir."

"What sort of assault?"

"Brutal assault," answered the boy with a smile on his face.[15]

On further questioning, it seemed to Churchill that many boys were imprisoned for quite trivial offences, if they could be called offences at all. Some had been sleeping rough. Others had been imprisoned for "obscene language", which turned out to be no more than sticking a tongue out at a policeman.[16]

Churchill inspired legislation that changed the treatment of young offenders. Young people – classed as those between sixteen and twenty-one – should be imprisoned only for serious offences and sentences should not exceed one month.

He also insisted that prisoners have access to books and that rules on solitary confinement were relaxed.

NW2
Brook Road

SECRET WARTIME BUNKERS

One proposal for a reserve government base in the Second World War was an extensive underground bunker in Dollis Hill. Winston Churchill refused to countenance the idea. Nonetheless, he did visit and inspect the site in September 1940, including the accommodation that was assigned to him at Neville's Court off Brook Road. It remained as back-up in the event of the Cabinet War Rooms receiving a direct hit.

The site's codename was the 'Paddock', inspired by a local nineteenth-century stud farm. The base had approximately forty rooms on two floors. It is now owned by the housing association Network Homes, and it is possible to visit the site two or three times a year.

A cabinet meeting was held at the Paddock in early October 1940, and each minister was invited to inspect the sleeping quarters to which they had been assigned. The meeting was followed by a slap-up lunch.

So secret was the site that in his war memoirs Churchill referred to it simply as being "near Hampstead" – which, in a way, it is.[17]

NW9
Grahame Park Way

THE ROYAL AIR FORCE MUSEUM

This airfield in Colindale, now occupied by the Royal Airforce Museum, dates from 1910. The site was bought by Claude Grahame-White in 1911, and he built a factory here for the design and production of aeroplanes. In those days, flying was seen as a rich man's sport, and the airfield saw displays of flying, parachuting and aerobatics.

Winston Churchill was enthusiastic about aircraft, and he learned to fly at Eastchurch in Kent. He quickly saw the military potential of aircraft and, in the years of the First World War, this potential was developed at a great rate. Both the army and the Royal Navy had flying branches, and these were combined on 1 April 1918 to form the Royal Air Force.

As First Lord of the Admiralty, Churchill inspected the factory in Colindale and placed orders there. After the First World War, however, aircraft production ceased and the factory was used to produce cars and furniture instead. But the RAF remained interested in the site, and they took it over in 1926. It became RAF Hendon.

In June 1940, Winston Churchill flew from here to France. It was the fourth time that he had visited the country in the six weeks since he had become prime minister. He was making a desperate attempt to shore up the morale of a collapsing France. He flew in a Flamingo plane with an escort of twelve Hurricanes and was accompanied by General Ismay and the secretary of state for war, Anthony Eden.

Churchill made a fifth and final flight shortly afterwards to see what he could do either to avert a French collapse or to prepare for a stiff resistance to German occupation. He arrived at Hendon airfield at eleven in the morning to be told that the flight should be postponed because of adverse weather conditions.

"To Hell with that," Churchill said. "I'm going whatever happens. This is too serious a situation to bother about the weather!"[18]

They flew.

Today, the site is home to the RAF Museum, which displays aircraft going back to the First World War. Huge hangars date from the early twentieth century and celebrate the history of the RAF, its achievements in both war and peacetime, its engineers and its culture.

NW10

Kensal Green Cemetery

DEATH OF DUCKADILLY

Officially the General Cemetery of All Souls, Kensal Green Cemetery was opened in 1833. It was seen as a London equivalent to Paris's Père Lachaise. Access is via the Harrow Road to the north. To the south is the Grand Union Canal, which was handy in the nineteenth century when coffins were sometimes brought to the cemetery by barge and other boats removed the earth extracted for interments.

In its first century, the cemetery became the final resting place of an A-list of writers, scientists and celebrities: the novelists W. M. Thackeray, Anthony Trollope, Wilkie Collins; the essayist Leigh

Hunt; the American historian J. L. Motley; the actor William Mac-ready; the businessman W. H. Smith; a large number of Fellows of the Royal Society; a minor royalty or two and a Duke of Portland. In the twentieth century, the playwrights Terence Rattigan and Harold Pinter were buried here, and Freddie Mercury and Christine Keeler were both cremated in the cemetery.

Tucked away near the canal is the unobtrusive grave of Marigold Frances Spencer-Churchill, daughter of Clementine and Winston Churchill, who died in August 1921 at the age of two years and nine months – just two months after the death of her grandmother, Lady Randolph Churchill. Her grave is sixty miles or so from where the rest of the family are buried in Bladon, Oxfordshire. It consists of a simple cross, a replacement of the original, on a plinth with lettering by Eric Gill.

Marigold was known in the family as 'Duckadilly' and, at two years old, was just developing her personality. She used to run as fast as she could around the dining room table while her parents were having lunch. She had a sweet singing voice and endlessly cooed the popular song 'I'm Forever Blowing Bubbles'. Unfortunately, Marigold was prone to catching colds and, in August 1921, a sore throat developed into septicaemia. At this time, she was in the care of a French nanny with her brother and sisters in Broadstairs, Kent. Her mother was staying with the Duke and Duchess of Westminster at Eaton Hall in Cheshire, attending the duke's annual tennis tournament; her father was working in London. When they realised how seriously ill she was, both rushed down. Marigold asked her mother to sing 'I'm Forever Blowing Bubbles'. She did so, choking back tears. But Duckadilly gradually faded away and died the following day.

Clementine Churchill periodically visited the cemetery to lay flowers on her daughter's grave.

SE15
Peckham

INSPECTING BOMB DAMAGE

During the Blitz in the autumn of 1940, Winston Churchill heard a heavy explosion coming from south of the River Thames. It came from Peckham. Along with the chancellor of the exchequer, Sir Kingsley Wood, and General Ismay, Churchill went to the scene of the air raid. Up to thirty houses had been destroyed. Little Union Jacks were newly planted in the rubble. When Churchill was recognised, a crowd of a thousand soon appeared. They cheered affectionately, and Churchill was reduced to tears. Ismay heard an old woman say, "But see, he really cares. He's crying." A little later the mood changed. "Give it 'em back," people cried harshly. "Let *them* have it too."[19] Churchill undertook to carry out their wishes.

SW6
Ranelagh Gardens, The Hurlingham Club

CHURCHILL'S FAVOURITE SPORT

The Hurlingham Club is an exclusive private club by the River Thames between Fulham and Kew, occupying forty-two acres of land around a Georgian mansion. It was once the headquarters of polo in the United Kingdom. A kind of hockey on horseback, polo was founded in Iran and reached Britain by way of India. The Club had a major polo ground from 1873 until the Second World War, when the grounds were compulsorily purchased for housing. The social and administrative headquarters of British polo then moved to Windsor, but the rules of the game are still those issued from the Hurlingham Club.

Winston Churchill was a passionate polo player from his teens until his late forties, including during his time as a young soldier in India. In the early years of the twentieth century, he spent many hours practising and playing polo at Hurlingham. He played his last match in 1927 at the age of fifty-two.

The political atmosphere of the Club was staunchly Conservative and when Churchill left the Conservatives to join the Liberals, he was blackballed – in effect expelled – from the Club. This was unprecedented, especially for a good polo player.

SW7
41 Cromwell Road

WARTIME HOME OF TWO BROTHERS

This end-of-terrace house on Cromwell Road faces the Natural History Museum, a two-minute walk from South Kensington underground station. The road was named after Richard Cromwell, son of Oliver, who is believed to have had a house here. Number 41 was Winston Churchill's London home for some of the First World War.

The house was already rented by Churchill's younger brother, Jack, when Winston Churchill moved in with Clementine and their children – at that time, two girls and a boy – in June 1915 after they had had to leave Admiralty House, the Whitehall residence that went with the job of First Lord of the Admiralty. The two families lived together amicably in the five-storey house, though Churchill was very depressed at the time. Dismissed as First Lord of the Admiralty with the unpopularity of the Gallipoli campaign, he had been given a sinecure and had no executive role in the management of the war. In his depression, Churchill took up painting. One of the first to give him guidance was the painter Sir John Lavery who, at the time, lived round the corner at 5 Cromwell Place, which is today adorned with a blue plaque. Both Lavery and his wife gave encouragement and indeed tuition to Churchill in his new venture. Lady Lavery was an Irish beauty; her image, based on a painting by her husband, appeared on Irish banknotes. The Laverys had good connections with Irish nationalists and introduced Churchill to Michael Collins, one of the leading IRA negotiators in the lead-up to the 1921 Anglo-Irish Treaty, which paved the way for Irish independence. Churchill and Collins got on very well. Both were men of action. Both, as Churchill observed, referring to his Boer War experience, had been soldiers and fugitives with a price on their heads.

While the family were at Cromwell Road, there were Zeppelin air raids on London. Churchill's six-year-old son Randolph found these fun. When the raids occurred at night, the children were wrapped up in blankets and taken down to the basement where grown-ups would be eating supper with glasses of champagne.

This was also the home from which Churchill set off for the Western Front, first with the Grenadier Guards and then as colonel of the Sixth Royal Scots Fusiliers. On the evening before he set off as colonel, Max Aitken, shortly to be Lord Beaverbrook, called on his friend. Churchill's secretary, Edward Marsh, was in tears and Churchill's mother, Lady Randolph, was in despair. Only Clementine Churchill seemed to be calm, collected and efficient.

Churchill left the Western Front the following year and hoped to get back into mainline politics. With gritted teeth, he and Clementine Churchill entertained the prime minister, H. H. Asquith – the man who had (they thought) humiliated Churchill – with an evening of bridge at Cromwell Road. The ingratiation failed, and it was not until several months after Lloyd George replaced Asquith in December 1916 that Churchill was invited back into government.

On 6 June 1916, Sir Ian Hamilton – a long-standing friend of Churchill and a general at Gallipoli – came here to discuss the evidence they were to submit to the Dardanelles Commission, which had been set up to investigate the unfortunate military campaign for which Churchill was largely held responsible. They suddenly heard a noise from the street and Kitchener's name being called out. Both men jumped up and went to the window, which Churchill threw open. Outside, Hamilton recalled, was a "newsvendor of solid and uncouth aspect. He had his bundle of newspapers under his arm and, as we opened the window, was crying out, 'Kitchener drowned! No survivors!'"[20] Lord Kitchener, the secretary of state for war, had been on a mission to Russia when his ship struck a mine in the Scapa Flow south of the Orkneys.

41 Cromwell Road today is one of a terrace that includes the French cultural institute and the French lycée. Most of the houses are vacant. Like many other streets in Kensington and Chelsea, Cromwell Road provides a good investment opportunity for those who have spare millions: number 41 was valued at £3.4 million in September 2018, its value having increased by £10,000 over the previous month alone. A shortage of housing in London means vacant properties increase in value; leaving them unoccupied also avoids the hassle and costs of tenants.

In spite of its illustrious former residents, the house has no plaque.

27 and 28 Hyde Park Gate

HIS FINAL DAYS

Hyde Park Gate is a prestigious address. Built in the early nineteenth century, this area is socially on the right (southern) side of Hyde Park and has been the home of the founder of the Boy Scout movement, Sir Robert Baden-Powell, the writer Virginia Woolf, the sculptor Jacob Epstein and one of Margaret Thatcher's chancellors of the exchequer, Nigel Lawson.

Above all, Hyde Park Gate was the last London home of Winston Churchill. The Churchills lost the 'flat above the shop' – 10 Downing Street – after Churchill's defeat in the 1945 general election. Their country house, Chartwell, had not been occupied by the family during the war and was not ready, and so they had had to stay with relations or at a hotel until they bought, for £24,000, number 28 in this secluded road.

The house was small for them, and in later years the Churchills bought the neighbouring house, number 27. They made a number of structural alterations, including the addition of a lift. In the last year or so of his life, Churchill aged rapidly. He took a bedroom downstairs in number 27, and the two properties were officially united.

For six years after 1945, Churchill was leader of the opposition – though this was more of an honorary role, as he spent months out of the country each year. His main preoccupation was, in fact, the writing of his war memoirs. Still, he often entertained Conservative Members of Parliament here. One, Henry Channon, MP for Southend-on-Sea and not always a fan, recalled being entertained in the dining room, which overlooked a small garden. Churchill talked about Southend and suddenly broke into "an old Southend music hall song of the eighties, singing two verses of it lustily".[21]

President de Gaulle called on him here in April 1960 when he was on a state visit to the country.

This was also where Churchill spent the most time in his last months. He retired from parliament in July 1964. On 28 July, the prime minister, Sir Alec Douglas-Home (who had been parliamentary private secretary to Neville Chamberlain at the time of the ill-fated Munich agreement), led a small delegation of MPs in an address of appreciation of the old man, who was then four months short of his ninetieth birthday. The delegation included the leader of the opposition Harold Wilson (whose father had canvassed for Churchill in Manchester in 1906), the leader of the Liberal Party Jo Grimond (son-in-law of Churchill's close friend, Lady Violet Bonham Carter), the Leader of the House Selwyn Lloyd, and two MPs who had supported or sparred with Churchill over the previous forty years: the Conservative Sir Thomas Moore and Labour's Emanuel Shinwell.

Over the next months, Churchill became increasingly frail. On his ninetieth birthday, 30 November, he was well enough to come to a window and greet well-wishers with a V-sign. His family had a celebratory dinner for him. He was just about aware of the occasion and beamed at his children and grand-children. Over the next few weeks, he spent hours sunk in silence, and on 15 January he suffered his eighth stroke and fell into a coma from which he never recovered. With a marmalade cat on his bed, he uttered a final sigh and expired on the morning of Sunday 24 January 1965 – seventy years to the day after the death of his father, Lord Randolph Churchill, at the age of forty-five.

The nation was awaiting the inevitable. The BBC changed programmes and played Beethoven's 'Fifth Symphony', with its four opening notes – da-da-da-daah – echoing V (for Victory) in Morse code: dot dot dot dash. Two days later, his body was moved to Westminster Hall for a lying-in-state.

Number 28 has a plaque noting that Churchill died here – actually it was next door in number 27.

SW15

Priory Lane, Roehampton, Templeton House

TEMPORARY HOME, THANKS TO RICH RELATIONS

Templeton House was built in 1786. It used to be a modest Georgian country house, but over the course of time extra wings were added. In 1905, it was bought by Winston Churchill's cousin, Ivor Guest, later the first Viscount Wimborne (Guest's mother was the sister of Churchill's father, Lord Randolph Churchill). Lord Wimborne was fabulously rich, his wealth coming from the biggest iron foundry in the world near Merthyr Tydfil in South Wales. The Churchill–Guest connection was a happy alliance of blood and money – the Churchills providing the blood and the Guests the money. The Guests followed Winston Churchill's political allegiances, originally being Conservatives and then switching to the Liberal Party for twenty years before returning to the Conservative Party from 1924.

In the months after the First World War, Churchill and his family left Lullenden in Surrey and lived at Templeton. The house had about twenty bedrooms and was in secluded grounds of thirty acres. It was not far from Richmond Park, which was suitable for horse riding. He painted a few pictures here, two of which are at Chartwell. They are both painted from the same spot at sunset. The grounds could be in the depths of the country. After the Guests sold the property in 1930, it was owned by the Froebel Institute. Today it is privately owned and can easily be missed. It is modestly called 118 Priory Lane and coyly hides behind tall brick walls. One of the reception rooms has been named after Winston Churchill.

SW17
Tooting Bec

A NARROW ESCAPE

The day before the 1945 general election, Churchill was canvassing in Tooting Bec. A young man threw a squib that all but exploded in his face. The father of the offender wrote a letter of apology, to which Churchill replied that if he had been injured or blinded there is no knowing how the crowd would have dealt with the young man.

W1
12 Bolton Street

FROM BACHELOR PAD TO MARITAL HOME

Bolton Street is a very smart address lying to the south of Piccadilly. Winston Churchill bought a house here in late 1905. Number 12 was split over four floors and was ample for an upwardly mobile young politician and his manservant; Churchill was shortly to be appointed to his first ministerial position as under-secretary of state for the colonies in the Liberal government of Sir Henry Campbell-Bannerman. The flat had facilities for entertaining guests but no garden. He also employed a couple, Mr and Mrs George Scrivings, to look after him. (Scrivings accompanied

Churchill on his African tour in 1907 but died in Khartoum. The widow received financial support from Churchill.)

The house in Bolton Street became the first marital home for Clementine and Winston Churchill. While they were on their honeymoon, his mother, Lady Randolph, did what she could to transform the house from a bachelor pad to a home for newly-weds. Like many of the upper class, Clementine and Winston Churchill had separate bedrooms; this practice continued for the rest of their fifty-seven years of married life. Nonetheless, they produced five children.

In October 1908, Charles Masterman, a journalist and radical Liberal MP, was a guest here. "Dinner talk did not flow from anyone but Winston, who poured out ideas in an undigested form," Masterman recalled.[22] Churchill had, in Masterman's words, "discovered the poor" and talked about the late Roman Empire, socialist writers and Napoleon.[23]

There is no plaque to commemorate Churchill's residence here, although there is one nearby for the eighteenth-century novelist Fanny Burney, who had lived next door at number 11.

Brook Street, Claridge's Hotel

A FAVOURITE LUXURIOUS REFUGE

Claridge's Hotel, where an overnight stay can put you back over £500, dates from the middle of the nineteenth century, when a Mr and Mrs Claridge took over a hotel and rapidly developed it into one of the smartest hotels in London. This status was confirmed when the Empress Eugénie, wife of Napoleon III, stayed here in 1860 and entertained Queen Victoria. The present building was erected at the end of the nineteenth century and has 203 rooms and 400 staff. The hotel is particularly popular with those Americans who can afford it.

Winston Churchill was fond of Claridge's and, in May 1932, arranged a dinner here to celebrate the twenty-first birthday of his son, Randolph. The theme was 'fathers and sons', and the guests were other distinguished men and their sons. These included the Marquess of Reading and his son; Lord Rothermere and his son Esmond Harmsworth; and Lord Hailsham and his son Quintin Hogg (father and son both became Lord Chancellors). One of Randolph Churchill's godfathers had been the Earl of Birkenhead, his father's closest friend. He had died in 1930, but his son, the second Earl, was present.

Three years later, when Churchill was campaigning against the government's policy of devolved authority in India, he hosted dinners here for sympathetic fellow parliamentary campaigners, such as Lord Rothermere and the Marquess of Salisbury from the House of Lords, and younger Members of Parliament, such as Alan Lennox-Boyd and Brendan Bracken.

After Churchill finally resigned as prime minister in 1955, he used Claridge's Hotel briefly as his London base, occupying a penthouse on the sixth floor. On one occasion, he was observed on the pavement outside waiting for a car, singing an old music hall song chirpily to the doorman.

I've been to the North Pole,
I've been to the South Pole,
The East Pole, the West Pole,
And every other kind of Pole,
The Barber Pole,
The greasy Pole,

And now I'm fairly up the Pole,
Since I got the sack
From the Hotel Metropole.[24]

48 Charles Street

CHURCHILL'S FIRST LONDON HOME

This was Winston Churchill's first home, although there is no plaque to celebrate it. The house was built in the middle of the eighteenth century in fashionable Mayfair. It was occupied by Churchill's parents before and after his birth. Diagonally opposite is the Footman pub – where, presumably, the below-stairs staff slipped out from the grand mansions for refreshment.

Down Street

AN UNDERGROUND BASE FOR THE WARTIME GOVERNMENT

Just off Piccadilly, on Down Street, is a red, glazed, terracotta façade that is the site of a disused underground station. It was opened in 1907 on the Piccadilly Line, but its proximity to Dover Street tube station, now Green Park, meant that it was not used a great deal, and it was closed in 1932.

At the beginning of the Second World War, the station was converted into an underground bunker and living quarters for the Churchills. One hundred feet below the ground, it was transformed into emergency offices for government operations during the Blitz. Winston Churchill used it occasionally – Clementine Churchill even hung up some pictures in the sitting room to give it a more personal appearance – but he did not really like it. He spent some nights here, but often returned to the Annexe at Storey's Gate before dawn.

Today it is maintained by the London Transport Museum, and it is possible to tour the bunker – though at great expense.

35A Great Cumberland Place

HOME OF HIS NEWLY WIDOWED MOTHER

This was the home of Winston Churchill's mother, Lady Randolph, in the first years after her (first) husband died. It stretched her financial resources to the limit.

46 Grosvenor Square

ANOTHER FAMILY HOME IN LONDON

Number 46 now seems to have been swallowed up by its neighbours, but this lofty Mayfair house was once the home of Winston Churchill's widowed grandmother, the Duchess of Marlborough. Churchill stayed here as a boy and friends of his parents looked after him. One, Sir George Wombwell, who had been present at the Charge of the Light Brigade during the Crimean War in the 1850s, used to take him to the music hall at Drury Lane, kindling a love of music hall songs that lasted for the rest of his life. In 1892, when financially hard pressed – as they often were – Churchill's parents doubled up with the dowager duchess. There was friction between the duchess and her fun-loving American daughter-in-law. Churchill also came to stay here when he was a cadet at Sandhurst.

There is no plaque to commemorate the Churchill/Marlborough association.

75 Grosvenor Street

CLEMENTINE CHURCHILL'S BIRTHPLACE

Clementine Hozier was born here on 1 April 1885 to Lady Blanche Hozier, the wife of Captain Henry Hozier – though whether he was the father is the subject of debate. Twenty-three years later, Clementine became the wife of Winston Churchill.

Hyde Park Corner

AN EARLY MOTORIST

Winston Churchill was always interested in the latest technology. He was keen to learn to fly, he recognised and encouraged the development of the tank, and he was eager to understand the technological advances of the Second World War.

Churchill was also an early motorist, and he bought his first car in 1901, selling some shares to make the purchase. He told James Stuart, Conservative chief whip during the Second World War, that he never took any driving lessons but simply worked it out for himself. While driving his first car, he was involved with a horse-bus at Hyde Park Corner – or, as he put it, had "a little trouble with a bus, resulting in some damage".[25]

105 Mount Street

HIS FIRST INDEPENDENT HOME

The family of the Dukes of Marlborough owned sections of Mayfair; Mount Street, however, was not one of the area's smartest streets. In the early nineteenth century, there was a workhouse on the south side. This would have lowered the tone.

From east to west, the road ran to Park Lane and Hyde Park. Its buildings were largely reconstructed in the last twenty years of the nineteenth century, but it was still a mixed residential and commercial area. There were shops and offices as well as flats in 1900 when Winston Churchill, then hoping to be elected a Member of Parliament for Oldham, was in search of a London home. His cousin, the ninth Duke of Marlborough, arranged for him to take over a lease at number 105. This was part of a block of flats with shops facing the pavement. It had been designed in what was known as a French Flamboyant style in red brick and terracotta. Churchill's mother helped him furnish the flat, though he was modest in his requirements. "So long as my table is clear, he said, and there is plenty of paper, I do not worry about the rest."[26] Modest he might claim to be, but he still had a uniformed servant who doubled as a chauffeur. Churchill moved in in September 1900 and became an MP in October. It was his home until the end of 1905, when he looked for larger premises.

There is no plaque to commemorate Churchill's residence here. However, since the 1970s, a cigar shop has rather appropriately occupied the ground floor. The owners have a small display of photographs and commemorative mugs related to Winston Churchill.

New Bond Street

WINSTON CHURCHILL AND FRANKLIN D. ROOSEVELT

On the pavement of New Bond Street is the Allies sculpture, life-sized statues of Winston Churchill and President Franklin D. Roosevelt sitting on a bench in amiable discussion. It was commissioned by the Bond Street Association – made up of the traders and businesses of the street – in 1995 to mark fifty years of peace since the Second World War, and presented to Westminster City Council. The sculptor was Lawrence Holofcener, who had dual US/UK nationality, and the seat was unveiled by Princess Margaret.

The sculpture lies in the heart of the Mayfair shopping area and is engagingly accessible. People like to take photos and selfies of themselves sitting between the two war leaders, or even sitting on the lap of one of them.

FDR was eight years younger than Churchill. They had first met in the summer of 1918, after the United States had entered the war. Roosevelt was assistant secretary of the navy and visited London on an extended tour of Europe. At the beginning of the Second World War, Roosevelt was deeply sympathetic to Churchill's pleas for US support but was politically constrained. Aid, known as Lend-Lease, was generously extended to the UK, but it was only after the Japanese raid on Pearl Harbor and Hitler's declaration of war on the United States that the country became one of the Allies wholeheartedly. Churchill paid several visits to the United States during the war and a warm friendship blossomed, cut short by Roosevelt's death in April 1945.

45 Park Lane

THE SASSOON LONDON HOME

The luxury hotel 45 Park Lane is actually on the site of 25 Park Lane, which was the London residence of Sir Philip Sassoon, the fabulously wealthy Conservative MP, between 1912 and his death in 1939. Sassoon never achieved the glittering prizes of the highest of political offices, but he was a minister for much of the 1920s and 1930s and was at the centre of political and social London. He was a generous host, and many were those who enjoyed his hospitality and friendship. Whenever there was a morning cabinet meeting, ministers adjourned to Sassoon's house for a "cabinet lunch".[27] One frequent guest was the Prince of Wales, the future King Edward VIII.

Sassoon was also a good friend of Winston Churchill, who often came here. Indeed, Churchill stayed here in early 1925 before he moved into 11 Downing Street on his appointment as chancellor of the exchequer; he reportedly enjoyed riding a mechanical horse simulator that was installed in the bathroom.

Two years earlier, Churchill was a guest at a party here, along with the former prime minister H. H. Asquith and the man who had displaced him, Lloyd George. Churchill wrote to his wife about seeing Asquith who was "heavily loaded".[28] Lloyd George "accompanied him up the stairs and was chivalrous enough to cede him the banister".[29]

Sassoon's house was originally built for Barney Barnato, the diamond magnate. Sassoon redesigned it, filling it with some of his collection of paintings – by Reynolds, Gainsborough and Zoffany – and Flemish tapestries. The ballroom was big enough for four hundred dancers.

After Sassoon's death the house was demolished and rebuilt.

Before it became a hotel, it was the home of one of Hugh Hefner's Playboy Clubs.

Piccadilly, Royal Academy of Arts

CHURCHILL AS A RECOGNISED PAINTER

The Royal Academy was founded in 1768 by King George III and had the objective of encouraging the arts and raising the status of artists. Its first president was Sir Joshua Reynolds, who introduced the practice of regular public lectures. Since the nineteenth century, it has been based at Burlington House on the north side of Piccadilly. To be elected a Royal Academician and to put the letters 'RA' after one's name is perhaps the highest social and professional honour for the aspiring artist.

Winston Churchill had an association with the academy for over fifty years. He first attended an annual banquet in 1908 and first gave a speech at one in 1912. In 1913, the prime minister, H. H. Asquith, was the main speaker. Asquith spoke on art and Churchill on naval policy: he was then the First Lord of the Admiralty. After the First World War, Churchill was invited back several times. By now he was a painter himself. In his banquet speech of 1927, he spoke with feeling about paintings being the fruit of "hours of pleasure, hours of intense creative enjoyment, bottled sunshine, captured inspiration, personal delight".[30]

Churchill got to know Sir Alfred Munnings, president of the Royal Academy, who restored the annual exhibitions and banquets after the Second World War. In 1947, Munnings persuaded Churchill to submit, anonymously, two paintings to be considered for exhibition. He did so, under the assumed name of David Winter. They were both accepted by an independent panel for display. The following year, Churchill was elected an Honorary Academician Extraordinary, a designation devised just for him.

Munnings was celebrated for his paintings of horses and hunting scenes. He deplored modern trends in art and hated Picasso. At his farewell address as president in 1949, broadcast live, he gave a drunken tirade against modern art, denouncing Cézanne and Matisse by name. He claimed Churchill agreed with him, saying that he and Churchill were walking in the street and Churchill said, "If we met Picasso or Matisse we'd give them a running kick, wouldn't we?"[31]

When he heard this, Churchill was upset. He admired Matisse, and was always tolerant of different art forms, even if they did not conform to his own. He had deplored the Nazis' burning of what they saw as decadent or degenerate art. "I was angry," he told the director of the Tate Gallery, Sir John Rothenstein on a visit to Chartwell. "I wrote to Sir Alfred. All quite untrue, and besides, I never walk in the street."[32]

In his retirement after 1955, Churchill often attended the annual banquets. In May 1956, he was cheered by people in the courtyard as he arrived. One of the other guests at the banquet, Sir Harold Nicolson, observed that Churchill looked very old. He cannot have been pleased with a portrait of him by Ruskin Spear that, in Nicolson's words, "makes him look like a village dotard from the Auvergne".[33]

One of Churchill's last public appearances was at the Royal Academy banquet of 1962, two and a half years before his death, when he was nearly eighty-eight.

52 Portland Place

WHERE WINSTON MET CLEMMIE

In March 1908, Winston Churchill and Clementine Hozier were reluctant guests at a dinner party hosted by a great aunt of Clementine, Lady St Helier. They had met four years earlier at a ball at Crewe House. Churchill, never described as a lady's man, was gauche, vain and awkward on that occasion. In 1908, Lady St Helier had wanted to make up the number of dinner guests to fourteen. Churchill had to be persuaded to go by his secretary, Eddie Marsh. Even then, he arrived late. The company (which included F. E. Smith, the First Lord of the Admiralty Lord Tweedmouth and the colonial proconsul Sir Frederick Lugard) had already sat down to dinner. Churchill sat between Lady Lugard and Clementine, and he devoted all his attention to the latter. So, it was love at second sight. When the gentlemen joined the ladies after dinner, Churchill – who usually lingered over port and cigars – was first into the drawing room and made a beeline for Clementine.

The young couple met regularly over the next few months, became engaged in August and married in September.

W2

2 Connaught Place

LORD RANDOLPH'S LAST HOME

Connaught Square and Connaught Place were early nineteenth-century developments. The houses of Connaught Place are multi-storeyed and architecturally undistinguished. Although they raised the social tone of the area north and west of Marble Arch and the Edgware Road, in terms of fashion – measured by physical access to the royal palaces and the Houses of Parliament – they were on the wrong side of Hyde Park. Winston Churchill's parents, Lord and Lady Randolph Churchill, took the end-of-terrace house for the last ten years of Lord Randolph's life. It was a London home for Churchill during holidays from boarding schools at Ascot and Harrow, though sometimes he spent time with his nanny's family on the Isle of Wight. Occasionally, Lord and Lady Randolph Churchill leased the house to others and stayed with his mother in Grosvenor Square.

The actual house is not numbered, but there is a plaque round the corner to mark the Churchill association.

Paddington Station

A WARM WELCOME AFTER TWO MONTHS AWAY

The station was the main terminus for the old Great Western Railway, which connected the capital with the west of England and south Wales. When it was first built in the 1830s, designed by Isambard Kingdom Brunel with the architect M. D. Wyatt, it was seen as an amazing engineering feat – with a triple roof of wrought iron and glass, supported on cast-iron pillars.

In January 1944, Winston Churchill had been away from Britain for over two months. He had been in Cairo and Tunisia and had met with Stalin and Franklin D. Roosevelt at Tehran. He had become seriously ill with pneumonia in Tunisia – so ill that Clementine Churchill had flown out. He recovered, sailed back to Plymouth and returned by train to London. Management of the war seems to have been suspended, as the whole of the cabinet along with the service chiefs came to Paddington station to greet the prime minister on his return.

2 Sussex Square

A LONDON FAMILY HOME

By the end of the First World War, Winston Churchill had overstretched himself in his house purchases. He had bought Lullenden during the war, but his London accommodation was unsettled. While he was First Lord of the Admiralty, he had had the use of Admiralty House. After that, he and his family camped out at houses belonging to his Guest cousins, including Templeton House, and they even shared a house with his brother Jack and his family in Cromwell Road. Then, in 1919, Churchill bought an early Victorian town house on the east side of Sussex Square. It was on the unfashionable side of Hyde Park, but it was just round the corner from the home of his mother in Westbourne Street. He also took over two mews flats, one of which was converted to a library and studio.

Churchill always liked to adapt his houses to his requirements. With the house at Sussex Square, to bring his ideas to life he employed the company Bovis, owned by Samuel Joseph (father of Margaret Thatcher's influential minister, Sir Keith). But there was a dispute about payment. Churchill never engaged Bovis again, though personal relations with Samuel Joseph – later a baronet and Lord Mayor of London – were undamaged.

2 Sussex Square became Churchill's London home for ten years during the 1920s. His daughter Mary was born here, and it was very much a family home. In contrast to his father, Churchill was an affectionate, "hands on" dad. He used to read stories to his children when they went to bed. He particularly enjoyed those by Rudyard Kipling (cousin of Stanley Baldwin) and *Treasure Island* by Robert Louis Stevenson. Churchill was sometimes so enthusiastic a reader that he would delay his

children's sleeping time by an hour and be himself late for a dinner party.

The house was irreparably damaged by enemy action in March 1941. It is the only one of Churchill's homes that so suffered. A plaque on the post-war brick replacement records Churchill's occupancy.

8 Westbourne Street

THE LAST YEARS OF CHURCHILL'S MOTHER

Winston Churchill's mother, Lady Randolph Churchill, lived at this house, though it has no plaque to record her time here. Her last decades were sad. Lord Randolph had died in 1895. She remarried twice, both times to men a generation younger than she was. The first was George Cornwallis-West. Lady Randolph Churchill wrote a play, and the principal actress in it was Mrs Patrick Campbell. Cornwallis-West fell in love with her, ran off and the marriage was dissolved. Lady Randolph later married another man, Montagu Porch, an exact contemporary of her son Winston. He was a colonial civil servant from Somerset. This marriage lasted for the rest of Lady Randolph's life. After the divorce from Cornwallis-West, she had reverted to the name Lady Randolph Churchill. It sounded better than Mrs Montagu Porch. It was as if she were living in the past, in those glorious days of late Victorian England when she was the lover of the Prince of Wales and seen as the dashing, witty, beautiful and talented star of English fashionable society. Over the course of her life, her successive residences told a story. They moved steadily away from the West End and Mayfair until she ended up here, on the unfashionable side of Hyde Park.

Churchill himself took a house round the corner in Sussex Square, and his mother lived her later life through her devoted son. It was at this home that Lady Randolph died in 1921, aged only sixty-seven, after a haemorrhage following a tumble down the stairs at Mells in Somerset.

W8

5 Lexham Gardens

CRAMMING FOR SANDHURST

This house was the home of one of the most celebrated 'crammers' of the 1890s, Captain Walter H. James, formerly of the Royal Engineers and known as 'Jimmy'. After he left Harrow, Winston Churchill failed at his first attempts to get into Sandhurst. Crammers were private tutors hired to train young men to pass the required exams. So, in the first months of 1893, Churchill was enrolled at this establishment. He was not a model student. He was seen as casual and easily distracted, "too inclined up to the present to teach his instructors instead of endeavouring to learn from them".[34] However, Churchill did well and, at his third attempt, obtained a place at Sandhurst.

Marmaduke Pickthall, a contemporary of Churchill at Harrow, describes life at a West Kensington crammer in his first novel, *All Fools*, published in 1900.

Number 5 Lexham Gardens is today occupied by the Embassy of Bosnia Herzegovina.

WC2
The Strand, The Savoy Hotel

CHURCHILL AND THE OTHER CLUB

When it opened in 1889, the Savoy Hotel was the last word in elegance and luxury. It had electric lights, lifts and nearly as many bathrooms as bedrooms. It was built by the owner of the adjacent Savoy Theatre, which used to specialise in the operas of Gilbert and Sullivan. Winston Churchill was a frequent patron.

In 1911, Churchill was Liberal home secretary. Although partisan in his politics, his friendships extended far beyond the Liberal Party. The High Church Tory Lord Hugh Cecil had been his best man three years earlier, and F. E. Smith, a Conservative firebrand, became his closest friend. But London gentlemen's political clubs tended to be allied either – like the Carlton – to the Conservatives, or – like the Reform Club and the National Liberal Club – to the Liberals. Churchill and Smith were keen for a venue where they could drink and socialise with men across the political divide.

There was, in fact, already a club that aimed to do just that: it was simply called The Club. The Club could trace its history back to the eighteenth century. Churchill and Smith decided to call their new venture The Other Club. The chancellor of the exchequer, Lloyd George – a few years older than Smith and Churchill, and politically senior – shared in the objectives.

The year 1911 was a particular acrimonious time for frontline politics. In 1909, Lloyd George had introduced a contentious budget that attacked the financial security of the landed classes – just those classes that had dominated British politics for the previous four hundred years. The budget's rejection by the House of Lords led to the Parliament Bill, the aim of which was to limit the power of the House of Lords to reject legislation passed by the lower House of Commons. In 1910, there had been two general elections. The massive Liberal majority was cut, and the Liberal government depended on the Irish Nationalists, who demanded an Irish Home Rule Bill as their price for support. Beyond parliamentary politics, the country encountered an increasingly militant suffragette movement, as well as industrial unrest.

Membership of The Other Club was to be restricted to fifty, with twelve Liberal and twelve Conservative MPs eligible for election. The balance was made up of some members of the House of Lords and other interesting chaps. One of the rules was that nothing "shall interfere with the rancour or asperity of party politics".[35]

The first dinner was held on 18 May 1911 at the Savoy Hotel in the Pinafore Room, which was named after the Gilbert and Sullivan opera *H.M.S. Pinafore*. There was an appropriateness about this, for one of the opera's principal characters, Sir Joseph Porter K.C.B., was believed to be based on W. H. Smith, who was First Lord of the Admiralty in 1877. Churchill was to hold that post twice and was a huge fan of Gilbert and Sullivan. (The then prime minister Asquith's musical tastes also did not extend much beyond Gilbert and Sullivan.)

Club dinners were usually held in the Pinafore Room, and members sat at a long table, with Churchill in the middle of the south side. He was very fond of oysters and Irish stew with plenty of small onions. He also liked Roquefort cheese and ended his meal with a peeled pear. All was accompanied by lashings of champagne and brandy.

Annual membership of The Other Club in 1911 was £5, and the dinner cost one guinea (£1.1.0d or £1.05). (To get an idea of today's value of this, one has to multiply the sum by nearly one hundred.)

The club took a while to get going, but it has continued to the present day. It became the main focus for Churchill's socialising. Members were effectively selected or approved by him. They included his loyal friends Professor Lindemann and Brendan Bracken, and many of his close political and wartime colleagues, such as Harold Macmillan and Hastings Ismay. Some, such as Anthony Eden, declined to join – he did not care for dinner clubs. One of his Second World War military heroes, Alan-brooke, was not a member, and Montgomery was only invited to join nine years after the end of the war. The original bipartisan composition of the club was eroded with the replacement of the Liberal Party by the Labour Party. The pool from which Labour politicians were drawn was far less socially advantaged, and few of the more patrician Labour MPs were keen to socialise with their political opponents. Attlee was not a member. In fact, in the late 1940s, when the Labour Party was in power, there were no Labour members. This was remedied in Churchill's last years with the election of Hartley Shawcross and Roy Jenkins (author of one of the best biographies of Churchill), Gerald – later Lord – Gardiner (who became a Labour Lord Chancellor) and the Earl of Longford.

The main common quality of membership was apparent 'clubbability' – and being acceptable to Winston Churchill. It included people who had crossed swords with him with "rancour and asperity".[36] John Seely, later Lord Mottistone, had been a vigorous defender of appeasement. Earl Winterton, a Conservative MP from 1904 to 1951, had frequently clashed with Churchill, including during the Second World War. David Margesson had been Neville Chamberlain's chief whip and had conspired to damage Churchill's political career in the late 1930s. Prudes, the self-righteous and the self-important were not welcome. Exclusively male, predominantly upper-class, the only member of the royal family who belonged was Earl Mountbatten. On one occasion, he turned up late saying he had been at a most important meeting of the Chiefs of Staff. He then left early, saying he was off to an important NATO meeting. As he was leaving, Churchill was heard saying mischievously, "Ought I to know him?"[37]

Churchill was a loyal member of The Other Club for the rest of his life, attending over three hundred dinners in the fifty years and outliving all the other founder members. The Club was a safety valve for his intense political life, and it gave him the chance to get to know colleagues and opponents personally.

On 30 September 1938, Churchill was at The Other Club with Robert Boothby, Lloyd George and others, including members of the Chamberlain government. It was the day Neville Chamberlain was seeing Hitler at Munich. Feelings were tense. The editor of the *Observer*, J. L. Garvin, took offence at something Boothby said and walked out. Duff Cooper, then First Lord of the Admiralty, slipped out to buy the last edition of the evening papers and read the details to the members. He kept his cool, but inwardly was full of anger and disgust. The following day, he was to resign from the government. Churchill left with Richard Law, a son of the former Conservative prime minister, Bonar Law, and they passed a restaurant full of people laughing merrily. "Those poor people!" observed Churchill. "They little know what they will have to face."[38]

Ten years later, the Conservative Party gave a dinner in honour of Churchill at the Savoy Hotel. In spite of his wartime leadership and the fact that he had been leader of the party for eight years, Churchill was still distrusted by many Conservatives who had been loyal to Chamberlain over Munich. One Conservative MP who was present, the diarist Henry 'Chips' Channon, observed that Churchill's "uninspired criticism of Munich and his pro-Zionism did not go down well with all the party".[39]

Churchill attended meetings of the Club throughout his eighties. His last appearance was in December 1964, a month before he died. He was accompanied by Sir William Deakin and was not quite with it but, as one who attended the dinner recalled, "all that could be said was that he knew where he was and was happy to be there."[40]

In the year after Churchill's death, Lord Moran – his doctor and a member of The Other Club for only four years – published his diaries. Many members considered Moran's intimate descriptions of Churchill's frailty in his old age a betrayal of trust, and they asked Moran to resign. He refused but did, in time, withdraw from meetings. Only Lord Longford had been ready to sit next to him.

The Savoy has been, along with Claridge's, a favourite central London watering-hole for Americans – especially film stars. On the steps up to the American bar is a gallery of signed portraits of Gary Cooper, Humphrey Bogart and others – and also a photograph of Churchill at the hotel. The Pinafore Room is on the ground floor and is used for private events. It is adorned with a bust of Winston Churchill, with cigar and V-sign, sculpted by Jon Douglas. The reproduction of a painting of Churchill is also on the wall.

3

HOME COUNTIES

BERKSHIRE, BUCKINGHAMSHIRE, HERTFORDSHIRE, KENT, MIDDLESEX, SURREY AND SUSSEX

Winston Churchill was a man from the southeast of England. He chose his homes outside London in the counties south of London. Other parts of the country were useful – as constituencies whose people could vote him into parliament, or places where he could relax and paint, or halls where he could give speeches.

The home counties – which, here, includes the counties of Berkshire, Buckinghamshire, Hertfordshire, Kent, Middlesex, Surrey and Sussex – were his political base; the people there gave him their support, especially in the last forty years of his life. Though many would include Essex in the home counties, it is included in this book in East Anglia as part of Central Britain.

And for Churchill, southeast England was the frontline of Britain's defence in the world wars. In the Second World War, fears of invasion made him focus on redressing the vulnerability of the Kent and Sussex coastline.

Berkshire
Ascot, St George's School

VICTIM OF A SADIST

Tucked away in woodlands to the south of the famous race-course is a tall Victorian building which, in the 1880s, housed a school for small boys. Winston Churchill was a pupil here from November 1882, just before his eighth birthday, until the summer of 1884.

The fashionable school was run by the Reverend Herbert Sneyd-Kynnersley, a sadistic bully who delighted in flogging the bare bottoms of small boys. The seclusion of the school probably concealed the boys' cries from neighbours.

The young Winston Churchill was thrashed for helping himself to sugar from the pantry. Far from being penitent, he took the headmaster's hat and kicked it to pieces. He was also seen as lowering the social tone of the school by repeating expressions and raucous songs he had learned from stable boys, that were not considered appropriate for young gentlemen.

It is probable that his nanny, Mrs Everest, saw the marks of the beatings and persuaded his parents to withdraw him from St George's. He was transferred to a more benign establishment, run by the Misses Thomson, at Brighton.

Sneyd-Kynnersley died in his late thirties, two years after Churchill left. In 1904, the establishment became a girls' finishing school. Today it is an independent girls' boarding school.

Sandhurst, The Royal Military Academy

FROM ADOLESCENCE TO RESPONSIBLE ADULTHOOD

The Royal Military Academy Sandhurst is the training base for British army officers. It occupies a magnificent site, in superbly landscaped gardens, between the small towns of Sandhurst in Berkshire and Camberley in Surrey. The academy is a working institution and not open to the public except by arrangement through the Sandhurst Trust. It is not even visible from nearby public roads any more.

In 1893, Sandhurst played a most important role in the development of the young Winston Churchill.

At his school in Harrow, Churchill wanted a career in the army and was in the Army Class. Entry into Sandhurst was for young men aged eighteen to twenty by competitive examination, and Churchill was only admitted on his third attempt. Like two-thirds of the entrants at the time, he had been trained to pass the exams by well-known crammers, such as Captain Walter H. James of Earl's Court, London. Churchill took exams in five subjects. Three were compulsory – Latin, mathematics and English – and he opted for French and chemistry.

Encouraged by his father, Churchill aspired to become an infantry cadet, but this required a higher grade in the exams and his performance fell short of the mark. However, because some cadets dropped out before the course started, Churchill entered Sandhurst as an infantry cadet in September 1893. This was a relief for his father. The costs of a cavalry cadet would have been much higher, and his parents' lifestyle was causing a cash flow problem at the time.

Churchill's father, Lord Randolph Churchill, had a low opinion of his son. Rather than congratulating him on passing the entrance exam, he wrote Churchill a witheringly scornful letter denouncing his son's "slovenly, happy-go-lucky harum-scarum style. Never have I received a good report from any master or tutor".[1] If there is no improvement, he went on, "you will become a mere social wastrel, one of the hundreds of the public school failures".[2]

The Sandhurst training consisted of three terms over sixteen months. In the first term, Churchill shared a room with two other cadets, their private quarters separated by a screen, "like stalls in a stable", as Churchill put it.[3] Conditions at first were spartan – no curtains, no carpets, no decoration, no hot water. But there was access to a billiard room, an anteroom with all the newspapers and "a capital library".[4] A dull uniform was worn for classes, but full dress – uniforms of scarlet and gold – was required for dinner each evening. Was this the start of his fascination with ostentatious uniforms?

He seems to have been happy from the start. "I shall like my life here," he wrote to his father within days of his arrival.[5] The 120 fresh cadets were divided into six companies, each under the supervision of a commander officer. In Churchill's case this was a Major Ball, a man described by Churchill as a "very strict and peppery martinet. Formal, reserved, frigidly courteous, punctilious, impeccable, severe, he was held in the greatest awe".[6] Because of the years of comparative Victorian peace, Major Ball had never actually seen any active service. This was not the case with the commandant of the college, General Cecil James East, who had been an officer in the Crimean War nearly forty years earlier.

Sandhurst provided a stable environment for Churchill. Over the three terms, his academic performance improved. Even his unpunctuality – regularly noted in his reports for the first year – was no longer a subject of reproof by the time he left. And his father was ready to concede that "Sandhurst has done wonders for him".[7] He read the textbooks with voracious enthusiasm and was particularly strong in tactics and military law.

In the 1890s, the Royal Military College consisted largely of the iconic white buildings of what is now called the Old College, with a grand columned façade overlooking the parade ground. It was designed by John Sanders, incorporating James Wyatt's original designs, and completed in 1812. The building would then have been visible from the London Road. Trees and bushes now screen the place from the road. It was different in 1894, but the lakes, formerly mill-ponds, linked by the Wish Stream which was (and is) the county boundary, were there. The grounds were dotted with small forts and ramparts used by the cadets for field exercises. Sandhurst in Berkshire was once a rural village, and Camberley and York Town in Surrey new settlements that grew up with the academy. These places serviced the academy providing supplies, servants, artisans and diversions for the cadets – from horses to whores.

During his second term, in April 1894, Churchill lost a valuable watch in the Wish Stream. It had been a present from his father. Lord Randolph Churchill was furious at what he considered to be his son's casual carelessness. Churchill, however, recovered the watch. He explained that the stream was very deep in places and, as luck would have it, that is where it dropped. But Churchill, showing early resourcefulness and an ability to mobilise people, arranged for the stream to be dredged and diverted until he found it. It is no longer possible to identify the location of this mishap. The course of the stream has been changed, and the deep water may have been landscaped into one of the lakes.

Lord Randolph Churchill's intemperate reaction to his son's

failings may be partly attributed to his degenerative illness. In his final term, Churchill was aware of the gravity of his father's condition. In late 1894, both parents set off on a world tour in the hope of a recovery. Churchill saw them before they left. In spite of these family concerns, he did well in his final term and finished twentieth out of a class of 130 – on entry he had been ninety-second out of a batch of 102.

Churchill left the Royal Military College in December 1894, just after his twentieth birthday. He saw his father on his parents' return from the world tour, "a swiftly-fading shadow".[8] Lord Randolph died on 24 January 1895. Churchill was conscious that he was now head of the family, with responsibilities for his mother and fourteen-year-old brother, Jack. But Sandhurst had matured him; he entered as a boy and passed out as a man.

Buckinghamshire
Bletchley, Bletchley Park

BRITAIN'S SECRET WEAPON

For thirty years after the Second World War, lips were sealed about what went on at Bletchley Park. People who worked there had signed the Official Secrets Act and that was that. But the undistinguished Victorian, mock Tudor, neo-Gothic mansion was the headquarters of the Government Code and Cypher School. Here a group of bright young (mostly) men and women succeeded in deciphering German codes, giving British strategists an extraordinary insight into German intentions. Bletchley Park produced daily decrypts, as they were called, and these were delivered in a battered old despatch box by Stewart Menzies – the head of MI6, responsible for overseas intelligence – to Winston

Churchill. This extraordinary advantage was probably the reason Britain was ultimately able to win the war.

Churchill took a great interest in Bletchley Park. In September 1941, he paid a visit to the school to praise and encourage staff. But it was only several years after Churchill's death that the general public became aware of the work carried out there. Accordingly, there is no mention of it in Churchill's war memoirs.

Today, Bletchley Park, with its main house and huts where people worked scattered around the park, is managed by the Bletchley Park Trust, and a quarter of a million people visit each year. One of the sights is a statue of the heroic Alan Turing, a leading cryptanalyst and pioneer of artificial intelligence who was hounded in 1952 as a homosexual, stripped of his security clearance and died by suicide in 1954. He received a royal pardon sixty years after his death.

Ellesborough, Chequers

THE PRIME MINISTER'S COUNTRY RETREAT

Chequers, or Chequers Court, has been the prime minister's country house since 1921. It lies forty-one miles northwest of Downing Street in the parish of Ellesborough in the Chiltern Hills. It was constructed in the sixteenth century and heavily restored in the nineteenth. In the early twentieth century, the house belonged to Lord Lee of Fareham and his wealthy American wife. They had no children and reflected that prime ministers were no longer from a wealthy landed class, with a tranquil estate to which they could retreat or where they could entertain foreign statesmen. They therefore arranged for the house to be given to the nation. The first prime minister to make use of it was David

Lloyd George. Since then, it has seen hundreds of distinguished visitors – from the Soviet foreign minister V. M. Molotov to Eleanor Roosevelt. The house is silent and deserted during the week, but it comes to intensive life at weekends when the prime minister is in residence.

Winston Churchill first visited Chequers in 1921 as a guest of the prime minister Lloyd George, but during his own wartime premiership he came here most weekends that he was in the country. Between 1940 and 1942, when Britain suffered targeted air raids and the threat of invasion, Chequers was seen as exposed and vulnerable. (On weekends when there was a full moon, Churchill, his family and guests went to Ditchley Park in Oxfordshire, the home of Ronald Tree and his American wife. Tree was a Conservative MP who had supported Churchill during the 1930s.)

It was hard to get domestic staff during the war, and Chequers was run by Miss Grace Lamont and members of the Army Training School and the Women's Auxiliary Air Force. It became a cherished weekend bolthole for Churchill and his family. His first grandson, Winston, the son of Pamela and Randolph, was born here. Grandson Winston was christened at Chequers on his grandfather's sixty-sixth birthday: 30 November 1940.

That Christmas, his daughter Sarah and her husband, the entertainer Vic Oliver, were among the guests. Oliver played Viennese waltzes and his wife sang. Churchill joined in the singsong, though he was not always in tune. He relaxed and danced on his own.

Churchill's taste in music was not very sophisticated. He loved music hall songs and military brass bands. His secretary, John Colville, observed disdainfully that he enjoyed the most vulgar kind of brass band songs. However, Churchill appreciated the significance of music, and he thought that recruiting drives for the army should be accompanied by "plenty of marching with bands through towns and industrial districts".[9] One evening at Chequers in 1941, Churchill was in a foul mood. Vic Oliver was a guest. At Clementine Churchill's suggestion, Oliver played a Beethoven piano sonata, hoping it would soothe her husband. But Churchill snapped at Oliver and told him to stop playing what he (Churchill) thought was a Handel march. There was no point in arguing.

In January 1941, Churchill arranged a party for Harry Hopkins, the personal envoy of President Roosevelt, before his return to the United States. For Churchill, the visit had been a success. After dinner, Hopkins brought in a box of gramophone records and many sentimental American tunes were played. Churchill was relaxed, and he danced in his self-centred way. He was very sentimental about the United States. He would quote lines of the nineteenth-century poet Arthur Hugh Clough, ending: "But westward, look, the land is bright."

Two months later, another presidential envoy came to Chequers: Averell Harriman. He was alleged – among others – to have had an affair with Randolph Churchill's wife, Pamela. A quarter of a century after the war, she was to marry Harriman as her third husband. Even later, under President Bill Clinton, she became the United States ambassador to France.

Churchill imposed his idiosyncratic lifestyle on his visitors. He had a daily bath and sometimes, after his afternoon sleep, a second one. He was very proud of his ability to lie in the bath and switch the taps on and off with his toes. After dinner in the evening and extended discussions of political or strategic issues over port and brandy, Churchill and his guests would go to the Long Gallery to watch a film, finally getting to bed between two and three in the morning. Anthony Eden, Churchill's foreign secretary during the war and his final administration (1951–1955), disliked these late hours and tried to avoid invitations to Chequers.

Other relaxations included croquet on the north lawn, when Churchill was not using it for rifle practice. In the winter of 1941, there was heavy snow and guests had fun tobogganing on nearby Beacon Hill. People were also brought in to entertain guests. The pianist Moiseiwitsch came on one occasion, and Noël Coward would also tickle the ivories and lead a singsong. Churchill's favourite Coward number was the newly composed 'Don't let's be beastly to the Germans'.

The house inherited a fine collection of paintings. One was a Rubens, *The Lion and the Mouse*, based on an Aesop fable. A huge canvas, it used to hang on the east wall of the Great Hall. Rumour has it that Churchill thought the mouse was too small for its significance in the story. He called for his paints and a step ladder, climbed up and painted on the canvas in order to make the mouse more prominent. In 1973, the painting was temporarily removed to be cleaned. It was brought back to Chequers minus Churchill's vandalism and now hangs in the Great Parlour, at a level where the mouse can be clearly seen.

When Churchill was at Chequers, the house and grounds were always full of people. Three secretaries would take turns to be on duty day and night, 24/7. In addition to the domestic staff and the gardeners, one or two private detectives or bodyguards, a valet, a film operator, an electrical engineer, three chauffeurs and a posse of London policemen would come to support and service the family and guests. When there was a threat of invasion, Coldstream Guards stayed in Nissen huts by the Lime Walk. Anti-aircraft guns were posted on nearby Beacon Hill, and an armoured car was always on standby in the event of an emergency.

There were air raids in the area. In August 1940, Churchill was host to Anthony Eden, Lord Ismay, Lord Wavell and others. After a strategy conference, a German raider flew over the house. "We all went out to look," John Colville recorded. Colville also noted how, on another weekend, Churchill strolled beneath the stars in the middle of the summer night. Though a moody man, he could be a genial host and become garrulous, comparing his role as prime minister to that of a farmer, "driving pigs along a road, who always had to be prodding them on and preventing them from straying".[10]

One permanent resident from 1940 was Nelson, the cat. His original home had been at Admiralty House, but he was moved to 10 Downing Street with the Churchills. He did not like the air raids – who did? – and was brought to Chequers. Churchill loved cats and cats loved him. Nelson used to spend the night on Churchill's bed, and hang around while Churchill – as he often did – worked on his papers from his bed until lunchtime. (Also a habit of the early-twentieth-century prime minister, Arthur Balfour.)

Churchill made several broadcasts from Chequers. In February 1941, he gave the speech with the words, "Give us the tools and we will finish the job."[11] It was also from here that he made his less inspiring 1945 general election broadcast, warning that a Labour government would bring in controls that would require introducing "some form of Gestapo".

During the war, it was the custom for other members of the War

Cabinet to broadcast a talk once a fortnight. In July 1940, it was the turn of Lord Halifax.

Halifax was a grandee and a Yorkshire landowner, devoted to hunting and the High Church, and quintessentially the man of Munich, for he had accompanied prime minister Neville Chamberlain as foreign secretary on his visit to Hitler in 1938. Halifax's Conservatism was very different from Churchill's. Halifax believed in "a world tranquil and well-ordered, and for a domestic administration that still hesitated to accept any much larger responsibility than that for enforcement of law and the maintenance of order".[12] By contrast, Churchill, with his father's Tory Democracy in his blood and his experience of the radical Liberal government of 1906, was more of an interventionist. But Churchill rarely bore a grudge and got on with people of all (or most) political persuasions and, when he became prime minister, he retained Halifax in his post. Still, there were tensions between the two men, for Halifax retained his bias towards appeasement even in the first years of the war. He was readier to give credibility to Hitler's peace offensives and to entertain the idea of Italy being a mediator between Germany on the one hand and Britain and France on the other.

Halifax prepared his broadcast talk but was not happy with the flow. He sought the prime minister's advice. Churchill invited Lord and Lady Halifax to Chequers for the weekend. Halifax read to Churchill the words he had drafted. It included the idea that whatever gains Hitler might make in Europe, he would have to confront the British navy, army and airforce. In his memoirs, Halifax recalled how Churchill listened carefully, acknowledged that the draft was awkward, walked up and down the long room in thought and then said, "Why not say, 'unless that man can sap the might of Britain'?"[13]

Churchill was at Chequers for the weekend of 21 June 1941. His house guests included the United States ambassador, John Gilbert Winant, and Anthony Eden. Churchill always slept well at night – or for the fragment of the night that was left after having worked through to the small hours. He instructed his secretary not to wake him before eight in the morning unless England had been invaded. That night, Germany invaded Russia, and he was given the news when he woke up.

"Tell the BBC I will broadcast at 9 tonight," he said.[14] From eleven, he spent the day working on what he would say. The idea of having a speech writer would have been unthinkable. It was a carefully crafted speech, for he had regarded the Soviet Union with bitter opposition for the best part of the previous quarter century. But, as he said to his secretary, "If Hitler invaded Hell I would make at least a favourable reference to the Devil."[15]

Winant was also staying at Chequers when it was announced that Pearl Harbor had been attacked by the Japanese in December 1941. It was a Sunday morning, and they were sitting together. Churchill had committed Britain to declaring war against Japan if that country attacked the United States. Churchill rose and headed for the office. Winant thought Churchill was about to declare war on Japan and was cautious. "Don't you think you should get confirmation first?"[16] he suggested. But within minutes, he was speaking with President Roosevelt and indeed got confirmation. War was declared against Japan the following day. For Churchill, "to have the United States at our side was to me the greatest joy".[17]

A contrasting guest at Chequers in May 1942 was the Soviet minister of foreign affairs, Vyacheslav Molotov, who was reinforcing the great alliance of the United States, the Union of Soviet Socialist Republics and the United Kingdom. Molotov was accompanied by Soviet police officers, who searched his room meticulously. Every cupboard, every piece of furniture and every wall was examined. The bed and mattress were prodded, and the sheets and blankets were rearranged. When their rooms were not occupied, they were kept locked and guarded by Soviet staff. The visitors had even brought two of their own cleaning women. When Chequers staff eventually gained access, they discovered pistols under the pillows.

In early 1944, while Churchill stayed away from London, convalescing after pneumonia, King George VI came here to lunch.

After the Conservatives' electoral defeat in 1945, the new prime minister, Clement Attlee, invited Churchill to spend the first weekend at Chequers. It was a sad occasion, and Churchill seemed quiet and despondent. Clementine Churchill went to bed after dinner, exhausted, but Churchill stayed up with some of his family and his two most loyal friends, Brendan Bracken and Professor Lindemann, now Lord Cherwell. They watched a film. There was no despatch box for Churchill to spend an hour or two working on. His daughter Mary tried to cheer him up with gramophone records of his favourite music – Gilbert and Sullivan, French and American marches – to little avail. Only the song 'Run, rabbit, run' and music from *The Wizard of Oz* brought any animation to his face.

When he left, he wrote under his name in the visitors' book, "Finis". But it was not so. Re-elected as prime minister in 1951, Churchill again used to come regularly to Chequers and use it for family occasions.

The public is unable to visit the house, and security in the surrounding area is, understandably, heavy.

Hertfordshire
Berkhamsted, High School for Girls

HAPPY YEARS FOR CLEMENTINE HOZIER

Clementine Churchill, then Miss Hozier, attended this school in 1900 and 1901. The school was on the high street. Clementine and her mother, sister and brother had a house on the same road. Though her father, Henry Hozier, gave his family an allowance, it was not enough for private education. Clementine's brother, Bill, had attended the elite preparatory school at Summerfields, Oxford. Most of his fellow pupils went on to Eton, Winchester or Harrow. He was mortified by having to go to Berkhamsted Grammar School – which was locally seen as a very smart place. He never seemed to recover from the shame, became a compulsive gambler and shot himself in a Paris hotel in April 1921. Clementine, however, flourished at this school. In 1901, she won a national prize for French, receiving a medal from the French ambassador. In 1903, she passed the higher school certificate in French, German and biology.

Clementine kept in touch with the headmistress, Miss Harris, over the next thirty or forty years, and made occasional visits to the school. In 1947, she returned for their Commemoration Day, fondly recalling happy days there. She was escaping the precious and secluded world of upper-class girls. "I felt I was out in the world," she said, "away from the fiddling little tasks of arranging the flowers, folding the newspapers and plumping up the cushions."[18]

Shenley, Salisbury Hall

LADY RANDOLPH ECONOMISING ON A STATELY HOME

This stately house was mostly built in the seventeenth century, but its history goes back to medieval times. In 1904, Winston Churchill's mother, not long married to George Cornwallis-West, twenty years her junior, took it as a house. The couple were strapped for cash, and taking a house in the suburbs was an economic measure. Seventeen miles from central London, it was handy, with its eight bedrooms, for entertaining at weekends. On the first weekend of occupancy, Churchill came to stay and help his mother settle in. The moat had to be weeded and Churchill, emotionally exhausted from just having left the Conservatives and joined the Liberals, lent a hand in this relaxing task.

Dukes and senior political figures were entertained here, and Churchill was a regular visitor. In 1906, King Edward VII was a guest.

During the Second World War, Salisbury Hall was occupied by the de Havilland Aircraft Company, who designed the Mosquito plane here. De Havilland left in 1947 and the house was neglected, but the company later returned to establish the de Havilland Aircraft Museum.

Kent
Biggin Hill

A HANDY AIRPORT FOR CHARTWELL

This airport occupies a high plateau on the North Downs, a dozen miles from central London, between the towns of Bromley and Westerham. Founded during the First World War, Biggin Hill was used for experiments in wireless communication and was one of the airports from which many pilots set off in the Battle of Britain.

In October 1940, Winston Churchill visited the airport to see the RAF Operations Room. It was not his first visit. Its proximity to his home at Chartwell was convenient, and he had made two or three visits in the late 1930s to find out about the latest technological developments. In June 1939, just after the outbreak of war, Churchill was shown around and became familiar with the latest advances in radar, being briefed by Robert Watson-Watt, the pioneer scientist. Britain's edge in this field was a huge advantage in the Second World War.

In 1959, when he was becoming frail, Churchill flew from Biggin Hill to Cambridge to plant a tree to mark the foundation of Churchill College.

In 2019, a museum was opened to commemorate, principally, the Battle of Britain. The airfield and site are owned by Bernie Ecclestone, business magnate and former chief executive of Formula One.

Chartwell

A DREAM REALISED

No place in the United Kingdom, in the world, expresses the multi-faceted personality or the range of Winston Churchill's enthusiasms as Chartwell does. It has been in the hands of the National Trust since 1946 and is open to the public for nine months of the year. Annually, it receives about 250,000 visitors.

The house of Chartwell lies two miles to the south of Westerham and looks over acres of Wealden countryside.

At the end of the First World War, Churchill already had a country house, Lullenden, ten or so miles southwest of Chartwell in Surrey. But for several reasons, this was not satisfactory. His old nanny, Mrs Everest, had been born in Chatham and always spoke highly of the county of her birth. When Churchill first saw the place, he was captivated – not by the house, which was architecturally undistinguished, but by the view. He entered into negotiations for its purchase with the estate agents Knight, Frank & Rutley, who had assigned Harry Norman Harding to accompany Churchill round the Home Counties and especially Kent. He saw Chartwell for the first time in July 1921. It was about to be put up for auction. Churchill brought Clementine to see it. She, too, was initially enthusiastic, but she later had misgivings. The house was not sold at the auction, and Clementine Churchill had a second look and harboured reservations. The house faced the road and not the splendid view. It would need a huge amount of money to adapt it for the family. Clementine Churchill, with her cautious Scottish background and her memories of a cash-strapped childhood, often placed a pragmatic check on Churchill's risky ventures.

Churchill had actually committed himself to buying the property with 100 acres in July 1921. The price agreed was £5,000. He did not tell his wife, but he brought the three older children on a mystery tour. They were thrilled by the sight. "Oh, do buy it, do buy it," they said.[19] He did not confess until they were almost home that he had already bought it.

The house had been largely built by the previous owners, the Campbell Colquhouns. For more than two years, Churchill oversaw considerable changes to the buildings and immediate grounds. The 1920s was a decade when – compared with the next decade – Churchill had few money worries. He had the reasonable salary of a cabinet minister for most of the time, and was receiving good royalties from *The World Crisis*, his account of the First World War. He hired Philip Tilden as his architect. Tilden had worked on Port Lympne, the Kent home of Philip Sassoon. He had also built Bron-y-de, Lloyd George's country house at Churt in Surrey. But the relations between patron and client were not smooth. Both had very firm artistic ideas, and the connection between Churchill and Tilden ended in bitter recrimination and threatened lawsuits. (This was not unusual in Churchill's relations with his architects.)

Churchill threw himself into expensive building projects at Chartwell, and took huge risks to the dismay of his wife. Reverses of a steady and sufficient income made Churchill twice consider selling the estate. But after the Second World War, the owner of the *Daily Telegraph*, Lord Camrose, had an idea. Bearing in mind that Blenheim Palace had been given by Queen Anne on behalf of the nation to the first Duke of Marlborough, he persuaded a group of wealthy men collectively to make a similar gesture by setting up a trust to purchase the Chartwell estate with the arrangement that the Churchills could live there for the rest of their lives, paying a modest rent. The names of Churchill's benefactors were kept secret during their lifetimes, but are now commemorated in a plaque in the garden terrace. After the deaths of Winston and Clementine Churchill, Chartwell would go to the National Trust as a permanent memorial. Clementine Churchill became more comfortable about Chartwell now there were no money worries. Indeed when, after Churchill's death, she was made a life peer, she chose to be Baroness Spencer-Churchill of Chartwell, identifying herself with her late husband's family and with his beloved home.

During his forty years of ownership, Chartwell was very much a family home. Churchill supervised the building of lakes and a swimming pool, and constructed with his own hands brick walls and a small cottage for his youngest daughter, Mary. He bought some of the neighbouring properties and became a gentleman farmer. He even bred swans and horses and had a collection of butterflies.

Churchill also wrote much of the life of his ancestor, the first Duke of Marlborough, at Chartwell. During the 1930s, he worked on another major literary work here, his *History of the English-Speaking People*. Work was resumed after he finally retired as prime minister and was published in four volumes between 1956 and 1958. For these literary works, Churchill relied on a team of younger professional historians. As in his painting, he was never afraid of seeking the advice of experts.

To the south of the main house is a building called the studio. In it are hundreds of Churchill's paintings. The studio is more or less as he left it. It is an overcrowded gallery – so much so, that the visitor gets no clear idea of his artistic development.

In 1928, Churchill wrote blissfully to the prime minister, Stanley Baldwin, that he was spending his time building a wall and writing a book – "200 bricks and 2,000 words a day".[20]

During the 1920s and 1930s, Churchill was a most generous host. The house put up weekend guests and he used hospitality as a strategy, winning friends, being briefed and sustaining alliances. He could certainly be entertaining. One guest in 1928 was James Lees-Milne. In his diaries, he described Churchill explaining the Battle of Jutland. He made barking noises to illustrate gunfire and puffed out cigar smoke to represent gun smoke.

In those days, there was a hierarchy of entertainment. Churchill was frequently a guest at ducal houses and at royal palaces. But such entertainment was not reciprocated. Similarly, Churchill was not a guest at the homes of most of the people whom he entertained. So it was exceptional that, in 1936, the Duke of Westminster – at whose homes in Cheshire, Scotland and the south of France the Churchills were frequent guests – turned up for luncheon unexpectedly.

Churchill always had an ample staff to assist him in entertaining. He was hopeless himself at domestic chores. He loved his food but did not cook. Though he did say that, if necessary, "I can boil an egg. I've seen it done."[21]

During the 1930s, three men were regular visitors at Chartwell. They formed what was like the court of an exile. One was Professor Lindemann of the University of Oxford, who was able to advise on all technical and scientific matters. A second was Desmond Morton, intelligence officer, who leaked numerous official documents dealing with Germany's rearmament programme to Churchill. (At one stage, Churchill was cautioned by the cabinet secretary, Sir Maurice Hankey, for receiving classified documents.) The third regular visitor was Brendan Bracken, the Irish-born adventurer, politician and financier. Bracken looked after Churchill's parliamentary and political visitors. Among these were politicians, ambassadors, relations and friends. They ranged from the scientist Albert Einstein to Charlie Chaplin, who delighted Churchill's children. In early September 1938, one visitor was the Soviet ambassador, Ivan Maisky, who clearly wanted Churchill – then not in office – to be a conduit for communication between the Soviet and British governments. He found Chartwell "large and tastefully presented".[22]

"You can observe all this with an untroubled soul!" his host told him. "My estate is not a product of man's exploitation by man; it was bought entirely on my literary royalties."[23]

Churchill was at Chartwell on the eve of war. He recorded in his war memoirs how he had completed laying bricks for a cottage kitchen.

During the Second World War, Churchill was only able to make occasional visits to Chartwell. In July 1940, he brought the Chief of the Imperial General Staff, Lord Ironside, here. The Field Marshal was bemused by the gentle affection Churchill showed to the animals: "he calls them all darlings, & shouts to the cat, & even the birds. The old swan on the lake knew his call, & answered back."[24]

Dover, Dover Castle

THE FIRST LINE OF ENGLAND'S DEFENCE

The stretch of coast between St Margaret's Bay and Dover is the closest to the European continent. The White Cliffs stretching to the east have symbolised the independence of the country. For a thousand years and more, Dover Castle has been the major fortification of the defence of England.

For Winston Churchill, the castle was of huge importance, and he regularly visited it during the Second World War. The evacuation of the British Expeditionary Force from Dunkirk in the early summer of 1940 was planned and directed from here.

In June 1940, Churchill paid the first of several visits that summer in order to inspect defences in the event of invasion. He ensured that the promontory was given guns that could fire across the English Channel to German-occupied France.

He would lunch at Dover, and wherever he went he was

greeted with cheering crowds, encouraging him with shouts of "Stick it!"

In January 1941, Churchill brought Harry Hopkins, President Roosevelt's personal envoy, to Dover. Hopkins was a frail man, and it was a grim winter, but Churchill took him wherever he went – from the far north of Scotland to the White Cliffs of Dover. A friendship grew which Churchill used as leverage on winning Roosevelt's sympathy and passive support. At Dover, Hopkins was able to see the heavy batteries facing the enemy.

In June that year, Churchill was back in Dover, inspecting anti-aircraft defences.

Dover Castle is open to the public and is managed by English Heritage.

Eastchurch

WHERE CHURCHILL LEARNED TO FLY

Eastchurch is a village on the Isle of Sheppey. It played a major role in the early history of aviation in Britain, and it was here that Winston Churchill learnt to fly in 1912 and 1913. The flat land, away from urban developments, was a suitable area on which to practise.

Aviation developed rapidly in the first years of the twentieth century. It was seen initially as a rich man's sport and only secondarily as a useful military tool, either for reconnaissance or for launching missiles. It was not until after the First World War that civil and commercial aviation developed, along with the aerial transport of passengers and freight.

The early aeronautical engineers the Short Brothers, who had been based at Battersea, moved their operations to Stone Pitts

Farm in Eastchurch, where they constructed workshops and conducted experiments. In 1909, John Moore-Brabazon made a number of pioneering flights. The same year, he flew from Eastchurch with a pig strapped to a wastepaper basket – proving that pigs could fly. Moore-Brabazon later entered politics and became a minister of transport. He was also minister of aircraft production in Churchill's wartime government.

Churchill always had an interest in the latest technology and, just as he pioneered tanks, so he pioneered the military use of aircraft. Between 1911 and 1915, Churchill was First Lord of the Admiralty and in charge of the Royal Naval Air Service. The latter had grown out of the Aero Club, which was based at Eastchurch and later absorbed into the admiralty. A flying school was added. The various admiralty elements united with the army's Royal Flying Corps to form the Royal Air Force on 1 April 1918.

As First Lord of the Admiralty, Churchill was a frequent visitor to Eastchurch. He made full use of the admiralty yacht, HMS *Enchantress*, and would sail down the Thames and watch the seaplanes flying from the nearby airstrip of Grain. The yacht docked at Sheerness, where Commander Samson would drive him over to Eastchurch. From here he flew – in a Short biplane, often at the controls – the few miles west to Grain. Later, Churchill made a number of training flights. His instructor was a young man called Gilbert Wildman-Lushington. On one flight, Churchill took the controls and flew over the Thames to Tilbury. On another visit, a small plane was despatched to Faversham to purchase some oysters for Churchill's lunch. Was this, perhaps, the first commercial flight?

But flying was a hazardous venture. The day after he had been instructing Churchill, Wildman-Lushington was killed during a solo flight; his plane fell into a landslip and crashed. There was a high casualty rate among those pioneer aviators, and Clementine Churchill was understandably nervous. She insisted that her husband, a man with a young family, should not take such risks. "Every time I see a telegram," she told him, "I think it is to announce that you have been killed flying."[25] To her relief, Churchill gave up learning to fly. In the latter part of the First World War, he resumed flying as a passenger on frequent visits to France. During his flights in the Second World War, he often joined the pilot in the cockpit and occasionally, under guidance, took over the controls.

There is a small but excellent museum of early aviation history at Eastchurch. About three thousand enthusiasts visit it each year. It occupies buildings from the 1920s that actually belong to the adjacent prison.

Manston

A FRONTLINE RAF STATION

RAF Manston is in the far northeast corner of Kent behind the Thanet towns of Margate, Broadstairs and Ramsgate. Its origins precede the birth of the Royal Air Force. During the Second World War, it was where the engineer Barnes Wallis developed specialist air bombs. Winston Churchill visited Manston in August 1940, when fears of a German invasion were at their height, to see the Air Force Operations Room.

Churchill was back at Manston one year later, accompanied by his wife. He inspected the 615 fighter squadron, of which he had been Honorary Air Commodore since 1939. He was shown a film of the squadron's recent attacks on German convoys in the

English Channel, and they were offered tea. "Good God no," he said. "My wife drinks that, I'll have a brandy."[26]

Margate

OPEN-ENDED COMMITMENTS FOR WAR DAMAGE

While southeast England was suffering air raids in the autumn of 1940, Winston Churchill visited Margate. There was an attack while he was there, and Churchill joined people in a shelter. When they emerged, they saw some of the damage. A small restaurant had been hit. "Nobody had been hurt," he recalled in his war memoirs, "but the place had been reduced to a litter of crockery, utensils, and splintered furniture. The proprietor, his wife, and the cooks and waitresses were in tears."[27] Churchill was moved and, on the way back to London, he dictated a letter to the chancellor of the exchequer saying that all damage resulting from enemy action should be compensated in full as a charge on the state – and at once. The chancellor was unsurprisingly worried at this open-ended commitment, but Churchill got his way.

Port Lympne

A RICH MAN'S INDULGENCE

Sir Philip Sassoon, Baronet, was a Gatsby-like character at the centre of a social world in the 1920s and 1930s. He was from the family of Baghdadi Jews who had moved to Bombay (modern-day Mumbai) in the nineteenth century and became fabulously wealthy. Sassoon was born at a Rothschild house in

Paris – his mother was a Rothschild – and sent to Eton and Christ Church, Oxford. From his father, he inherited the estate at Lympne near Hythe as well as the Folkestone parliamentary constituency where he was the Conservative MP from 1912 until his death at the age of fifty-one in 1939. Siegfried Sassoon – a poet admired by Winston Churchill – was a second cousin.

Philip Sassoon was generous with his wealth – he also owned a great mansion in Park Lane, another estate in Enfield, twelve miles north of central London, as well as a lodge in the Scottish Highlands – and Churchill was one of many to enjoy his friendship and hospitality. Others included Lloyd George, the Mountbattens, Charlie Chaplin, Noël Coward and T. E. Lawrence. Sassoon and Churchill shared an enthusiasm for polo, as did the Prince of Wales, the future King Edward VIII. Sassoon was also keen on flying and used to fly his own planes.

Although Philip Sassoon never achieved high office, he was always close to members of the royal family and leading politicians. He was the private secretary of Douglas Haig, the leading British general in the last part of the First World War, and of Lloyd George when he was prime minister of the coalition government between the end of the war and 1922. He was a minister – though not in the cabinet – in Conservative and National governments in the 1920s and 30s. He was also a member of the government at the time of the Munich crisis – though his friendship with Churchill was unaffected.

Churchill completed over twenty paintings at Port Lympne, including some of the interiors of the house and also – one of his best – a landscape overlooking the Romney Marsh, now kept at Chartwell.

The house was designed by Sir Herbert Baker before the First World War, and Sassoon worked on the interior design with

Philip Tilden – whom Churchill recruited to do extensive work on Chartwell in the early 1930s. (Tilden also completed work on Lloyd George's country house at Churt, Surrey.) The style at Port Lympne was exuberant, even garish. Lady Honor Channon, the wife (for a few years) of the diarist and Conservative MP Henry Channon, described the decor as like "a Spanish brothel".[28] Commentators have wondered how extensive her experience of Spanish brothels was. This is unkind and unfair. Many of the rooms, and certainly the gardens, reflect a Spanish Moorish influence – the Alhambra at Granada was obviously an inspiration. One particular room that might have inspired her observation has a number of darkened, tapestried recesses, which could be used for intimate encounters.

Another room of great distinction was designed by Rex Whistler. It is made to give the impression that you are in a tent, with glimpses of landscapes outside appearing between the folds of the canvas.

Sassoon only occupied the mansion for six weeks during the summer and for the New Year. Lympne was renowned for its annual New Year parties, when guests often stayed for several days. Both Churchill and Lloyd George were guests for the New Year party in 1921. There was a singsong round the piano and Churchill surprised many with his extensive repertoire of the music hall songs of his youth.

Guests at Lympne extended beyond politicians and show-business celebrities. They included writers such as George Bernard Shaw and H. G. Wells, as well as artists like Sir William Orpen. Sassoon also had his own fleet of light planes, based at an airfield close by with pilots in residence. There is a story that, on one occasion in the 1920s, he decided to take his guests to call on Diana Guinness, who lived on the Wiltshire–Hampshire border. The guests, who included Clementine and Winston Churchill, climbed into seven planes and off they all flew in elegant formation – Churchill and Sassoon taking over the controls occasionally.

After Sassoon died in 1939, the house was used to accommodate airmen and the Free Czechoslovak Army. The house and gardens fell into disrepair, and the site was uninhabited for nearly thirty years until it was bought by John Aspinall in 1973. He had already developed a zoo in the surrounding area. Today access to the mansion, now a luxury hotel, is through a safari park.

Walmer, Walmer Castle

WHERE THE GALLIPOLI CAMPAIGN WAS CONCEIVED

Walmer Castle was one of a series of coastal forts constructed during the reign of King Henry VIII in the sixteenth century as a defence against possible invasion from France. It was built according to the latest ideas of military fortifications. Low and circular with very thick walls, it was less exposed to the latest naval artillery. It has, since the eighteenth century, been the official residence of the Lord Warden of the Cinque Ports, an honorific title given to a distinguished military or political figure. Former Lord Wardens have included prime ministers William Pitt, the Earl of Liverpool, Duke of Wellington, Viscount Palmerston and the Marquess of Salisbury. And Winston Churchill.

From 1913 to 1933, the Lord Warden was Earl Beauchamp, a Liberal politician. He offered the castle to prime minister H. H. Asquith as an occasional country retreat, and it became a favourite bolthole. He entertained friends and colleagues here. In January 1915, Churchill and his wife were guests. Churchill was just forty, and Asquith's wife recorded that he was no longer interested in being viceroy of India. But another eastern venture was discussed: a diversion from the deadlock of the Western Front with an attack on the Ottoman Empire. It is feasible to claim that the Dardanelles, or Gallipoli, campaign was conceived at Walmer Castle. A room on the first floor was the location for these discussions, and a red Admiralty despatch box that had belonged to Churchill is on display on the table.

The Dardanelles campaign was a turning point in Churchill's life. It was not exclusively Churchill's idea, and it had the support of the secretary of state for war, Lord Kitchener, the First Sea Lord, Admiral Fisher, and prime minister Asquith. The idea was to storm through the Dardanelles, occupy the Ottoman capital Constantinople (modern-day Istanbul) and put the Ottoman Empire out of the conflict. It was thought that this would ease the pressure on Britain's ally, Russia, win over Balkan neutrals, divert Germany's attention from the Western Front and bring an early end to the First World War. It seemed a good idea at the time.

But it all went horribly wrong. The campaign necessitated a landing on the Gallipoli peninsula. The Turkish resistance was ferocious. There had been poor intelligence about both the enemy and the terrain where Allied troops – including soldiers from Australia and New Zealand – landed. Casualties were high, and Churchill was held personally responsible for what was seen as a major disaster. He received insufficient backing from the prime minister. Kitchener turned lukewarm and Fisher claimed he was always against the project.

In May 1915, Asquith was forced to head a government that was no longer solely made up of Liberals (plus Kitchener): the Conservative opposition was brought into a coalition. One of the Conservatives' conditions was the removal of Churchill from a position of authority. Churchill was deeply unpopular with the Conservatives. He was a renegade of the party, which he had publicly abused in the most virulent terms. Churchill was himself a man with little rancour and could not understand the bitterness against him. After all, he retained close friendships with Conservatives such as Lord Hugh Cecil and F. E. Smith.

Churchill resented the lack of sympathy from Asquith, who described him to his wife one weekend at Walmer Castle: "Oh! He is intolerable! <u>Noisy</u>, longwinded and full of perorations."[29] Asquith demoted him from being First Lord of the Admiralty – a post he loved – to the sinecure of Chancellor of the Duchy of Lancaster, the main responsibility of which was the appointment of Justices of the Peace in Lancashire.

The Dardanelles campaign fizzled out and it was decided to abandon it at the end of 1915. A commission of enquiry exonerated Churchill from exclusive responsibility for the disaster, but he went through a period of deep depression. For the first time in his career, he suffered a major reverse. He felt bitter about Asquith, and it took him time to recover his bounce. He served as a soldier on the Western Front and, in 1917, was brought back by Asquith's replacement as prime minister, David Lloyd George, as minister of munitions.

The albatross of the Dardanelles hung round Churchill's neck for the rest of his life. But some who had served in the campaign were less critical: Major Attlee and Colonel Wedgwood became Labour politicians and Churchill always retained a friendly appreciation of them.

Churchill became Lord Warden of the Cinque Ports in 1941, during the Second World War. Enemy artillery fire could, with the right wind, be heard across the Channel, and the castle was closed down during the war years. Churchill made visits but not as many as other Lords Warden; after all he had his own excellent home at Chartwell at the other end of the county.

The Castle is open to the public and is managed by English Heritage. The current (2020) Lord Warden, Admiral of the Fleet Lord Boyce, regularly comes here with his family to stay.

Middlesex
Enfield, Trent Park

PHILIP SASSOON'S OTHER COUNTRY HOUSE

Winston Churchill was a regular visitor to Trent Park, a property belonging to the seriously rich Sir Philip Sassoon, whose Jewish family were originally from Baghdad. Sassoon's mother was a Rothschild, and Philip became a Conservative MP and one of the most celebrated social and political hosts between the wars. He was a second cousin of the poet Siegfried Sassoon, much admired by Churchill.

The house was an undistinguished Victorian building set in extensive grounds designed by Humphry Repton. Sassoon inherited the property but took it over only in 1922 and in the next few years transformed it. He brought some bricks and stonework from the recently demolished Devonshire House in the West End. The house was filled with Chinese cabinets, Flemish tapestries and Persian carpets. The blue swimming pool was heated and surrounded by a profusion of lilies with an overpowering scent. Flamingos stalked the grounds. There were also ducks and black swans, some of which were sent as presents to Churchill's own country house, Chartwell.

Every July, Sassoon hosted a series of garden parties here. Robert Boothby described how the "white-coated footmen" served "endless courses of rich but delicious food" to guests who included members of the royal family and stars of politics, literature and art.[30] "Philip himself flitted from group to group, an alert, watchful, influential but unobtrusive stage director."[31] Churchill brought his palette and paint brushes and did several paintings of the house and gardens, which are on display at Chartwell. Along with Churchill, Duff Cooper, Anthony Eden and Samuel Hoare were regular visitors. Charlie Chaplin, on a visit to England, was once a guest. But not all senior, usually Conservative, politicians were regulars. Stanley Baldwin preferred to relax in Worcestershire or at Aix-les-Bains.

Sassoon died in 1939, and his ashes were scattered over the park – not from an ornate urn but from a cardboard box marked 'Lipton's Tea', dropped from a low-flying plane. The house was commandeered during the Second World War and used as a prison for high-ranking German officers. Since the war, it has been a campus of Middlesex University.

Today, Trent Park is the property of Enfield Borough Council and part of London's Green Belt. It is possible to wander around the 400 acres of woods, lakes and meadowland. The house is in the hands of property developers. There are plans (in 2019) to provide luxury flats, but the park will continue to be open to the public.

Harrow on the Hill, Harrow School

AN AWKWARD SELF-WILLED TEENAGER

In the 1880s, Harrow was a rural town surrounded by fields. There was a green belt between the town and the great metropolis. On a fine day, you could make out Windsor Castle to the west. The small town was physically, economically and socially dominated by Harrow School, which had been founded by a local farmer and landowner in 1572. By the nineteenth century, it had become one of the most celebrated public – that is, non-governmental, private boys' boarding – schools in the country. It was the school of Sir Robert Peel, Lord Palmerston and Stanley Baldwin as well as Winston Churchill. As well as, one might add, Lord Byron and Sir Terence Rattigan. It has always had an appeal for the wealthy and well-connected in countries influenced by the British Empire. Jawaharlal Nehru and King Hussein of Jordan were alumni. In recent years, Harrow has also been a popular choice of affluent families from Russia and Asia.

Today, Harrow on the Hill is a small, detached town, cut off from the suburban sprawl of western London. Views in all directions are over wooded and open land, on which housing or industrial development is not permitted. It has the appearance of a Home Counties market town. The school itself is not hidden from the world behind walls or within extensive grounds; rather, its buildings lie on both sides of a narrow main road. During term time, young men can be seen moving from one part of the school to another, smart in their dark 'bluers' – their suits – and wearing straw hats. (Hats, not boaters: the latter are what they wear at Eton College.)

Male members of the Churchill family tended to be sent to Eton. That was the school of Lord Randolph Churchill, and was where Winston Churchill sent his son, Randolph. The idea had been for Winston to be sent to Winchester College. His cousin – known as 'Sunny', three years older than Winston, who later became the ninth Duke of Marlborough – was sent there. But a chilling of the relationship between Lord Randolph and the rest of the family over the sale of art treasures from Blenheim Palace dissuaded him from sending Winston to Winchester. Eton was rejected because, with its fogs and the low-level damp climate on the River Thames, it was regarded as unhealthy for the (then) delicate Winston, who had been seriously ill at his school in Brighton.

So Winston Churchill was sent to Harrow in April 1888 when he was thirteen and a half, appearing in the register as Spencer-Churchill, W. L. His parents did not, as is customary, take him themselves because they were about to set off on a seven-week tour of Russia. Churchill's first impressions of the school were positive: there was a swimming pool, a gymnasium and a carpentry shop. But eighteen months later, he was miserable. "I hope you don't imagine," he wrote to his mother, "that I am happy here. It's all very well for monitors and Cricket Captains but it's quite different for fourth form boys. Of course what I should like best is to leave this hell of a place but I cannot expect that at present."[32]

Churchill stayed for fourteen terms, leaving in December 1892 when he had just turned eighteen. The headmaster all this time was a youngish (mid-thirties) bachelor, the Reverend James Welldon, who went on to become Bishop of Calcutta and Dean of Durham. Welldon was a reformer, and he improved conditions for the assistant masters. He took a pastoral interest in his charges and appreciated Churchill's qualities, although he was obliged to flog him on one occasion for an act of vandalism.

Churchill was in the Head Master's house for all but his first three terms. His school career was not as abysmal as some biographers have suggested – following Churchill's own (uncharacteristic) modesty. It is true that he was seen as a self-willed rebel and worked hard only at the subjects that interested him, namely history and literature. But he was well above the average in achieving prizes and recognition. He won form history prizes. He showed a photographic memory in learning poetry, reciting 1,200 lines of Macaulay's *Lays of Ancient Rome* for a prize. And he won a house prize for a poem on the subject of influenza (there had been a global pandemic in 1890):

> *Oh how shall I its deeds recount*
> *Or measure the untold amount*
>   *Of ills that it has done?*
> *From China's bright Celestial land*
> *E'en to Arabia's thirsty sand*
>   *It journeyed with the sun.*[33]

Four teachers in particular had an influence on him. One was Robert Somervell, whom Churchill remembered as a delightful man. Churchill responded to the teaching of English literature and entered for the school Shakespeare prize, coming fourth out of twenty-five contestants. Somervell inspired Churchill with the essential structure of "the ordinary British sentence – which is a noble thing".[34] Somervell kept one extended essay that Churchill wrote in 1889 about an imaginary invasion of Russia twenty-five years in the future, in 1914. In 1945, Somervell's son, Donald, presented the manuscript of the essay to the school. Donald was born at Harrow while Churchill was a pupil. He later became Solicitor General and Attorney General in governments between 1933 and 1945, and he was home secretary in Churchill's caretaker government of 1945 before retiring as Lord Somervell of Harrow.

On his arrival at Harrow, Churchill joined the Officers' Training Corps and, in his last two years, he was in the 'Army Class' of which L. M. Moriarty was master-in-charge. Moriarty taught history, and in his adult life Churchill told him that his love of history had been acquired or developed in Moriarty's Army Class. Both were keen fencers and even fenced with each other. In 1892, aged seventeen, Churchill became the public schools' fencing champion. His father was always dismissive of his elder son, and Churchill craved for his parents' affection and approbation. The finals were at Aldershot, and Churchill was very anxious that his father should attend. But Lord Randolph had better things to do. "I cannot possibly get to Aldershot on the 7th as it is Sandown races which I must go to."[35] But he did send a postal order for £1.

Churchill studied French with a Monsieur Minssen and spent some holidays in France with him, meeting French army officers. Churchill was fairly fluent in French, though purists mocked his accent. In early letters to his mother, who had very good French, he sometimes dropped into accurate French, and in one he frenchified his name as "Winston de Montéglise".[36] In 1940, he addressed the French nation in a broadcast in French ("Français, c'est moi, Churchill, qui vous parle") and, in old age, his French was good enough for him to read Balzac in the original.

Churchill also appreciated his teacher of mathematics, C. H. P. Mayo, who made the subject interesting.

His first (English) publications were in the school magazine, *The Harrovian*.

Churchill, however, was not a model student. He did not enjoy team sports, preferring activities – such as fencing – in which he relied on his own prowess. He augmented his funds by getting his celebrity parents to send him lots of samples of their signatures, which he sold off to his fellow pupils. His parents were probably happy to oblige, as it reduced the pressure on their son's constant demands for extra pocket money. Churchill was also seen as disorganised – one early report wrote that he was "regular only in his irregularity"[37] – and cocky; on one occasion he was given six strokes of a cane, curiously called 'six of the best', from the head boy. After the punishment, he told his senior, "I shall be a greater man than you".[38] The response was two more strokes. Against the regulations, he kept two dogs, which were kennelled at a house in the town, and exercised them on walks. He also loved swimming in the pool, known as the Ducker. It was here that Churchill pushed the older, but diminutive, L. S. Amery into the water. Amery later became a political ally of Churchill and served as secretary of state for India in Churchill's 1940 government. Among Churchill's other contemporaries at Harrow were the historian G. M. Trevelyan and the novelist Marmaduke Pickthall, who later became a Muslim and translated the Qur'an.

Churchill was always distressed that his parents visited him so infrequently. On one occasion, he defied schoolboy convention by hosting his beloved nanny Mrs Everest, who came by train and with whom Churchill walked round the town arm in arm while other boys jeered. When she left, he gave her a warm embrace.

His brother, Jack, to whom he was much attached in spite of the six-year age difference, was at a preparatory school at Elstree eight miles away. Winston would walk there to see him. Jack joined his older brother at Harrow in Winston's last year, where they shared a room.

When he became famous after the South African War, having hit the headlines of the world by dramatically escaping from a Boer prison, Churchill achieved distinction as a lecturer on his experiences. His first lecture, in 1900, was at his old school.

Over the following years, Churchill rarely spoke of the school – and then only with dislike. This dislike was probably reinforced by an incident that took place in 1912, a time of intense political bitterness between Conservatives and the governing Liberals over the Parliament Act and the issue of Home Rule for Ireland. Churchill was then a minister in the Liberal government, but his best friend was a combative Conservative, F. E. Smith. Churchill and Smith were driving in the area and Churchill had the idea of showing Smith his old school. They entered the grounds as boys were assembled. They recognised Churchill and booed him loudly. Churchill was taken aback, humiliated and angry, resolving never to have anything more to do with the place.

Even so, ten years later he arranged for his son, Randolph, to visit both Eton and Harrow as possible options for his secondary education. Randolph chose Eton.

Churchill's attitude changed during the Second World War when he heard that Harrow had been bombed. A missile fell on the Speech Room. The school authorities decided to take advantage of the open space created, and, thinking that it resembled the Globe Theatre, used it for the production of Shakespeare plays with the audience surrounding the actors. Churchill respected the cool resourcefulness shown by his alma mater.

During the Second World War, Malvern School in Worcestershire was requisitioned by the military, and Churchill suggested that the boarders and staff be transferred to Harrow.

By the time of Churchill's first premiership, his connections with the school had warmed even more. His secretary, John

Colville, also an Old Harrovian, suggested a visit there. He agreed and, in December 1940, accompanied by his wife and Old Harrovians in his administration, was cheered by up to five hundred boys. He joined in the singing of school songs, for which he always had a great affection. He seemed, as Colville recorded in his diary, to remember most of the words without referring to the book. To one song, 'Stet Fortuna Domus', a new verse was added:

Nor less we praise in darker days
  The leader of our nation,
And Churchill's name shall we acclaim
  From each new generation.
While in this fight to guard the Right
  Our country you defend, Sir,
Here grim and gay we mean to stay,
  And stick it to the end, Sir.[39]

Churchill recommended that "darker" in the first line be replaced by "sterner". This suggestion was accepted.

When Churchill spoke informally to the boys, Colville observed, he was never patronising.

In later years, although he did not think he had distinguished himself at school, his nostalgia for the place grew and grew. He used to pay an annual visit into his eighties, lustily joining in the Harrow songs.

Today, the school remains a private working institution and is not normally accessible to the public. However the Gallery, in the Old Speech Room, serves as a museum and is often open to the public during term time afternoons and on special occasions. (The Harrow School website gives details of when it is accessible.) It exhibits aspects of the school's history and includes one of

Churchill's paintings, 'Distant View of Venice', a gift from Lady Churchill after her husband's death. There is also a maquette of a bust of Churchill clad in the heavy Garter robes he wore at the coronation of Queen Elizabeth II in 1953, sculpted by Willem Verbon, and a portrait of Churchill photographed by Cecil Beaton, another Old Harrovian.

On the eastern side of the high street are three large buildings belonging to the school with which Churchill would have been familiar. On the left as you face them is the Vaughan Library, and then the chapel. To the south is what used to be the Head Master's house. Churchill spent much of his time at Harrow in this house. His room is the second on the left on the third floor. Gardens and open space cascade eastward to a lake. Did Churchill have this in mind when he landscaped the grounds at Chartwell?

Uxbridge, Battle of Britain Bunker Museum

CHURCHILL'S FAVOURITE PORT OF CALL

Dowding Park, to the east of Uxbridge's Victorian St Andrew's Church, used to be the grounds of Hillingdon House, home of one of William III's Dutch lieutenants, the Duke of Schomberg. In the First World War, the estate was bought by the government and it became two RAF sites: Hillingdon and Uxbridge. They were later merged as RAF Uxbridge. There was no airstrip: it was a base for land operations, workshops and training. In 1922, one of the men serving at RAF Uxbridge was aircraftman 352087 Ross, better known as T. E. Lawrence. He had just left working for Winston Churchill at the Colonial Office and was seeking anonymity. While here, he recorded his daily experiences. These were published posthumously as *The Mint*.

The park was named after a Scottish air force officer, Hugh Dowding, who built up the London defences. He was based at Uxbridge. The bunker was constructed here in 1938 and 1939. The principal room was sixty feet below the ground, with heavy, thick stone roofing. After the outbreak of war, it was the base of the No 11 Group RAF Fighter Command. The task of this unit was to monitor activity in the air. A number of young women, from "good families", had volunteered to join the Women's Auxiliary Air Force, the WAAF. With the help of professional RAF staff, they received information about the movements of enemy aircraft and plotted their locations on a huge map of southeast England, which took up most of the bunker. A number of rooms looked down on the map room, like balconies at a theatre. These provided opportunities for visitors to inspect and oversee the work. King George VI and Queen Elizabeth were among those who came to see what was going on. The work in this bunker became crucial during the Battle of Britain, from July to October 1940.

Churchill made several visits to the bunker during the Battle of Britain; it was conveniently located between central London and the prime minister's country retreat at Chequers. Lord Ismay said it was Churchill's "favourite port of call".[40] According to my late mother-in-law, who was one of the young lady plotters, the ban on smoking in the operations rooms was relaxed during his visits. Churchill described one visit in detail in the second volume of his war memoirs. He was able to monitor closely how the air battle raged. Pilots from both sides were being shot down, and all this activity was recorded on the large map. Churchill was deeply moved. On one visit, in August 1940, he was accompanied by his wife. They were taken down to the bomb-proof basement, which he described as being like a small theatre. On another occasion, Lord Ismay recalled how, as they left to be driven to Chequers, Churchill said, "Don't speak to me; I have never been so moved."[41] As they drove off, Churchill leaned forward and said, "Never in the field of human conflict has so much been owed by so many to so few." These memorable words had an echo of Shakespeare's play *Henry V*, in which the king addresses his troops before the Battle of Agincourt with the words, "We few, we happy few, we band of brothers." Churchill later uttered these words in a formal speech in the House of Commons. It illustrates his power of rhetoric – using short, familiar words to memorable effect.

The site was disused after the war, even forgotten, but it was restored and opened to the public as a museum in 2018, with a visitor centre next door. As much as possible of the earlier equipment has been restored, and there are photographs and recorded memories of the people who worked here.

Surrey
Croydon, Ashcroft Playhouse

CHURCHILL'S LAST PUBLIC APPEARANCE

Formerly the Ashcroft Theatre, this playhouse in the Fairfield Hall cultural complex was named after the actress Peggy Ashcroft, who was born in Croydon. It was opened in 1962.

Winston Churchill made his last public appearance – outside the House of Commons – on 25 April 1964 when he came to see his daughter Sarah act in a play, *Fata Morgana*, here. Churchill was mentally frail and clearly did not follow what was going on.

Dormansland, Lullenden

THE FIRST COUNTRY HOUSE

Tucked away in the rolling countryside where Surrey, Kent and Sussex meet is a fine seventeenth-century house, which became Winston Churchill's rural retreat from early 1917 to late 1919. Churchill had known Dormansland from his childhood. His father had been friends of the Spender-Clay family who lived here.

The house, Lullenden, dates back to the 1620s. It has a great hall with a vaulted ceiling and a fireplace with an iron fire-back dated 1582, presumably from an earlier building. Churchill bought it for £6,000 and shared the house with his brother, Jack, his wife and children. In 1917, Winston Churchill had three spirited young children. They and their cousins slept in the outbuilding fifty yards to the northwest. Churchill only spent weekends here, but his family stayed during the week and the children went in a pony trap to a primary school at Dormansland a mile or so away.

At this school, Churchill's son, Randolph, learned for the first time that his father was an important man. He went up to another small boy asking if he would be his "chum" and was rebuffed with the words, "No, your father murdered my father".[42] Randolph asked for an explanation and was told that the boy's father had been killed "at the Dardanelles".

Randolph, who was eight years old when they left, remembered playing hide-and-seek in the neighbouring woods. He also recalled the Union Flag being raised on his school's flagpole on Armistice Day in 1918.

There were extensive grounds at Lullenden, including a potato field and gardens. Churchill enjoyed strolling around the garden with the blood-red Britannia rhododendrons, which were among his favourite flowers. A path leading through the woodland to a small lake is still known as Churchill's Walk. Three of the paintings he did at Lullenden are now at Chartwell.

Churchill found the property too expensive to run and, in 1919, sold it to his army friend Sir Ian Hamilton, whom he had known in India in the 1890s and during the Boer War and who had been a Gallipoli general.

Hascombe, Hoe Farm

THE START OF HIS PAINTING CAREER

Hascombe is a village in the wooded hills south of Godalming. It is home to several houses designed by prestigious architects towards the end of the nineteenth century. To the northwest of the village, at the end of Hoe Lane in a secluded valley, is a sixteenth-century farmhouse that was converted into a spacious residence at the end of the nineteenth century by the architect Edwin Lutyens. Winston Churchill and his brother Jack rented the house for the summer of 1915 for their families as a country retreat.

It was comfortable and possessed what Churchill called the essentials of life: "hot baths, cold champagne, new peas, and old brandy".[43]

Unlike his own detached father, Churchill used to play with his children. In 1915, Churchill's eldest two children, Diana and Randolph, were six and four respectively. His third, Sarah, was just a baby. One favourite game at Hoe Farm was 'Gorilla'. Churchill chased after the children, who would climb up trees. The father would then climb up after them.

Churchill had just been dismissed from the post of First Lord of the Admiralty. The Gallipoli expedition with which he was associated had turned out to be a disaster, costly in human lives, and all the blame seemed – unfairly – to be dumped on Churchill personally. He now had the underwhelming task of being Chancellor of the Duchy of Lancaster. Churchill was still in the cabinet but felt very uncomfortable – he knew everything but had no power to do anything. Since 1899, his career had gone from one triumph to another. Now, at the age of forty, it seemed to have plummeted. Churchill was acutely depressed. He spent much of his time at Hoe Farm pacing up and down between a small copse of trees and a summer house at the end of the garden.

One day in May 1915, his sister-in-law, Lady Gwendeline (known as 'Goonie'), set up an easel and started painting. Churchill was fascinated. Lady Gwendeline offered him her sons' watercolours. He responded at once, and noted that there was a lot to paint: the garden, the sloping lawn, the house with its jumble of roofs and chimneys, the winding tree-lined drive, the woods and the pasture land rising behind the house.

One can see the house from a gate at the end of the lane, but the property and its gardens are private.

The following morning, he sent Clementine Churchill to Godalming to buy some paints. (Yes, why could he not have gone himself?)

The next month, back in London, Churchill opened an account at the art suppliers Robersons in Long Acre and bought his first easel, a mahogany palette, oils and turps, paints and brushes. Thus he started on a pastime that would be a solace from the cares of office for the rest of his life. He found he was able to concentrate intently on the task of painting, with nothing else to distract him.

The first of his paintings completed at Hoe Farm are at the

studio at Chartwell. One early painting is of Lady Gwendeline herself at her easel.

When, later that year, Churchill went to the Western Front to serve as colonel of the Sixth Royal Scots Fusiliers, he took his paints and easels with him and completed four paintings at Ploegsteert ("Plug Street").

Over the next forty years or so, he produced over five hundred paintings – mostly landscapes, but also portraits and still lifes. If you discount the ten years he served as prime minister, this works out as one every three weeks. Churchill was never interested in abstracts. His paintings are of grand houses where he stayed but also of places abroad. He loved the strong lights of the Mediterranean – southern France, Italy, Morocco. In spite of his intense interest and experience of war, he never painted any pictures of battles, tanks, battleships, bombers or the machinery of war. Painting was obviously an escape from all that. Even the paintings of Ploegsteert, were essentially landscapes. The fact that it was a war zone was incidental.

Churchill threw himself into this activity. Although he was forty years old when he started, he had often doodled in the past and was a good draughtsman. He may well have inherited some talent from his mother – though he did not inherit her musical talents. His friend Violet Asquith, later Lady Violet Bonham Carter, observed that it was the only activity that Churchill undertook in which he was totally silent. He was modest about his efforts, referring to his paintings as "my daubs",[44] but was nonetheless pleased when they attracted the attention of leading artists and critics such as Sir John Rothenstein and Kenneth Clark. Just as he was ready to take advice from professional historians in writing his life of his ancestor, Marlborough, so he was ready to seek and obtain advice from professional painters such as Sir John

Lavery, Walter Sickert and Paul Maze. He admired the Impressionists and the work of Henri Matisse and J. M. W. Turner, but he had his own distinctive style and was not derivative.

Churchill celebrated his passion for painting in a long essay, 'Painting as a Pastime', in two articles published in the *Strand Magazine* in December 1921 and January 1922. It was later revised and published as a small book in 1948, becoming a bestseller. In it, he wrote about his first experiments and his enduring love for painting. "When I get to Heaven," he wrote, "I mean to spend a considerable part of my first million years in painting."[45]

He was uninterested in selling his paintings and kept many of them at Chartwell. Others he gave to members of his family or to friends. But when they have reached the auction rooms, they have sold well. In 2014, after the death of his daughter Mary, the widow of Christopher Soames, fifteen of the canvases were sold. Two of them – one of Chartwell and one of Blenheim – were sold for over one million pounds each.

It so happens that two key protagonists of the Second World War, Adolf Hitler and Winston Churchill, were painters: as Sir David Cannadine says, one was a failed professional, the other a successful amateur.

It all started at Hoe Farm.

Lingfield, Newchapel Stud, West Park Road

A NEW CAREER IN HIS EIGHTIES

In May 1955, the month after retiring as prime minister, Winston Churchill embarked on a new venture. He bought a forty-two-acre stud farm for £6,500 and, in partnership with his son-in-law Christopher Soames, bought four or five high-quality mares.

He installed a vet as manager and, over the next years, bred colts that became successful runners, notably High Hat and Vienna.

The stud farm was sold after Churchill's death for £38,000.

Newchapel is a hamlet north of East Grinstead and to the west of Lingfield. The stud has been renamed the Churchill Stud and is south of the West Park Road. It was on the market in November 2019 for an asking price of £950,000.

West Molesey, Hurst Park

CHURCHILL, RACEHORSE OWNER

All that is left of the Hurst Park racecourse are the starting gates, incongruously visible in a post-war housing development. It was a racecourse for over seventy years, closing in 1962.

In May 1951, Winston Churchill was the owner of a racehorse, Colonist II, which won the Winston Churchill Stakes. It was an early triumph in Churchill's enthusiasm for the turf.

Churchill had always enjoyed horses. As a young cavalry officer, his career depended on the ownership and welfare of horses. Until the 1920s, he had also been a keen player of polo at home and abroad. It was only in 1949, when he was the leader of the opposition and aged seventy-four, that, with the guidance of his son-in-law Christopher Soames, he bought his first horse, Colonist II. Clementine Churchill was mystified and not altogether enthusiastic. "Before he bought the horse (I can't think why)," she wrote to a friend, "he had hardly been on a race-course in his life".[46] He kept it at Epsom in the care of Walter Nightingall.

In 1950, the horse won eight out of nine races he was in. In his career, Colonist II raced at Kempton Park, Salisbury, Sandown Park and Windsor. After he retired from racing, he was put to stud. As Churchill put it, "He has given up racing; he is now rogering."[47] Colonist II was the first of a number of horses Churchill bought and sold over the next few years. He was not able to be present at each event: his horses won seventy races over the years.

Churchill, the wordsmith, derived pleasure in naming his horses. One was named after his favourite champagne, Pol Roger.

Racing and talking about racing brought him close to the royal family. Both King George VI and Queen Elizabeth II were enthusiastic followers of the sport. On some occasions, Churchill's horse beat the queen's.

Sussex
Brighton and Hove

HAPPY SCHOOLDAYS AND A MEAL WITH MONTY

Winston Churchill always had a soft spot for Brighton. He was happy at his second prep school here, a contrast to his previous school at Ascot. Many of the very wealthy had houses in Brighton, including the Dukes of Marlborough. After his accident at Bournemouth in December 1892, Churchill came to stay here with his grandmother, 'Duchess Fanny', to convalesce.

Brunswick Road, Hove

A HAPPY PREP SCHOOL

At numbers 29–30, tall houses at the junction of Brunswick Road and Lansdowne Road, two spinster ladies – the Misses Thomson – ran a boarding preparatory school in the 1880s. Winston Churchill came here in the summer of 1884 after a disastrous year or so at St George's School Ascot, which was run by a sadistic clergyman who delighted in beating small boys. Churchill stayed at Brighton until he went to Harrow School in 1888. Another advantage of the school was that the Churchills' family doctor in London, Robson Roose, mostly practised in Brighton.

Things were looking up for young Churchill; the school "was smaller than the one I had left. It was also cheaper and less pretentious".[48] Indeed, it was so unpretentious that it did not even have a name. Here, he was able to learn things that interested him, such as history and French. He also had the opportunity to learn poetry by heart and to go swimming and riding, sometimes three times a week. He spent Sunday afternoons poring over old volumes of *Punch*, enjoying the political cartoons.

It was not just riding and swimming that got him out of the school; the pupils were also taken to chapel and to the theatre. Churchill had a deep affection for his parents, though this was not manifestly reciprocated. Lord Randolph came to Brighton to attend the races, and Churchill was distressed that his father could not find time to visit him. His father was at the height of his political celebrity at the time, and Churchill was a huge fan of his Tory Democracy. In 1887, he went to a pantomime that featured a sketch of Lord Randolph Churchill; actors and people in the audience hissed at his name. One who hissed was sitting behind young Churchill, who turned round and expostulated, "Stop that row, you snub-nosed Radical."[49]

Churchill's time here was blighted in 1886 when he suffered seriously from pneumonia. Dr Roose was fortunately around and attended him constantly at the crisis of the illness.

His residence in Brighton is commemorated by a plaque on the Lansdowne Road wall. Unfortunately, the Thomsons' name is misspelt, and the dates of Winston's attendance at the school are wrong.

Chapel Royal

CHURCHILL, UNCHARACTERISTICALLY, AT PRAYER

The son of King George III, the Prince Regent – later King George IV – was an art lover and voluptuary. From the 1780s, he would periodically escape the responsibilities of the capital and stay in Brighton. He had a modest villa, the Marine Pavilion, prepared for his use. But he incurred criticism for not attending any church; he thought the parish church of St Nicholas was too far away. The Vicar of Brighton decided to build a chapel nearer the centre of the emerging fashionable quarters of Brighton. The prince went along with the idea and the Chapel Royal was built in the 1790s; the prince and his wife, Princess Caroline, attended the inaugural service in August 1795.

The chapel was a fashionable place in which to worship (or to be seen worshipping), and it underwent much restoration in the middle years of the nineteenth century. When Winston Churchill was a pupil at the school owned and run by the Misses Thomson, he and his fellow pupils walked from the school in Brunswick Road to the service at the Chapel Royal. The pupils were seated in rented pews that ran from east to west. On reciting the Apostles' Creed, pupils turned east. The young Churchill received no apparent religious instruction from his parents, but he seems to have absorbed some Low Church instincts from his nanny, Mrs Everest. When everyone turned east, Winston "was sure Mrs Everest would have considered this practice Popish, and I conceived it my duty to testify against it".[50] He remained facing across the church, causing a sensation. There was no response, but after that the boys were seated in pews that faced east. Churchill faced a dilemma. How should he respond? By facing west when the Creed was recited? He did what the rest of the boys did – becoming, in the words of his granddaughter, Celia Sandys, "a passive conformist".[51]

Since then, the Chapel Royal has seen further restoration, and the pews that Churchill would have known have been removed.

Royal Albion Hotel

GETTING TO KNOW MONTGOMERY

In June 1940, Winston Churchill spent one day a week inspecting the landward defences of the country on the south and eastern coasts. An early visit was to the Third Division, commanded by General Bernard Montgomery, whose headquarters were at Lancing College. After the inspection, he and Montgomery drove through Shoreham and Hove "to the familiar Brighton front, of which I had so many schoolboy memories".[52] They had dinner at this hotel. It was the first time the two men had met. Each was impressed by the other.

Churchill asked Montgomery what he would like to drink.

"Water," he replied.

Churchill seemed astonished, and Montgomery explained that he neither smoked nor drank and was 100 per cent fit.

Quick as a flash, Churchill came back: "I both drink and smoke and am 200 per cent fit."[53]

(Montgomery lived to the age of eighty-eight. Churchill to ninety.)

Churchill was amused to see a sandbag machine-gun post being installed on a kiosk on the pier "like those where in my childhood I had often admired the antics of the performing flea".[54]

4

SOUTH WEST
ENGLAND

BRISTOL, DEVON, DORSET,
HAMPSHIRE, THE ISLE OF WIGHT
AND SOMERSET

The Churchills originally came from the West Country. The father of Churchill's illustrious ancestor the Duke of Marlborough traced the family to a Wandrell, Lord of Courcelle, whose younger son came over to England with William the Conqueror in 1066. In the course of time, they had property in Somerset, and it has been claimed – though not universally accepted – that the village of Churchill, fifteen miles south of Bristol, was named after them.

Winston Churchill, beyond quoting this in his life of Marlborough, showed little interest in his earlier ancestors and seemed not to be drawn to the counties of the West Country. He did, however, have sustained links with the city of Bristol, where he was a long-serving chancellor of the university. His first political speech was delivered in Somerset. Some of the significant days of his childhood were spent on the Isle of Wight and, in his earlier political life, he was close to his Guest cousins, who owned extensive property near Bournemouth.

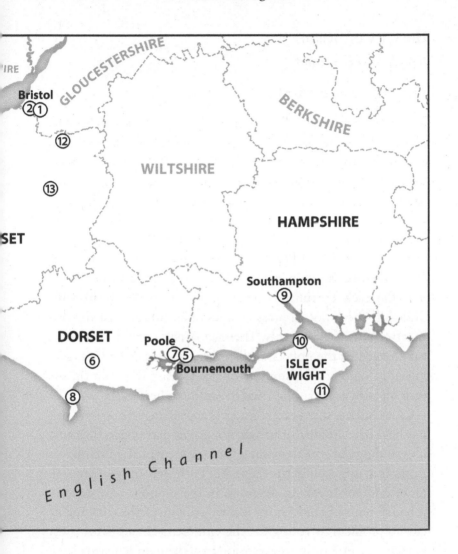

The City of Bristol
Temple Meads Station

WHIPPED BY A SUFFRAGETTE

On 14 November 1909, Winston Churchill arrived with his wife Clementine at the main railway station in Bristol. He was due to address the Anchor Society. As they came off the train, they were greeted by local Liberal Party officials. A young suffragette then broke through a police cordon and started striking Churchill with a dog whip. "Take that, you brute, you brute," she shouted.[1] The whip came down on Churchill's head and face, which were partly protected by a hat. Churchill seized her wrists and was able to remove the whip from her but, in the mêlée, he nearly fell on to the track. Fortunately, he was grabbed to safety by his wife. Churchill chose not to press charges of assault against the suffragette, but the young lady, Theresa Garnett, aged twenty-one, was charged by the police for disturbing the peace and was sentenced to one month's imprisonment. During that month, she went on hunger strike and tried to set fire to her cell.

Churchill became a target for militant suffragette action. This may have been unfair, for he was not unsympathetic to the cause of extending the vote to women, and Clementine Churchill was certainly a supporter of the cause. But both were opposed to militancy and law-breaking. In 1904, in the House of Commons, he had supported a motion for women to be given the vote, and he had no problem in voting for the enfranchisement – for most women – in 1918 or in its extension to all women ten years later. Churchill was, however, seen as the epitome of male privilege. He was certainly more at home in smoke-filled rooms discussing political strategy and tactics with other men than in the drawing room. He appointed only two women to junior positions in his wartime governments – Florence Horsbrugh and Ellen Wilkinson; the former he made his only female cabinet minister in his 1951 government. But Clementine Churchill was highly political, as was Violet Bonham Carter – the daughter of the prime minister, H. H. Asquith – who was one of his oldest friends. With both, he discussed politics without any condescension, and he sometimes took political advice from his wife.

But in 1909, as one of the most prominent Liberal ministers, he attracted attention – such was the flipside of self-promotion. And after he became home secretary in 1910, he was obliged to enforce the law as it was. This meant supporting action against suffragettes who deliberately set out to break the law. This polarised feelings between him and militant suffragettes and has somewhat distorted history.

University of Bristol

A LONG-SERVING UNIVERSITY CHANCELLOR

The University of Bristol grew out of the city with support from its business leaders, especially the Frys (manufacturers of chocolate) and the Willses (makers of cigarettes). Outside Oxford and Cambridge, universities tended to be middle-class endeavours, catering for local students and with an atmosphere of earnest endeavour. Often, in order to give the university some status and dignity, a local aristocrat might be chosen to be chancellor. Selection was made locally and not imposed by the government.

In 1929, Winston Churchill was appointed chancellor of Bristol University, and he was to hold the position for the rest of his life. This was an honorific rather than executive role. It was the vice-chancellor who was chief executive officer. Churchill was a curious appointment for – apart from being whipped by a suffragette in 1909 – he had no connection with the city.

The idea of Churchill as chancellor seems to have come from Sir William McCormick, an academic and a higher education administrator. Like Churchill, McCormick had a Dundee connection: he had taught at Queen's College there, though several years before Churchill represented that city in parliament. More recently, McCormick had been chairman of the University Grants Committee, the body that channelled public funds to universities. As such, he had been in regular contact with Churchill during his years as chancellor of the exchequer. After initial hesitation on the grounds that he had no academic qualifications – at that time, he still had a complex about not having been a university student himself – Churchill accepted the honour. He would become one of the longest-serving chancellors in the history of British universities.

Before his appointment, the chancellor had been Lord Haldane, a Liberal statesman who had sat around Asquith's cabinet table with Churchill. With the implosion of the Liberal Party at the end of the First World War, Haldane had moved to the Labour Party and was Lord Chancellor in Ramsay MacDonald's first Labour government of 1924. Although Churchill had moved from the Liberal Party in the opposite political direction, Churchill always had a warm affection for the older man, who died in 1928.

Churchill paid eleven visits to the university between 1929 and 1954. He was a little casual in the first decade, often calling off a visit at a late hour. But from wartime onwards, he took his role seriously. He was conscientious in nominating people for honorary degrees and in presiding over university occasions with panache – even showmanship. He did not wear the gown of a university chancellor but the robes worn by his father, Lord Randolph Churchill, when he had been chancellor *of the exchequer* in 1886. Churchill's mother had kept the robes, and Churchill also wore them on formal occasions when he himself was chancellor of the exchequer.

During his first graduation ceremony in December 1929, Churchill nominated and awarded an honorary degree to the then Labour chancellor of the exchequer Philip Snowden, for whom Churchill had a quixotic regard – Snowden was a subject in his book, *Great Contemporaries.*

Churchill was appreciative of the city and the university during his 1930s "wilderness" years, and during the war paid two ceremonial visits to the city. Two of his senior Labour Party colleagues in his war administration had close connections with the city: Ernest Bevin, minister of labour, was born in Somerset and had been a trade unionist in Bristol, and A. V. Alexander, First Lord of the Admiralty, had been born in Weston-super-Mare, not far from the city.

In November 1940, Bristol suffered badly from German bombing, and Churchill wrote to the Lord Mayor of Bristol expressing solidarity with the people of the city. As chancellor of the university, he wrote, "I feel myself united to them with a special bond of sympathy".[2] During these raids, the Great Hall of the Wills Memorial Building at the university was bombed.

Four months later, Churchill came to Bristol in person. The university had decided to hold no graduation ceremony for the duration of the war, but Churchill persuaded them otherwise. The prime minister of Australia, Robert Menzies, the new United States ambassador, J. G. Winant, and the president of Harvard, J. B. Conant, were all in Britain. Churchill had the idea of showing them how a provincial city was facing up to German bombing raids. Moreover, the United States had not yet entered the war, and such a visit might help to sway American public opinion.

On 11 April 1941, the day before Churchill's scheduled visit to Bristol, the city was subject to one of the most intensive air raids of the whole war. Over two hundred people were injured. During the raid, Churchill's train was on its way to Bristol and was held up in a siding to the east of the city from where they could see and listen to the raids on the docklands and residential areas. The following morning, Churchill, accompanied by the Lord Mayor, toured the most devastated areas and talked to survivors. "God bless you all," he said. "We will give it to them back."[3]

The graduation ceremony took place in the afternoon of 12 April 1941. Outside, buildings were still smouldering. Churchill made a stirring speech in the presence of professors whose academic gowns were worn over stained fire-fighting uniforms. When he left the university, Churchill was cheered by crowds in the street. He was in tears when the train pulled out of the station.

Understandably, Churchill was too busy to come to Bristol again until April 1945, when the country was on the brink of victory. The City Council gave him the Freedom of the City. That year, honorary degrees were awarded to Ernest Bevin (who had left school at the age of eleven) and A. V. Alexander. Churchill made a triumphant progress through the city.

He was able to visit the university more frequently after the war. More of his wartime colleagues received honorary degrees: the former secretary of the cabinet, Sir Edward Bridges, Field Marshal Lord Alanbrooke, the Marshal of the Royal Air Force, Lord Portal of Hungerford, and Sir Stafford Cripps – incidentally a Bristol MP.

Churchill came again in November 1954, the month of his eightieth birthday, and five months before he was finally persuaded to retire as prime minister. It was a festive occasion, with a feeling that this might be Churchill's last visit – as indeed it was. There were honorary degrees for Churchill's chancellor of the exchequer, R. A. Butler, and for his minister of labour, Sir Walter Monckton (who had also been a Bristol MP). To undergraduates, he seemed not an old man but a man with a puckish humour. They greeted him with cheers. One person present told Churchill's doctor, Lord Moran, that he had seen him a few days earlier at Buckingham Palace, "sitting on a sofa, apparently too weary to listen to anybody... he seemed a very old man who had not long to live. But at Bristol, he was pink, his expression was full of animation, and his eyes twinkled".[4]

The last ten years of Churchill's life were a decade of sad, unrelenting physical and mental deterioration, but there was never any question of hinting that he withdraw from his chancellorship in favour of a more active person. The city and university were immensely proud of the association.

A Churchill Hall was built to honour him. It was opened in 1956.

Devon

Devonport, Forum Cinema

RANDOLPH CHURCHILL VERSUS MICHAEL FOOT

The dockyard quarter of the city of Plymouth used to be a separate town. Although as a port it dated back to the Middle Ages, Plymouth was not built up as a naval dockyard until the nineteenth century.

In February 1950, Churchill came to Devon during the general election to speak on behalf of his son, Randolph, who was the

Conservative candidate for Devonport. The Labour candidate was Michael Foot, who had arranged for Aneurin Bevan to come and speak on his behalf the same day. Churchill loathed Bevan, who had been an eloquent thorn in his flesh during the Second World War.

Churchill spoke at the Forum Cinema, Devonport, which was built in 1939 and is still standing. It now serves as a bingo hall.

Churchill began his speech by recalling two previous visits to Plymouth. He came in 1940 when, as First Lord of the Admiralty, he welcomed HMS "Exeter after her glorious victory in the Battle of the Plate".[5] The second time was after an air raid when he and Clementine Churchill drove through the streets and "I was inspired to see the high morale which everyone in the city and in the dockyard maintained".[6]

Randolph Churchill lost.

Plymouth Railway Station

TWO CONTRASTING WARTIME VISITS

Winston Churchill arrived at Plymouth from London in May 1941 after a heavy air raid on the city. He had travelled by sleeper, having spent a few hours at a Devonshire siding. He walked with his entourage for miles around the quays, the barracks and the workshops and drove round the city, which had suffered more devastation than the dockyards. They saw a bus that had been projected by the force of the explosion on to the roof of a building 150 yards away. The visit depressed him greatly, and he repeated constantly to his secretary, "I've never seen the like."[7]

Churchill was back in Plymouth nine months later in very different circumstances. After the United States entered the war following Japan's assault on Pearl Harbor, he went to America for a second wartime visit to see President Franklin D. Roosevelt, spending Christmas Day at the White House. He flew by a Boeing flying boat south to Bermuda. He made friends with the chief pilot, Captain Kelly Rogers, and even took over the controls for a bit.

"What about flying from Bermuda to England?" Churchill asked him. "Can she carry enough petrol?"

"Of course we can do it," Rogers answered with excitement. "The present weather forecast would give a forty mile tail wind behind us. We could do it in twenty hours."

"How far is it?"

"About three thousand five hundred miles."[8]

At Bermuda, he raised the matter with the First Sea Lord, Sir Dudley Pound, and the Chief of the Air Staff, Sir Charles Portal, who had accompanied the Prime Minister on the transatlantic visit. They initially thought the risks too great, but they were ready to come with him. There was also room for Lord Moran, his doctor, and Lord Beaverbrook as well as one or two others.

After Churchill addressed the Bermuda Assembly, the party went by launch to the flying boat, which took off ponderously. Churchill had a comfortable bed in the plane's bridal suite. (What about the others?) They set out in the afternoon and the next morning Churchill sat with the pilot. There had been heavy cloud, and the crew were anxious. Wireless navigation was restricted in 1942, and the crew felt they should be above the Scilly Isles. In short, the crew did not know where they were. Portal studied some charts and said they should turn north. Within half an hour they sighted England and, in due course, reached Plymouth.

What had happened, Churchill later learned, was that the flying boat had strayed seriously off course. Had they continued another five or six minutes before changing direction, they would have been within range of German batteries at Brest – or so the story goes. They then had to approach Plymouth from the southeast instead of from the southwest. They were coming from the direction of the enemy, were suspected as a hostile bomber and six Hurricanes were ordered to shoot the flying boat down. Their mission failed, and Churchill and his party landed safely – having dodged being shot down by either side.

Dorset
Bournemouth, Alum Chine

A FIRST BRUSH WITH DEATH

Shortly after Winston Churchill's eighteenth birthday, he, his mother and younger brother Jack were staying at Canford Manor House, the home of his aunt, Lady Wimborne. The Canford Estate extended for thousands of acres, including woodlands that stretched down to Poole Bay on the western side of Bournemouth. The estate had been bought in the middle of the nineteenth century by Sir John Josiah Guest, who had built up what was then the largest iron works in the world at Dowlais, outside Merthyr Tydfil in South Wales.

The Guest family was seriously rich, but they lacked aristocratic blood. They made up for this with good marriages. Sir Josiah's son married the sister of Lord Randolph Churchill. Her husband became the first Lord Wimborne.

The pine woodlands behind the cliffs were cut by deep gorges called chines. In December 1892, the Churchill boys and Lionel, a son of Lady Wimborne, were playing in the woods, chasing each other through this wilderness. Across Alum Chine was a "rustic" bridge. Winston was being pursued by the younger boys and found himself on the middle of the bridge with a pursuer at each end. Winston was cornered. He saw that there were lofty fir trees, whose branches touched the bridge. He decided in an instant to leap onto the upper branches and somehow slither down to the ground thirty feet below. He "plunged, throwing out my arms to embrace the summit of the fir tree".[9]

But he fell to the ground, knocking himself out. Lionel and Jack rushed to find Lady Randolph. "He jumped over the bridge and he won't speak to us," they reported.[10] Winston returned to consciousness three days later and was convalescent for two months, with injuries including a ruptured kidney.

This was one of a number of near escapes from death in Churchill's early adulthood. It gave him a sense of immunity and added to the notion, which he expressed during the time of his soldiering abroad in his early twenties, that he was somehow being preserved for greater things.

The rustic bridge was replaced in the early twentieth century and is now a pedestrian bridge accessible from West Overcliff Road on the east and Studland Road on the west. Although there has been some dispute about the actual spot of this adventure, a walk over the bridge gives you a clear idea of what happened. All the local details fit in with the account of the accident.

During the twentieth century, most of the Canford Estate was sold for millions. Villas and comfortable houses have replaced much of the woodland. Canford Manor House, to the west of Wimborne Minster, became a public school, one of the most expensive in the country.

Moreton

CHURCHILL AND LAWRENCE OF ARABIA

In the cemetery of this quiet village lies the grave of T. E. Lawrence, so-called 'Lawrence of Arabia'. Although Lawrence had, in 1923, changed his name to T. E. Shaw, the headstone bears the name by which he has been better known. In 1935, when he was killed in a motorcycle accident at Bovingdon nearby, his mother was still alive and probably insisted on the name Lawrence being used.

Winston Churchill attended Lawrence's funeral on 21 May 1935 along with many other mourners, including Sir Ronald Storrs, the poet Siegfried Sassoon, the artist Augustus John, the military theorist B. H. Liddell Hart and Nancy Astor MP. Churchill had admired Lawrence for his courage and heroism in the campaign in Arabia and Transjordan and in his role in the liberation of Damascus from Ottoman rule. Lawrence had had a remarkable career, in both scholarship and intelligence. He was an interesting man – vain, original, secretive, flamboyant, tortured and erudite. But there were parallels in the careers of both men. Both became British war heroes at a time of military disaster. Churchill was a self-publicist and gave lectures in Britain and in the United States about his adventures; Lawrence relied on an American journalist, Lowell Thomas, to trumpet his cause. Both had a heroic story that raised the spirits of a public depressed by news of the grimmer realities of war.

Churchill and Lawrence were both fluent writers and their stories became classic works of war literature. Both accounts have been subject to scrutiny and some scepticism, but there are few doubts about the literary quality of the writings of both men.

Lawrence was a hero only to the British – and, to a lesser

extent, the Americans. In France, he was seen as a malign anti-French agent. He gets few mentions in German military records of the Levant campaigns, and in Greater Syria he is seen as exclusively concerned with British – not Arab – interests.

In early 1921, Churchill was appointed secretary of state for the colonies and immediately set up a Middle East Department within the Colonial Office, uniting a British policy that had been a responsibility shared by the Foreign Office and the India Office. In doing so, Churchill popularised the term 'Middle East'. He appointed T. E. Lawrence as an adviser and they both went off to attend a conference in Cairo with imperial proconsular officials who settled the borders of the region.

Lawrence had no love of bureaucracy and had misgivings about the post-war settlement. He gave up advising Churchill after one year, instead seeking anonymity in the Royal Tank Corps and the Royal Air Force. He later retired to live reclusively at Clouds Hill near Moreton. But he maintained a correspondence with the great and the good (including Churchill) until his death.

The Moreton Tea Rooms in the village caters for Lawrence pilgrims. The café has the bier on which his coffin was borne, and displays photographs taken at the funeral, including one of Churchill following the coffin.

The funeral took place in St Nicholas's parish church, an eighteenth-century Gothic building with glass engraved by Laurence Whistler.

Poole, Salisbury Road, Upper Parkstone

THE POLITICAL INFLUENCE OF THE GUESTS

Tucked away off the Ashley Road and near a supermarket at number 1, Salisbury Road, is the handsome large Liberal Club. A foundation stone tells us that it was laid in 1909 by Lady Wimborne. It was opened the following year by Winston Churchill, then Home Secretary in H. H. Asquith's Liberal government.

Lady Wimborne was Churchill's aunt, the sister of Lord Randolph Churchill and daughter of the seventh Duke of Marlborough. The Guests owned much land locally and wielded great social and political influence in the area. One of Lady Wimborne's sons, Frederick ("Freddie"), was a very close friend of Churchill's.

The Club still thrives, with a bar and billiard table on the ground floor and the offices of the constituency's Liberal Democratic Party upstairs. Displayed prominently is a photograph of the opening with Winston Churchill and Frederick Guest.

A hundred yards away on the corner of Churchill Road and Ashley Road is a pub called The Churchill.

Portland, Naval Base, Castletown

FROM WHERE THE D-DAY LANDINGS IN NORMANDY WERE LAUNCHED

For centuries, Portland was a major element in the defences of England. The peninsula, with its hills, is linked to the rest of Dorset by a narrow isthmus, like Gibraltar. The bay to the east is sheltered. King Henry VIII had a castle built here, and it was a major naval base until the mid-1990s. Torpedoes were developed in the bay.

In the days leading up to 6 June 1944, Portland was busy with the arrival of half a million troops and thousands of vehicles and tanks, ready for the invasion of Normandy. Castletown D-Day Centre – a museum with replica aeroplanes and army vehicles as well as waxwork models of soldiers – gives a feeling of what those days were like.

On 15 June 1938, Winston Churchill visited Portland's naval base and was shown how asdic worked. This was an early mechanism for detecting the movements of submarines, and it became of great importance for the defence of convoys bringing essentials into the United Kingdom during the war. Churchill stayed overnight on a flagship.

After he became First Lord of the Admiralty on the outbreak of war in 1939, he toured all the naval bases in the country. Very little escaped his attention, and he was always concerned with the welfare and recreation of the ordinary sailors.

On completing his tour of Portland, he spoke to the commander in chief.

"Not much entertainment here for the men, is there?"[11]

He immediately engaged in details and, by the time he left, arrangements had been made for entertainments for officers and ratings.

Hampshire
Southampton Docks

SEEING TROOPS OFF AS THEY HEADED FOR NORMANDY

Churchill wanted to accompany the soldiers who were to invade France on D-Day in June 1944. It was only on the express instructions of King George VI that, loyal monarchist that he was, he was made to change his mind. (And he did cross the Channel six days after the first Normandy landings.) But he came to Southampton with Ernest Bevin, the minister of labour, to see the soldiers off. He was overcome with emotion at the sight and called out, "Good luck, boys."

One soldier approached him.

"Have you got your ticket, Sir?"

"What ticket?"

"One like this," said the soldier, holding up a piece of paper. "It entitles me to a free trip to France."

"I wish I had," answered Churchill, holding back tears. "If only I were a few years younger, nothing would have kept me away."[12]

Isle of Wight
Cowes, Rosetta Cottage, 57 Queen's Road

WHERE RANDOLPH MET JENNIE

Cowes Week is one of the world's major regattas for amateur yachtsmen. It has traditionally taken place at the beginning of August and dates back to 1826. As well as a sporting fixture, Cowes Week is a major social event, and it was during the regatta that Winston Churchill's parents met in August 1873.

Lord Randolph Churchill was twenty-four, the second son

of the seventh Duke of Marlborough. He had been educated at Eton College and Merton College in the University of Oxford, and had not yet launched himself on his brief but dazzling political career.

Jennie Jerome was nineteen years old, the eldest daughter of a wealthy American businessman, Leonard Jerome. The Jeromes were a Huguenot family that had emigrated to the United States from the Isle of Wight in the early eighteenth century. Leonard was a major shareholder of the *New York Times* and owned property in that city. A keen sportsman, he was particularly interested in horseracing and was a patron of racing in New York. The Jerome Stakes race is named after him, and he was co-founder (with a Vanderbilt) of Coney Island Jockey Club. There are avenues named after him in both Brooklyn and the Bronx. He had three daughters (a fourth had died as a little girl) who spent most of their girlhood in Paris. Jennie, christened Jeanette, was fluent in French, was an accomplished pianist – she was able to play Beethoven piano sonatas – and dancer, and had aspirations to write. All accounts report that she was stunningly attractive and beautiful. For the Cowes Week, the Jeromes rented Rosetta Cottage for the family.

One evening, a ball was held on one of the ships, a wooden screw frigate with the name HMS *Ariadne*. Lord Randolph saw the vivacious young Jeanette, in a white tulle dress decorated with freshly picked flowers, at the centre of a group of admirers. And so their eyes met across a floating ballroom. Randolph and Jennie danced a quadrille – but Randolph was not a natural dancer, and they more appropriately sat the next dance out. They talked for the rest of the evening. The following evening, the pair had a (chaperoned) dinner together. And the next evening. Randolph, still besotted, proposed in the garden of this cottage. In some ways, it was a convenient marriage for both of them. The Marlboroughs were very rich in assets but, compared with other ducal families who owned large parts of central London and tracts of Scotland, they were not well-endowed with ready cash. For two generations, the British aristocracy had sought brides from wealthy families in the United States.

Initially, the news of the proposal and the acceptance was not good for either family. "Under any circumstances an American Connection is not one we would like," wrote Lord Randolph's father, the duke.[13] And Mrs Jerome, on hearing the news, refused to acknowledge any engagement. But love was persistent and ultimately triumphed. It suited status-conscious Americans to be associated with a family like the Spencer-Churchills. Both families entered into negotiations as if preparing for an international treaty, and Mr Jerome agreed to settle £50,000 on the couple and give an annual allowance of £1,000. The duke matched this with an annual allowance of £1,100. (For an idea of the value in 2020, one must multiply the sums by a hundred.) The couple, who were big spenders, managed to 'scrape by' on this financial basis without having to worry about earning their own living.

Lord Randolph set a family precedent. Two decades later, his nephew – the ninth duke and Churchill's great friend and cousin, "Sunny" – was to marry a Vanderbilt. This marriage, enthusiastically promoted by Consuelo Vanderbilt's mother, was to end in tears and a divorce.

Randolph and Jennie finally married the following year, in March 1874. Jennie soon became pregnant and Winston Leonard Spencer-Churchill was born at the ducal Blenheim Palace on 30 November.

Lady Randolph entered the social whirl of upper-class London with grace and enthusiasm. Randolph was less outgoing, but they were both preoccupied with the social and political world. Lady Randolph had many admirers, including the Prince of Wales, later King Edward VII. Fifteen years after they married, Lord Randolph became seriously ill with a nervous disease – some say it was syphilis – that affected him mentally and physically. He died in 1895 at the age of forty-five. Lady Randolph married twice after that. Both subsequent husbands were at least twenty years her junior.

They were awful parents to Winston Churchill, but he worshipped both from afar. When he was an adult, the relationship between mother and son became much closer. Lady Randolph used all her charms and connections to further her son's career as a military correspondent. Churchill was also more loyal to his father than Lord Randolph had been to Winston. In 1906, Churchill published a generous two-volume life of Lord Randolph, which has become a classic of political biography. He often saw himself as the political heir of his father, seeing a continuity in his own career.

Winston Churchill, his younger brother Jack and his parents are all united in the family grave at Bladon churchyard in Oxfordshire.

Lady Randolph's two sisters also married on the eastern side of the Atlantic. One married a wealthy Anglo-Irish baronet and the other an Anglo-Irish writer, a gambler and spendthrift, called Moreton Frewen, known to the family as "mortal ruin";[14] their daughter, Clare Sheridan (Winston Churchill's first cousin), became a sculptress and a supporter of Communism.

Rosetta Cottage, a mile to the west of the centre of West Cowes, is now owned by the National Trust and it is possible to rent it. A plaque commemorating the meeting of Winston Churchill's parents has been placed in the pavement across the road.

Ventnor, Wheelers Bay Road, Ventnor Holiday Villas (*formerly Flint Cottage*)

WITNESSING A NAVAL DISASTER

Until the middle of the nineteenth century, Ventnor was a small fishing village at the foot of a terrace of cliffs. The Isle of Wight was a place of escape for those who were much in the public eye. Queen Victoria had Osborne House built between 1845 and 1851, and she died there in 1901. In 1853 the poet laureate, Alfred, Lord Tennyson, bought a house near Freshwater in the west of the island and wintered there for the rest of his life. Charles Dickens escaped for a summer to Bonchurch near Ventnor. It was already becoming a resort by the time the railway was extended to Ventnor in 1866, though the station was inconveniently located on the Newport Road, six hundred feet above the town.

The busy social and political life of Winston Churchill's parents often meant that they did not have time for him when he came home for the school holidays. Instead his nanny, Mrs Everest, had to look after him. Her sister had married John Balaam, who had a succession of jobs on the Isle of Wight: an official at the Ventnor Gas and Water Company, a warder at Parkhurst Prison on the outskirts of Newport, and a rates collector. It is believed that, between 1878 and 1888, Mrs Everest brought the young Churchill to Ventnor five times. The first visits were to Flint Cottage. These trips gave him an interesting exposure to an unfamiliar provincial, lower-middle-class world. Indeed, throughout his life, Churchill was never a social snob and always had the ability to relate to the lives and needs of people brought up in completely different social circumstances.

Flint Cottage looks down a cliff to the seashore. Today, it is named Vine Lodge, and there is a faded plaque recording

Churchill's association with the place. It is now one of the Ventnor Holiday Villas.

Although it has none of the grandeur of either Blenheim Palace or the smart West End houses he and his parents were accustomed to, Churchill was happy here. Ventnor was acquiring a reputation as a resort for the wealthy and well connected; indeed it was known to some as 'Mayfair on Sea', though there is no evidence that the boy Churchill had any connections with people of his class here. He first visited in March 1878 at the age of three while his family was based in Dublin and before he was sent off to school. The Balaams had a son, Charles, who was about the same age as Churchill. On that first visit, while being walked down the steep path from Flint Cottage to the sea, young Winston saw the ship HMS *Eurydice*. This was a corvette, a training ship, that was returning from a winter in the West Indies. A sudden squall sent them back to the house. When they went out again, they could see only three masts protruding from the sea. The ship had capsized in the ferociously stormy seas. All but two of the 319 on board had perished, either from drowning or from exposure. It was one of the worst naval disasters in British peacetime. Then Churchill saw boat after boat bringing corpses ashore.

Ventnor, 28 Mitchell Avenue (formerly 2 Verona Cottages, Newport Road)

DID WINSTON CHURCHILL MEET KARL MARX?

This was another home of the Balaams, the sister and brother-in-law of Winston Churchill's nanny, Mrs Everest. Churchill stayed here as a lad when his parents were apparently more concerned with their social life than their son.

The cottage is the middle of a group of three. It is now privately owned and has no plaque. It is small and cannot have more than three bedrooms. Did the young Winston share a room with the Balaams' son, Charles?

A hundred yards to the west are the offices of the Gas and Water Company where Mr John Balaam worked. Perhaps the modest cottage belonged to the company? The offices are next to a modern industrial estate that includes the site of the former railway station.

Across the road are the St Boniface Downs, steep and wooded. When he was older, on holiday from Harrow, Churchill used to walk on these downs with John Balaam, who would tell him tales of shipwrecks and prison mutinies. John also had a set of Macaulay's *History of England*. At Harrow, Churchill learnt hundreds of lines of Macaulay's poetry by heart and, a decade later, Macaulay would become one of his literary inspirations: Macaulay's rich narrative prose style had a marked influence on his own. The historian had, however, been critical of the great soldier the first Duke of Marlborough, and Churchill's biography of his military ancestor was written partly as a corrective to Macaulay.

From Ventnor, too, Churchill would see and be thrilled by the sight of ships of the Royal Navy.

Midway between Verona Cottages and Flint Cottage is St Boniface Road. During the winters of 1881–1882 and 1882–1883 the ageing Karl Marx – who died in 1883 – wintered at number 1. With his portly corporation and his ample beard, he was a striking figure in his old age, and it is quite possible that he would have attracted the attention of a curious and observant red-headed seven- or eight-year-old boy.

Somerset
Claverton

HIS FIRST POLITICAL SPEECH

Claverton is a sparsely populated village four miles south-east of Bath, overlooking the River Avon and the Kennet and Avon Canal. The local Claverton Manor is a magnificent house, designed by Jeffry Wyatville, that today houses the American Museum in Britain. In July 1897, Winston Churchill made his first political speech here.

As a young man, Churchill always aimed to get into politics; he wanted to continue the work of his father, Lord Randolph Churchill. The Conservative Party was the natural vehicle for his aspirations, but he first wanted to see the world, experience some military action and earn some money. (By the time he was twenty-five, he had achieved all three ambitions.)

In the summer of 1897, Churchill was on leave from his army duties in India and made contact with the Conservative Central Office, saying he wanted to be a parliamentary candidate. He was told he should speak at a party function first. The Primrose League, a Conservative organisation celebrating the memory of Benjamin Disraeli, was holding a rally in the park of Claverton Manor, the home of Henry Skrine, then in his eighties. Churchill was invited to speak there. He was twenty-two.

Churchill travelled to Bath by train. He was very nervous and had meticulously prepared his speech, committing it to memory. He shared a compartment with a reporter from the *Morning Post*. They chatted to each other and he "tried one or two titbits on him, as if they had risen casually in conversation".[15] As his speech was much about the Workman's Compensation Bill, the journalist must have been bemused at the young man's eloquent earnestness.

They reached Bath station and travelled on to Claverton. Churchill collected his official badge and gave his speech, arguing that "British workmen have more to hope for from the rising tide of Tory Democracy than from the dried-up drainpipe of Radicalism".[16]

Within two days, Churchill was back on a ship returning to India. In his anxious confusion, he found he had forgotten to return his Primrose League badge to old Mr Skrine.

A plaque on the western wall of the house memorialises the speech.

Mells

CELEBRITY GRAVES, ARTISTS AND LADY RANDOLPH'S MISHAP

Mells Manor was the home of the Horners from the sixteenth century. Sir John Horner (1842–1927) was a barrister who became commissioner of Woods, Forests and Land Revenue. He married Frances Graham, a lively Scottish lass, who made Mells Manor a major social centre for artists, writers and politicians. In the parish church and the village can be found work by Edwin Lutyens, Edward Burne-Jones, Alfred Munnings, William Nicholson and Eric Gill.

Winston Churchill stayed at the house in the hot summer of 1911. He was preoccupied by the international crisis, with the Germans rattling their sabres off Agadir in Morocco, confronting France's reinforcement and expansion of its North African possession. The crisis presaged war. Churchill did get away from the manor and recalled in *The World Crisis* how he sat "on a hilltop in the smiling country"[17] with lines from Housman's *Shropshire Lad* running through his mind:

On the idle hill of summer,
Sleepy with the flow of streams,
Far I hear the steady drummer
Drumming like a noise in dreams.

Ten years later, in May 1921, his mother was staying at the manor. She was wearing some new Italian high-heeled shoes and, coming downstairs, she slipped, fell and broke an ankle. (Had her maid failed to sand-paper the slippery leather soles?) A doctor came out from the neighbouring town of Frome and set the broken bone, but she was taken to her London home. The injury worsened, gangrene set in and her leg was amputated. She seemed to improve but then suffered a sudden haemorrhage and died at the end of June. She was sixty-seven.

Her (third) husband, Montagu (Monty) Porch – twenty-three years her junior – originated from nearby Glastonbury. At the time of her death, Monty Porch was away in Africa earning some money to help pay for Lady Randolph's way of life. He was unable to attend the funeral.

Sir John and Lady Horner had two sons, both of whom predeceased them. The youngest child, Katherine, married Raymond, the son of the prime minister H. H. Asquith. Raymond was killed in the First World War, and his widow inherited Mells Manor on the death of her parents. The prime minister, who became the first Earl of Oxford and Asquith, died in 1928, passing his title to his infant grandson, who became the second Lord Oxford for over eighty years. *His* son, Raymond, also inherited both the title and the manor.

In St Andrew's churchyard, adjacent to the manor, are three graves with Churchill connections.

Siegfried Sassoon, despite being regarded as an anti-war poet, was much admired by Churchill, who sought him out at the end of the First World War through his secretary, Eddie Marsh. Sassoon was also a second cousin of Philip Sassoon, who frequently hosted Churchill. Although originally from a Baghdad Jewish family, Siegfried Sassoon became a Roman Catholic under the influence of Monsignor Ronald Knox, whose last years were spent at Mells Manor. It was Sassoon's wish to be buried near the grave of Knox. And so he is, for Knox is buried a few yards away.

Also within a few yards of Sassoon's final resting place is the grave of prime minister Asquith's daughter, Violet. She married her father's principal private secretary, Maurice Bonham Carter. After Asquith became an earl, Violet became Lady Violet Bonham Carter, by which name she was best known. She was very close to Winston Churchill when he was a Liberal MP (1904–1922), and they remained on excellent terms for the rest of his life. She twice stood for parliament as Liberal Party candidate. In 1945, she stood in the Somerset constituency of Wells, and in 1951 for Colne in Lancashire. In the latter election, Churchill persuaded the Conservative Party not to put up a candidate against her. It was reckoned that, had she won, Churchill would have tried to bring her into his cabinet. For her, Mells was "a place of magical beauty".[18] She came frequently to stay at the manor. In December 1964, Lady Violet – now a widow – became a life peeress and she reverted to her maiden name for her title, becoming Baroness Asquith of Yarnbury. Churchill died the following month and the new peeress's first speech in the House of Lords was to pay a tribute to him. She was also a frequent broadcaster. One of her daughters married Joseph Grimond, who became leader of the Liberal Party. A son became the father of the film actor Helena Bonham Carter.

At the northeast of the churchyard is a sadly neglected grave, flanked by four Turkey oaks and designed by Sir Edwin Lutyens.

Here lies the Liberal politician Reginald McKenna. In his middle age, he married a niece of Sir John and Lady Horner. The prime minister, Asquith, was very fond of the young Mrs McKenna. The McKennas lived at Mells Park in the village, a house designed by Lutyens. McKenna preceded Winston Churchill in the Liberal cabinets of Campbell-Bannerman and Asquith as president of the Board of Trade and as First Lord of the Admiralty, and also succeeded him as home secretary. But they were not close. McKenna was seen as uptight and prissy.

5

CENTRAL BRITAIN

EAST ANGLIA, THE MIDLANDS AND WALES

Central Britain is made up of East Anglia, the Midlands and Wales. If we count Oxfordshire as part of the Midlands, then it includes where Churchill was born and where he was buried.

His constituency for the last forty years of his political life was in Essex, but Churchill had also stood for parliament at Leicester. He never lived in the Midlands or took holidays there or in Wales, though his family spent time at the seaside in Norfolk.

Unlike Scotland and Ireland, Wales has few intimate links with Winston Churchill. He came to the country to give speeches, visited the major cities after bomb damage in the Second World War and attended the Conservative Party conference at Llandudno in 1948. In those days, the Conservative leader would only attend for the last day to give a rallying speech.

Nevertheless, one controversial story connects Churchill with Wales: that he sent in the army to crush a miners' strike in the south of the country.

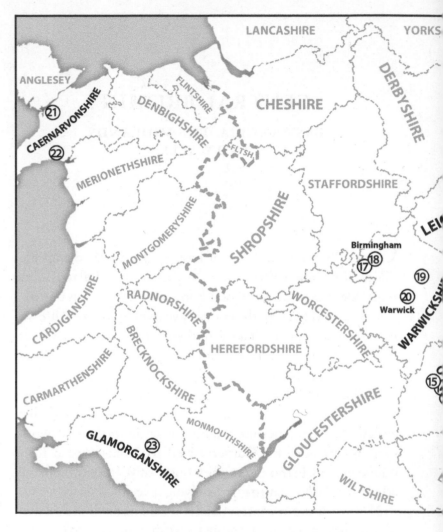

Cambridgeshire
Cambridge, Churchill College

A MAJOR LEGACY

Six weeks before his eighty-fifth birthday, Winston Churchill flew from Biggin Hill, five miles from Chartwell, to Cambridge to plant an oak tree. This was a symbol of laying the foundation stone for the college that was named after him. He was accompanied by Clementine Churchill and was met at the airport by Sir John Cockcroft, nuclear scientist and master designate of the college. The Churchills had lunch at King's College before going to the site of the proposed college. Among those present at the tree-planting was Frank Cousins, general secretary of the Transport and General Workers' Union (T&GW). The union was donating £50,000 to the college for a library to commemorate the life and work of Ernest Bevin, the leading trade unionist of his generation and a member of Churchill's war cabinet. Churchill was very fond of Bevin, who was born out of wedlock in Somerset, had minimal education but, through drive and personality, created the T&GW and, after the war, became foreign secretary in Attlee's Labour government.

Churchill's spadework as he dug a space for the tree was vigorous, and the soil flew. Some of the distinguished spectators had to retreat to avoid their shoes being filled. He gave a speech in which he welcomed research in technology that would be the basis for mankind "to probe ever more deeply into the mysteries of the universe in which we live".[1] He then attended a short meeting of the trustees of the college.

Churchill College was intended to devote seventy per cent of its efforts to science, engineering and technology. Churchill's interest in the idea had been stimulated by the complaints of

Professor Frederick Lindemann, later Lord Cherwell, known as 'the Prof'. He had bemoaned the fact that Britain lacked the equivalent of the Massachusetts Institute of Technology. The college's first students were admitted in 1961. It started with sixty fellows and 540 undergraduates.

Churchill College houses the Churchill Archive Centre, the most comprehensive resource for Churchill studies: his works, his papers and everything related to him. The college also stores the papers of a later Conservative prime minister, Margaret Thatcher.

Cheveley

A CHERISHED CHILDHOOD HOME

Winston Churchill had a peripatetic childhood. He was born at his grandparents' house, Blenheim Palace. His parents had no permanent address, instead renting houses in the West End of London, and he was shipped off to boarding school at the age of eight. There was no place he could call home. Holidays from school were spent in the austere splendour of Blenheim Palace or at boarding houses in Norfolk, and elsewhere. The London homes revolved not around the children but around the busy political and social lives of his parents. On more than one summer he was sent off to the Isle of Wight to stay with the family of his nanny, Mrs Everest.

Lord Randolph Churchill was keen on horseracing and took a country house for a few years until 1892 at the village of Cheveley, four miles south of Newmarket. The house, Banstead, was big enough for family and guests. The grounds were large enough for Churchill and his younger brother, Jack, to run around as they liked. On one occasion, Churchill had been unwell on his way by train to Newmarket but became better on arrival at Banstead and danced around all evening. Next morning, he was up before breakfast, going out to shoot rabbits with the keeper.

One summer, the teenage Churchill had the idea of building a den in the garden for himself, his brother and his cousins. He got some estate workers to construct a large hut, with mud and planks. It was carpeted with straw and had a moat and draw-bridge. The den was guarded by a large catapult that propelled apples, sometimes hitting unwitting cows.

Lord and Lady Randolph Churchill liked to host parties to coincide with the racing season. In 1891, they planned a big party – so big that there was no place for their sixteen-year-old son. They delegated passing on the news that he was not wanted to Mrs Everest, who wrote to Winston, "Well, my dearest the reason Mamma cannot have you home is the house is to be full of visitors for the race week."[2]

In the late summer of 1892, Churchill – seventeen at the time and about to go for his final term at Harrow – was shooting at rabbits and fired off below windows of the house. His father was disturbed and was furious. Churchill admired his father from afar, but Lord Randolph had never shown any understanding of or empathy with his son. On this occasion, however, Lord Randolph repented his anger, called his son in and apologised and then chatted to him "in the most wonderful and captivating manner" about life, the army and public affairs. "I listened spell-bound to this complete departure from his usual reserve, amazed at his intimate comprehension of all my affairs."[3]

In that year, Lord Randolph's financial difficulties obliged him to give up Banstead Manor.

Churchill inherited Lord Randolph's interest in horseracing late in life and adopted his colours for his own horses.

The house Churchill knew was burnt down in the 1920s. Its replacement is now the base for the Juddmonte stables, belonging to Prince Khalid bin Abdullah of Saudi Arabia.

Essex
Chigwell, The King's Head

IN THE STEPS OF BARNABY RUDGE

A hostelry that Churchill got to know here was the King's Head, made famous in Charles Dickens's novel *Barnaby Rudge*, where it featured as the Maypole Inn. In early 1939, a meeting of the Chigwell branch of the Conservative Party met here, under the chairmanship of Colin Thornton-Kemsley. This man organised a campaign against Churchill in the constituency. Churchill, he argued, was disloyal to the party leader, Neville Chamberlain. Thornton-Kemsley issued a press statement declaring his intransigence towards Winston Churchill's "unhelpful attitude towards the man at the helm in these times when national unity is a prime necessity".[4]

Attitudes towards their MP were quite different six years later, immediately after the war, when Churchill made a triumphant tour of his constituency and had lunch here. The proprietor found a spare room for Churchill to have his customary afternoon shut-eye.

Chingford, Royal Forest Hotel

SCENES OF TRIUMPH

The Royal Forest Hotel was a regular venue for speeches delivered by Winston Churchill to his constituents when he was MP for Epping. It was the site of victory rallies after the general elections of 1924 and 1929. In the late 1930s, he addressed crowded meetings here warning of German rearmament and the need for Britain to respond in kind. At the time, he was trying to extend his message beyond the ranks of the Conservatives. In December 1938, he addressed a meeting of the local branch of the League of Nations Union. On this occasion he was heckled by local fascists who cried out, "Mind Britain's business", to which Churchill answered back: "We are minding our own business. We don't want organisations which seem chiefly to be minding Germany's business."[5]

Epping, Epping Forest

HIS CONSTITUENCY FOR TWENTY YEARS

Epping Forest lies ten or so miles to the northeast of central London. According to H. G. Wells, the presence of the forest was one of the reasons why what he called "villadom" did not spread into Essex. This county was more plebeian than those to the south and west. But the area around the forest had some smart residences inhabited by smart people.

In the spring of 1924, Churchill had fought and lost a by-election in Westminster. He had presented himself as a Constitutionalist and anti-socialist, disassociating himself from the imploding Liberal Party that had been his political home for the previous twenty years. At the Westminster by-election, he had attracted support from individual Conservatives, though the official party put up a candidate against him. Nevertheless, Churchill was shuffling towards the Conservatives. In the summer of 1924, he was approached by a senior member of the Epping constituency Conservative Party – Sir Harry Goschen, businessman and banker – suggesting he put his name forward as candidate. Although he was not yet a member of the party, he accepted. There was much in it for Churchill. Unlike Dundee, where he had been MP for fourteen years until 1922, it was handy for London and only eighty minutes by car through the Blackwall Tunnel from his new Kent home at Chartwell.

There was an interesting and symmetrical family connection with the Goschens. In 1886, Lord Randolph Churchill abruptly resigned as chancellor of the exchequer from the government of the Marquess of Salisbury. He thought he was indispensable, but Salisbury appointed George Goschen in his place. Goschen had financial and government expertise in previous Liberal administrations, but he had broken with his party over Home Rule for Ireland. Like Winston Churchill forty years later, Goschen was in the process of shifting from the Liberals to the Conservatives. Lord Randolph Churchill was taken aback by the appointment and is alleged to have said that he had "forgotten Goschen".[6]

The constituency was partly rural and agricultural and included the expanding suburbs around the forest: Woodford, Wanstead, Waltham Abbey, Buckhurst Hill, Chigwell, Chingford, Theydon Bois and Loughton. It included villages like Harlow – not yet a new town – and among its constituents was the Labour MP for Limehouse, Clement Attlee. Over the next decade, other constituents were to include the captain of the England cricket team, J. W. H. T. Douglas, who lived in Theydon

Bois, the sculptor Jacob Epstein who lived at Loughton and the actor Laurence Olivier. There were also a number of retired military and naval officers, including Brigadier General R. B. Colvin (who had been MP for the constituency from 1917 to 1923) and Admiral Sir Roger Keyes (who, as an MP in 1942, supported a vote of censure on Churchill's conduct of the war in the House of Commons). Many of the salariat worked in the City of London, for whom the Central Line of the London underground provided an easy commute.

Churchill was duly elected at the general election of 1924 on 29 October. The count took place at the Church Rooms, St John's Road, Epping. After victory was declared, his supporters towed his car with a rope – the twentieth-century version of replacing horses by supporters and physically towing the coach of the hero.

The local party was in general pleased with their celebrity MP. He was reasonably conscientious in keeping local Conservatives happy with regular visits. But he had to work at it, and it was not all plain sailing. The newly returned Conservative prime minister, Stanley Baldwin, surprised many in his party by appointing Churchill as chancellor of the exchequer. After the Conservatives lost their majority in the next general election in 1929, Churchill became a member of the Conservative Party's business committee, the predecessor of the shadow cabinet. The following year, he resigned over differences on Conservatives' support for the Labour Party's policy on India. This was, for Churchill, the beginning of ten years in the political wilderness. In joining the Conservative Party, he had tried to bring in some Liberal values and saw some of his budgets as a continuation of the social reforms of the Liberal government of the years when he was president of the Board of Trade. He had the sympathy of younger and more left-wing Conservatives like Robert Boothby and Harold Macmillan. But in opposing moves towards self-government in India, he found himself allied to the more reactionary members. People in the Conservative Party – while acknowledging his talents, his oratory and his industry – suspected his judgment. This scepticism became acute in 1936 when he spoke up for King Edward VIII during the abdication crisis. He was even hissed at when he spoke in the House of Commons. This cloud of suspicion undermined the impact of his warnings about Nazi Germany.

Churchill used to pay two regular annual visits to the constituency in the 1920s and 1930s, giving speeches in the towns and villages. He would often stay with one of the grandees, though in 1929 Clementine Churchill rented the Wood House in Epping, a large and elegant dower house, for the duration of the election campaign. Churchill would additionally attend garden parties and fêtes.

In 1935, Churchill's son Randolph, aged twenty-four, fought a by-election in Wavertree Liverpool as an Independent Conservative without his father's approval, representing the elder Churchill's dissident views. Some of the party faithful in the constituency were not happy and thought the father was as culpable as the son. Randolph split the right-wing vote, letting in a Labour man. The Nazeing branch of the local Conservative Party was particularly loyal to the Conservative-dominated National government. Led by Major Ralph Bury, they passed a resolution at a meeting in the Chapel Hall deploring "Mr Churchill's consistent opposition"[7] to the government. The constituency party deplored this, but there was more to come.

Churchill had managed to carry most Conservatives in his constituency over India, but it was a different matter when he made a fierce attack on the prime minister, Neville Chamberlain, after a House of Commons debate on the Munich agreement in September 1938. There was strong general local opposition to Churchill's stand and his disloyalty. This time, much of the opposition in the winter of 1938/39 was led by Colin Thornton-Kemsley, who had political ambitions of his own. Thornton-Kemsley thought that many "of the branches are in practically open revolt... They demand a candidate who will support the Prime Minister and the National Government".[8] As he saw it, their member was sheltering under the benevolence of the party whose actions he was criticising. A groundswell of complaint rumbled throughout the winter and into the spring of 1939, with collaboration from Conservative Central Office. Presiding at a meeting of the Nazeing branch of the Conservative Party, again at Chapel Hall, Major Bury resumed his baiting of Churchill. Thornton-Kemsley was a guest speaker and argued that Churchill should resign and stand for re-election as an Independent. A resident grandee, Sir Thomas Fowell Buxton, fifth Baronet, was even approached to stand as the official Conservative candidate against him; Churchill declined the invitation. Thornton-Kemsley had his own parliamentary ambitions and became MP for Kincardine and West Aberdeenshire at the end of March 1939. For him, as a serving MP, it was inappropriate to seek to undermine a colleague. He remained an MP until 1964 but was never given office by Churchill.

Once the war broke out and Churchill joined the government and later became prime minister, all was forgiven. He was not often able to visit his constituency, but the local Conservatives' support for him was intense. Thornton-Kemsley later rued his actions.

The constituency grew in population and the Boundaries

Commission decided that, in the 1945 election, it would be split into two: Epping and Woodford. Churchill was adopted as candidate for Woodford. In the 1945 general election, Epping was won by the Labour candidate, Leah Manning.

Loughton, Lopping Hall, High Road

HOW TO DEAL WITH A HECKLER

Until the nineteenth century, the people of Loughton had the right to 'lop' trees in Epping Forest for fuel. The Epping Forest Act deprived them of this right in 1878, but the people of Loughton were still allowed to graze their animals in the forest. The forest became the responsibility of the City of London Corporation, and, in compensation for the loss of rights, the City arranged for a large public hall to be built in the middle of Loughton. Hence Lopping Hall.

The hall was a frequent venue for political meetings, and Winston Churchill addressed crowded gatherings here several times when he was the local Member of Parliament.

Churchill was nearly always good-humoured when he addressed meetings. Although he prepared his speeches meticulously, he was quick-witted and enjoyed repartee. However, during an election meeting in November 1935, he displayed an unaccustomed annoyance at a heckler. He was talking about the persecution of Jews in Germany and the need to be aware of German rearmament, when someone sitting on the platform behind him called out, "Why tell us so much about Germany? Let's hear more about Great Britain."[9] Churchill turned to face his interrupter and stamped his foot.

"How dare you, Sir! I will not be interrupted from my own

platform! I decide what is important for me to tell my constituents and neither you nor anybody else will stop me."[10]

Today, the hall occupies the corner with Station Road (which provides the main entrance), and it is still used by the public – namely for local dramatic and recreational activities. It is closely surrounded by shops but has some fine Victorian Gothic windows. A plaque records its singular origin.

Waltham Abbey

BAD WEATHER STIMULATES GOOD ORATORY

This old abbey town has been overwhelmed by suburbia. An attractive centre has been preserved near the massive and magnificent abbey where King Harold, defeated by William of Normandy at Hastings in 1066, is thought to be buried.

Monkhams Hall lies a mile north of the town. In the 1920s, it was the home of Brigadier General R. B. Colvin, who had been Unionist (Conservative) MP for Epping between 1917 and 1923. His gardens were host to Conservative Party events, such as the local Conservative Party's summer fête on 16 July 1927. Churchill addressed the crowd from the back of a lorry. The weather was cold and damp, but Churchill made light of it. This climate, he said, "with all its shortcomings, disappointments, menaces and surprises has nevertheless enabled us over the centuries to rear in these islands a race of men and women who have written their names indelibly upon the history of the world".[11]

Woodford Green

THE STORY OF A SUBURBAN STATUE

Just south of Broadmead Road, on the corner of Woodford High Road and Wensley Avenue, is a bronze statue on a rough stone plinth of Winston Churchill, who represented the area in parliament for forty years. The statue is on a small strip of grass ambitiously called 'The Green', an acre or two of common land that was once part of Epping Forest. Sometimes, especially on the anniversary of his birth and death, wreaths and bouquets are laid at the foot of the plinth.

The initiative for erecting the statue came from Churchill's local supporters. Money was raised and, in 1958, a Scottish sculptor called David McFall was commissioned to produce the work. McFall went to the south of France where Churchill was staying. The model gave the sculptor some sittings, and the work was erected in 1959 and formally unveiled in October that year, a few days after Churchill had been re-elected as a Conservative MP for the constituency and six weeks before his eighty-fifth birthday.

The unveiling ceremony was performed by Field Marshal Lord Montgomery of Alamein in the presence of Winston Churchill and his family. Montgomery delayed the proceedings by inspecting a guard of honour. He spoke a few words, ending by saying that Woodford was Churchill's political Alamein. He gazed at the unveiled statue, paused and then saluted it. He then turned to Churchill and saluted him.

Churchill was a man of so many moods and with so many aspects to his personality that no one work of art – be it a photograph, portrait or sculpture – will satisfy everyone or bring out all the features of his life, work and character. In this statue, Churchill himself thought that his feet were made too big. He was curiously proud of his small feet (he took size 6). His bodyguard, Edmund Murray, recalled that it "depicted a pudgy-faced Churchill, a huge head thrust forward, the left hand sweeping back the jacket, and the shoulders stooping. One could see that it was Churchill... and yet it was not he. It was almost as if the sculptor had produced a very good likeness of a Churchill stand-in".[12] The New York *Daily Times* reported that it made Churchill look moronic and as if wearing "an old suit of clothes a couple of sizes too big for him".

1959 would be Churchill's last general election. He came to make a speech earlier in the year to announce his readiness to stand and spoke for twenty-two minutes. His announcement was received "with tumultuous applause".[13] Although he was increasingly frail, both physically and mentally, the constituency was honoured by having him as their Member of Parliament. But he was incapable of carrying out constituency duties; these were dealt with by his constituency association and by neighbouring Conservative MPs.

A few yards to the east of the statue is Broomhill Walk. Here was the home of Sir James Hawkey, who dominated Woodford Conservative politics and local government for most of the first half of the twentieth century. He was a successful local businessman, with a bakery and bread distribution business. For Churchill, Hawkey was a constant tower of strength, "my ever faithful and tireless champion".[14] Close to Hawkey's house was 26 Broomhill Road, which housed the headquarters of the constituency Conservative and Unionist Party. From here, Churchill's first local campaign was managed. When the constituency was divided in 1945 and Epping and Woodford became two separate constituencies, this house was sold for £975.

A few yards away in Broomhill Road, north of Broadmead Road, is the Sir James Hawkey Hall, low, expansive and constructed of brick. It was built to commemorate the great man of Woodford politics. The hall was formally opened by Winston Churchill in 1955, ten days before he finally resigned as prime minister. Four years later, on 29 September 1959, he gave one of his last political speeches here during that year's general election. The result was announced in the hall. In spite of his frailty, he was reluctant to withdraw – even passively – from political life. He announced in April 1963 that he would retire at the end of the parliament; this gave the local party eighteen months to select a new candidate.

Norfolk
Breckles, Breccles Hall

WHERE CHURCHILL PAINTED

Breccles Hall is a fine Tudor mansion, a private house and therefore not open to the public. It is surrounded by extensive gardens, designed by Edwin Lutyens, better known as an architect – he designed the Cenotaph in Whitehall. Breckles is the modern name of the village, but the hall retains an earlier name.

After the First World War, Breccles Hall became the country home of Edwin Montagu, a Liberal politician, and his wife, Venetia. Venetia was a first cousin of Clementine Churchill and a friend of Violet Asquith (later Lady Violet Bonham Carter). Back in 1912, the prime minister H. H. Asquith and Edwin Montagu had gone on holiday to Sicily. Asquith took his daughter, Violet, and Violet took her friend Venetia. Asquith and Montagu both fell in love with Venetia. Over the next few years,

Asquith wrote almost daily to Venetia, intimate letters but also about his views on politics, his colleagues and wartime strategy. Meanwhile, Montagu was also pursuing her – and succeeded in winning her hand. Asquith was emotionally shattered. He was unable to cope politically. The emotional crisis coincided with a political crisis when the exclusively Liberal government was obliged to bring in Conservative ministers to form the first wartime coalition government. Winston Churchill was, at Conservative insistence, removed from the post of First Lord of the Admiralty. Montagu continued to be a government minister.

Eighteen months later, Asquith was forced out and David Lloyd George became prime minister. A few months later, Lloyd George brought Churchill back into the government. Edwin Montagu continued in office. Montagu was Jewish, but he strongly disapproved of the Balfour Declaration, which promised British support for a national home for Jews in Palestine; Churchill, on the other hand, was an enthusiastic supporter. This did not affect their friendship, however. Churchill knew both Edwin and Venetia well, and he was a regular visitor to Breccles between the wars. He painted several pictures of the interior of the house, of the gardens and the Breckland landscape of the area.

In the end, the Montagu marriage was not a happy one. It was childless, and Venetia had close relationships with, among others, Lord Beaverbrook, to whom she handed over the intimate letters she had received from Asquith. Edwin died in 1924, but Venetia stayed on at the house and entertained the Churchills and others. Indeed, Asquith stayed there a few weeks before he himself died.

The gardens at Breccles also had an influence on the design of the gardens at Chartwell. Some of the gardening staff were even loaned to Chartwell.

Venetia lived on until 1948. She is buried in a wood behind the house in a shared grave with her husband, reunited in death.

Today, Breccles Hall can be just glimpsed at the end of a long drive through a security gate.

Cromer

A CHILDHOOD HOLIDAY AT THE SEASIDE

Cromer, famous for its crabs, is still a popular resort for day trips from Norwich. Several of the old hotels have survived, but these were not for Churchill's nanny.

Cromer had two bursts of being fashionable. The first was at the beginning of the nineteenth century; a character in Jane Austen's *Emma* held it to "be the best of all the sea-bathing places". The coming of the railway was delayed but, from the 1880s to the First World War, smart hotels catered for the well-to-do. In 1885, Winston Churchill was sent here with his nanny, Mrs Everest, to holiday for some weeks in the summer. They stayed first at Tucker's Hotel on the seafront and then at Chesterfield Lodge in West Street.

Overstrand, Pear Tree Cottage, The Pleasaunce

A FAMILY HOLIDAY INTERRUPTED BY WAR

The village of Overstrand became a fashionable resort for the wealthy at the end of the nineteenth century. There were two grand houses and several smaller places to rent for the summer. A Christian Endeavour Holiday Home as of 2019, the Pleasaunce was a moderately stately home built for Lord Battersea, who had married a Rothschild. Pear Tree Cottage had six bedrooms and, in July 1914, Clementine Churchill brought her children here – Diana aged six, and Randolph aged three – plus a nanny and a maid, for the summer. They were unaware of the impending war. Winston Churchill, then First Lord of the Admiralty, came for weekends.

Leicestershire
Leicester, De Montfort Hall

CHURCHILL'S LAST LIBERAL STAND

Overlooking Victoria Park to the south of the city centre is De Montfort Hall, a large concert and events venue built by the City Corporation and named after the thirteenth-century statesman Simon de Montfort, Earl of Leicester.

It was here that the votes were counted in the general election of December 1923 when Winston Churchill stood for the last time on the Liberal Party ticket.

Churchill was no stranger to Leicester. He had spoken here in September 1909 – four years before the De Montfort Hall was built – and dealt with the Conservatives in scornful tones. "Do not let us be too hard on them," he proclaimed. "It is poor sport – like teasing goldfish... These ornamental creatures blunder on every hook they seek, and there is no sport whatever in trying to catch them."[15]

In 1923, though, he had a difficult fight. There were two Leicester newspapers, neither of which gave him any support, though the local paper of the rival city of Nottingham, thirty miles away, championed him, thanks to a word in the editor's ear from Churchill's latest friend, the twenty-two-year-old Brendan Bracken.

Churchill's appearances at meetings were greeted with both groans and hoots. But Churchill was nearly always good-humoured and spoke with a conviction that silenced objectors.

His campaign was supported by his wife, Clementine, who confronted a heckler who said Churchill was "unfit to represent the working classes". Clementine Churchill turned on him. With the exception of David Lloyd George, she answered back, her husband had been responsible for more legislation "for the benefit of the working class than any other living statesman".[16]

His principal opponent was the Labour candidate Frederick Pethick-Lawrence, who also had a formidable wife, Emmeline. He was a wealthy Old Etonian, and both husband and wife had been at the forefront of the campaign for women's suffrage. Both had been imprisoned; he had even been on hunger strike and force-fed. Pethick-Lawrence, moreover, had been a conscientious objector in the First World War. He was not Churchill's kind of chap.

Emmeline wrote a song for the election that went:

Vote, vote, vote for Pethick-Lawrence!
Work, work, work, and do your best!
If all workers we enrol,
He is sure to head the poll,
And we'll have a Labour man for Leicester West![17]

Children sang it in the streets, and the local press reported that it was chanted in Churchill's ears as he toured the constituency.

The result was a defeat for Churchill, though he managed to return to parliament a year later, winning Epping with Conservative Party backing. He was consoled in his Leicester loss by an aunt who lived not far from Leicester. "We always thought they were beastly people," she wrote to him.[18]

Oxfordshire
Bladon, St Martin's Church

A SECLUDED FINAL RESTING PLACE

Just outside the estate of Blenheim Palace, this parish church-yard contains the grave of Winston Churchill. His father's body lies nearby with his mother – who was still known as Lady Randolph Churchill, even though she married twice after Lord Randolph died and was, officially, Mrs Porch at the time of her death in 1921. There is no mention of her later two husbands; they are airbrushed out of history.

Churchill's grave is inscribed simply with his full name and his years of birth and death: no honours, no titles, no mention of his achievements. At one stage he thought of being buried at Chartwell, but he later chose to come to the parish of his birth and the graves of his parents.

Other members of the family buried in the Churchill plot at Bladon include four of Churchill's children, Diana, Randolph, Sarah and Mary; Randolph's son Winston; his brother John and nephew Peregrine.

Blenheim Palace lies in the parish of Bladon. The Dukes and Duchesses of Marlborough are buried in the palace chapel and some other members of the family in the Bladon churchyard. One duchess – or rather ex-duchess – born Consuelo Vanderbilt, lies in the Churchill churchyard plot. She was the American first wife of the ninth duke, the cousin of Winston Churchill. She later married a French flying pioneer. The duke married another American, but they drifted apart and the duke ejected the second duchess from Blenheim and became a Roman Catholic.

Blenheim Palace

AN AWESOME BIRTHPLACE

Blenheim Palace is one of the most magnificent stately homes of England. It had been a medieval park belonging to the Crown but, in 1705, Queen Anne gifted the manor of Woodstock to the first Duke of Marlborough after his military victory over French forces at Blenheim (or Blindheim) in Bavaria. The estate spanned 2,500 acres. The architects were John Vanbrugh (who had earlier been a playwright) and his assistant, Nicholas Hawksmoor, who was later to design the western towers of Westminster Abbey. Work proceeded slowly – partly because funding dried up after the Duchess of Marlborough fell out of favour with Queen Anne. The duchess also quarrelled with the architects, so it was not until 1719 that the house was sufficiently ready for the duke and duchess to move in. The duke died only three years later; the duchess lived on for another twenty-two years and supervised work on the estate.

The first duke was a great collector of paintings, but many were sold off by Churchill's grandfather, the seventh duke, between 1884 and 1886. These included works by Raphael, Bruegel, Rembrandt and Holbein.

Work on the palace and the park continued throughout the eighteenth century, for in the 1760s the fourth duke commissioned Lancelot 'Capability' Brown to turn the parkland into the semi-natural landscape that the visitor encounters today. The Great Bridge was originally built not over a lake but over marshlands, which were later flooded to form the present lake. He also added an artificial river with cascades.

To enter the grounds from Woodstock, you pass under a triumphal arch designed by Hawksmoor.

Lord Randolph Churchill and the nineteen-year-old American Jennie Jerome met at the Cowes Regatta on the Isle of Wight in August 1873. It was love at first sight. Jennie was very beautiful and from a wealthy New York family. Randolph was twenty-four, the younger son of a duke; the family had ample assets but not the steady income to which they felt their social station entitled them. They became engaged days after meeting, but the marriage was delayed while the families negotiated a financial settlement. The marriage took place in the chapel of the British Embassy in Paris in March 1874.

Lord and Lady Randolph Churchill had a home in London, and it was expected that their first child would be born there. They were staying at Blenheim Palace in late November. Lady Randolph had been horse riding during the day and went into labour prematurely. She was rushed back to the palace, and a downstairs room was prepared for the birth; this firstborn was Winston Churchill, who appeared at 1.30 a.m. on Monday 30 November 1874. The anticipated children's clothes were in London, so the future prime minister's first clothes had to be borrowed from a family in Woodstock.

The infant was baptised in the font of the chapel on 27 December 1874 by the chaplain of the Duke of Marlborough. His family name was officially Spencer-Churchill, and he was christened Winston Leonard. An unusual name, Winston was called after the first duke's father, who had first brought the family on to the national stage after relative West Country obscurity. Leonard was the name of his American grandfather.

Religion was not a significant element in Churchill's intellectual or spiritual make-up. There is no evidence that he received any formal guidance from his parents. His nanny, Mrs Everest, was Low Church, and he seemed to have imbibed some ideas from her. Although he frequently invoked the Almighty and felt that he had been chosen by Him for great things, Churchill never, in the millions of words he had published, referred to Jesus Christ. He did write an essay on Moses, whom he saw as a national leader, and in old age gave a copy of this to the Israeli prime minister, David Ben Gurion. His religious views seem to coincide with those he attributed to Savrola, the eponymous hero of his youthful novel: "His religion, like that of many soldiers... was merely a jumble of formulas, seldom repeated, hardly understood, never investigated, but a hopeful, but unauthorised belief that it would be well with him if he did his duty like a gentleman."[19]

Blenheim Palace was a constant in Churchill's life. The connection with the Dukes of Marlborough gave him a sense both of emotional security and entitlement. There was never any social ambiguity that is so often the cause of snobbery. Indeed, he was a friend of other dukes (Abercorn, Sutherland and Westminster), but his closest friends were from a variety of class backgrounds. Lindemann was the son of an immigrant German engineer and businessman. F. E. Smith was from a lower-middle-class Merseyside family. Brendan Bracken's father was an Irish builder.

Churchill regularly returned to Blenheim, often for holidays from school or for family Christmases. It was ideal for a child – riding in the grounds, fishing in the lake, putting on plays with cousins. As a young man, he frequently hunted. In the early years of the twentieth century and before he was married, Churchill stayed at the palace for long periods, working on the biography of his father. He was allocated a set of rooms and was able to work through the thirty-two volumes of Lord Randolph Churchill's political papers, bound in handsome morocco leather.

The chapel houses the graves of the Dukes and Duchesses of Marlborough. They include the first duke, the subject of a biography by Churchill, as well as the dukes whom Churchill would have known personally: his grandfather, uncle and first cousin. This cousin, the ninth duke, was, in spite of political differences, a constant and close friend. Three years older than Winston Churchill, he was always known as 'Sunny' – not as a result of his disposition but from the courtesy title he had as a child, the Earl of Sunderland. (The son and heir of the Duke of Marlborough has the courtesy title of Marquess of Blandford; *his* eldest son is known as the Earl of Sunderland.) Sunny had a political and military career, serving as a junior minister in the governments of the Marquess of Salisbury and as an officer in the Boer War.

Blenheim is also the location of Churchill's courtship of his future wife, Clementine Hozier. Clementine was from a broken home. Her father had been a soldier who was also, like his son-in-law, a military historian. He was separated from his wife, Lady Blanche, a daughter of the Scottish peer the Earl of Airlie. Lady Blanche and her daughters were far from well off and lived in genteel poverty for many years in France. This became useful when they were back in London, for Clementine Hozier was able to earn some money by giving French lessons.

Churchill was already in his thirties and a government minister when he met his future bride at a dinner party in London. He had had flings and one serious romance before. In 1901, his offer of marriage to Pamela Plowden was rejected. She married the Earl of Lytton the following year, but she and Churchill remained on the best of terms for the rest of his life (she outlived him). Churchill had the reputation of being socially rather gauche with women, either ignoring them or lecturing them.

But Clementine Hozier was different. She was twenty-three in 1908 and had already had proposals of marriage. She became friends with Churchill, and they began an extraordinary correspondence. Clementine Hozier was invited to Blenheim to meet Churchill's cousin, the ninth duke, in early August 1908. By this time, Churchill had made up his mind to propose. He always had a sense of theatre and planned his moves carefully: it was fitting that the proposal would take place with many happy family and personal associations. The duke was informed of the plan. A small dinner party was arranged for Monday 10 August. Churchill's mother was present, as well as Churchill's close friend the Conservative MP F. E. Smith, and his wife.

Before they retired, Churchill made an arrangement to have a walk around the Rose Garden with Clementine after breakfast the following morning. Clementine came down to breakfast the next day, but there was no Winston – who was never very good at getting up in the morning. Clementine felt embarrassed. She wondered if her imagination had made a terrible mistake and was prepared to return to London straightaway. The duke detected her discomfort and sent a note up to Churchill's room, offering to take Clementine for a ride round the park while he performed his morning toilette. She agreed and, on their return, found Churchill up and dressed. They went off for their walk. A shower of rain obliged them to take shelter in the Temple of Diana, a small Grecian building designed by Sir William Chambers. There they paused. Clementine had a shrewd idea about what was coming, but Churchill seemed to dither. Clementine looked down at the paving stones and watched an insect slowly crawling across the floor. If it reaches that crack without Winston popping the question, she said to herself, then he is not going to at all. But Churchill did propose, and she accepted – but on the condition that it should not be made public until after her mother was informed.

They walked back to the main palace and met the duke and his guests on the lawn. Churchill could not contain his gleeful and triumphant excitement and burst out with his news, breaking his promise to his new fiancée within minutes. She forgave him.

Clementine was due to return to London the following morning. Churchill wrote a letter to Lady Blanche for Clementine to deliver. He was to see her off at Woodstock station and return to the palace; he had brought work (and a civil servant) to the palace. But, at the station, he changed his mind and went to London with Clementine. They both brought Lady Blanche back to Blenheim.

Churchill and Clementine were married at St Margaret's Church Westminster a month later, on 12 September, and started the first days of their honeymoon at Blenheim Palace.

Beatrice Webb, the socialist and socialite, thought Clementine was "a charming lady". She was not rich, and it "was by no means a good match which is to Winston's credit".[20]

Fifty years after the engagement, Clementine and Winston Churchill returned to Blenheim to celebrate. One of the guests was the historian A. L. Rowse, who noted how he was unsteady on his feet but beaming happily. "It was sad to see him," Rowse recorded in his journal. "Still the centre of all our attention, the embers of a great fire, all the force gone. Very deaf now, and rather impenetrable, apparently he had asked for me to sit beside him at dinner, the ladies' talk being like 'the twittering of birds' to him."[21]

Inside the Temple of Diana is a plaque to commemorate the site of the proposal. It was unveiled by Clementine Churchill herself, then ninety years old, in 1975. Nearby is a Churchill Memorial

Garden with a windy paved path, ninety yards in length, marking the ninety years of his life. Halfway along is a large bust of Churchill sculpted by Oscar Nemon.

Blenheim was a site for Conservative Party rallies, which were attended by Churchill when he was not a Liberal. When he wooed and married Clementine, he was seen as on the left wing of the Liberal Party. Clementine remained a Liberal all her life, though she loyally supported her husband in his political career, even speaking on Conservative platforms. Churchill's cousin, however, the ninth duke, remained a Conservative. Blood was thicker than political water, but there was a slight temporary estrangement in 1912. Churchill had been a vociferous defender of the social reforms of the Liberal government and a close ally of the chancellor of the exchequer, David Lloyd George, who was accustomed to rail against the aristocracy in general and dukes in particular. Churchill, too, had strong words to say about the upper classes and primogeniture. This did not go unnoticed at Blenheim.

Clementine Churchill and her sister were staying at Blenheim without their husbands when Lloyd George gave a speech at Swindon, castigating large landowners. The duke and his guests were reading the press reports with contrasting reactions. Then, at a mealtime, Clementine received a telegram from Lloyd George. She moved to draft a telegram to reply. The duke came up. "Please, Clemmie," he said, "would you mind not writing to that horrible man on Blenheim writing-paper?"[22] Clementine Churchill was greatly offended, left the room and prepared to leave. The duke intercepted her in the Great Hall, but Clementine insisted. It took two years for the quarrel to be made up and the Churchills did not, as customary, stay at the palace for Christmas. Relations improved during and after the First World War.

After his depression in 1915 when he took up painting, Churchill brought his painting gear to Blenheim and made several paintings of the palace and grounds – some landscapes of the Great Lake, but also the Great Hall, tapestries and the boathouse.

As well as holidays, Churchill often returned to Blenheim for a fortnight each year where the Imperial Yeomanry, a precursor of the Territorial Army, used to camp for manoeuvres. Churchill was a captain in the Queen's Own Oxfordshire Hussars (QOOH, sometimes mockingly referred to as 'Queer Objects On Horseback'), when Blenheim was one of their venues. Churchill was a regular volunteer in the fifteen years before 1914, as was his personal friend and parliamentary opponent F. E. Smith. Consuelo Vanderbilt, the divorced wife of the ninth Duke of Marlborough, thought these exercises were good fun, "with dinners and dances and sports".[23]

The state rooms of the palace are open to the public and, when the duke's family is not in residence, visitors can view the private rooms. The building itself is austere, a touch impersonal and intimidating, but arrangements for visiting the palace are superbly efficient, with a helpful and friendly staff. The facilities – from the shop and restaurants to audio guides – are excellent. 700,000 people buy tickets to visit the palace each year. For many, the ticket can be converted to an annual visiting season ticket.

There is a host of interesting things to see relating to the Dukes of Marlborough. And there is plenty of Churchilliana, with portraits of the statesman in various rooms.

One of the food outlets is by the Water Terrace and used to be the Arcade Room, which Churchill used when writing his two family biographies – of his father Lord Randolph and his ancestor, the first duke.

A special Churchill exhibition leads up to the room where he was born, featuring the bed to which Lady Randolph Churchill was rushed. Some of Churchill's paintings adorn the walls, and above the bed is a lock of the child Churchill's hair. Nearby are articles that belonged to Churchill or with some other intimate association: a siren suit, in which he was happy to work in a relaxed way, and a faded red despatch box, used for official papers, which Churchill used when he was secretary of state for war from 1919 to 1921.

The exhibition also features a video of some of Churchill's greatest moments. His great speeches can be heard, and video clips show his funeral and the transporting of his body from St Paul's Cathedral to Bladon churchyard. A certificate records the pealing at the church of a plain Bob Major: 5,040 strikes on the bells, carried out on the day of the interment at Bladon, on 30 January 1965.

Ditchley

CHURCHILL'S SIR FRANCIS DRAKE MOMENT

Ditchley Park was the grand home of a wealthy Conservative Member of Parliament, Ronald Tree, and his even wealthier American wife, Nancy. Ronald Tree was parliamentary private secretary to Brendan Bracken, a close ally of Winston Churchill, and worked in the Ministry of Information in the early part of the Second World War.

It is a magnificent mansion, designed by James Gibbs in the 1720s.

During the Second World War, Britain was subject to German air raids. The prime minister's country residence, Chequers, was

considered too exposed and a potential target for air strikes –
especially when there was a full moon. Ditchley, not far away,
was surrounded by woodland and so less visible to the pilots of
possible bomber planes. Ronald Tree made the house available
to the prime minister as his country retreat on weekends with a
'high moon'. Churchill took full advantage of this, and he used
to bring his family, his domestic staff, his secretaries and typists
– plus a detective or two – and hosted official guests (including
Edvard Beneš, former and future president of Czechoslovakia).
Churchill visited frequently between November 1940 and September 1942, after which there was a reduced threat of air raids
and Chequers was not seen as so much at risk.

Churchill also brought to Ditchley his mobile cinema, and
one Sunday evening in May 1941 he listened to news reports of
heavy raids on London. There was nothing he could do about
it, so he watched a Marx Brothers film. He paused periodically
to find out what was happening in the capital. "The merry film
clacked on, and I was glad of the diversion."[24] Brendan Bracken,
one of the guests, then interrupted him to give the news that
Rudolf Hess, a close colleague of Adolf Hitler, had flown his
own plane to eastern Scotland, landed and sought out the Duke
of Hamilton, imagining he was politically important. Churchill
insisted on watching the rest of the Marx Brothers film. Hess
was duly arrested and interrogated and spent the rest of his
life in detention – first in the Tower of London and latterly in
Spandau in Germany, until he hanged himself in 1987 at the age
of ninety-three.

The Tree marriage broke up and Ronald remarried. His second
wife did not like the place, and it was sold to the tobacco magnate
Sir David Wills. He created the Ditchley Foundation, which

hosts (very) high-level conferences on international affairs, especially relating to US–UK relations. Its board of governors includes former prime ministers and former foreign secretaries.

Wolvercote

THE PROF'S FINAL RESTING PLACE

The Oxford City Council's Wolvercote cemetery lies on the west side of Banbury Road. Among many dons and city notables is the grave of Professor Frederick Lindemann, first Viscount Cherwell. Cherwell – the first syllable rhymes with car – is the name of the river that flows from the north into the River Thames at Oxford. Lindemann was, from the 1920s to his death in 1957, one of Churchill's closest friends. It was an unusual friendship: Lindemann was a bachelor, a vegetarian, a non-smoker and tee-totaller, though Churchill occasionally tried to tempt 'the Prof' to have a glass of brandy.

Lindemann was born in Germany to a German Alsatian father and an American mother, though his family had by then already migrated to Britain where they became naturalised. He was educated at universities in Berlin and Paris and became professor of experimental philosophy – that is to say, physics – at the University of Oxford in 1919. Lindemann was a first-rate pianist and a fine tennis player, and it was through a charity game of tennis, in which Lindemann played against Clementine Churchill in 1919, that he first met Churchill.

Churchill had a strong interest in – but a layman's understanding of –engineering and scientific warfare. (Chemistry had been one of the subjects he took for his Sandhurst entry examination.) Lindemann, on the other hand, had the great gift of explaining these topics and other complex scientific matters with concision and clarity. During the 1920s and 1930s, he was the most frequent visitor to Chartwell, where he became known as 'the Prof'. Unprepossessing in appearance, he had very narrow far-right views, believing in eugenics and the sterilisation of what he called the insane. Churchill, however, who for a time believed in eugenics – as did H. G. Wells – was devoted to Lindemann and defended him against anyone and everyone. Churchill was reported to have said that they did not, in general, disagree.

In 1941, Lindemann was raised to the peerage and made paymaster general, a government sinecure. When Churchill became prime minister again in 1951, Lord Cherwell was given the same post and brought into the cabinet.

He died in his sleep at the age of seventy-one. The funeral service took place in Christ Church, the college of which Cherwell was a 'student' (equivalent to a fellow). Churchill attended and insisted on coming on to the interment. "I must go to the grave," he said.[25]

The grave lies, without ostentation, eighty yards west of the chapel.

Warwickshire
Birmingham

A KISS IN EXCHANGE FOR A BOX OF CIGARS

Birmingham suffered heavy bomb damage in November 1940. A day or two later, Winston Churchill visited the city to see the damage and to raise morale. A pretty young factory girl came up to the car and threw a box of cigars into it. "I won the prize this week for the highest output," she told him. Churchill was touched and was "very glad (in my official capacity) to give her a kiss".[26]

Castle Bromwich, Spitfire Island

WHERE SPITFIRES WERE MADE

Along the Chester Road, in the village of Castle Bromwich, there used to be an airfield. Attached to it was the Castle Bromwich Aircraft Factory, which produced hundreds of military aircraft during the Second World War.

In September 1941, Winston Churchill visited the site and watched a display of aerobatics. The factory's chief test pilot, Alex Henshaw, gave a display, flying a Spitfire upside down forty feet above the ground.

Airfield and factory are no more. The roundabout, called Spitfire Island, is just about all that recalls this history. The island is also home to a sculpture that pays homage to this part of history. It was designed by a great-nephew of J. R. R. Tolkien

Coventry

ARMAMENTS PRODUCTION CENTRE

The city of Coventry probably suffered more devastation from air raids in the Second World War than any other British city. It was targeted for its concentration of munitions and armaments factories. Raids in November 1940, which the Germans called 'Operation Moonlight Sonata', also hit many residential areas – 4,000 houses were damaged or destroyed – and the historic centre. The cathedral was left a shell.

In September 1941, Churchill, accompanied by his wife, came to the city by train. He visited the Armstrong Siddeley factory, where aircraft parts and torpedoes were produced. As he entered the workshops, workers clanged their hammers in welcome. He also visited the Whitley bomber factory. Although the workers there had a reputation for militancy with Communist shop stewards, his appearance with cigar and V-sign led to a rousing reception. He went on to the cemetery where victims of the air raid were buried.

Warwick, Warwick Castle

A PROPOSAL REJECTED

In 1901, Winston Churchill and his mother were guests of the Countess of Warwick at Warwick Castle. (Both the Countess of Warwick and Lady Randolph Churchill had been intimate friends of the new king, Edward VII, when he was Prince of Wales.) Churchill was a newly elected MP, and one of the other guests was Pamela Plowden, whom Churchill had known and wooed in India. There, in Hyderabad, they had travelled together around the city on the back of an elephant. On a boat on the river, he proposed marriage to her. He was turned down. Pamela was a popular young lady, and, according to Churchill's brother, at least three other young men imagined that they were informally engaged to her.

In spite of this rejection, Churchill remained on good terms with Pamela, who married the Earl of Lytton the following year, becoming chatelaine of Knebworth House, Hertfordshire. The Earl of Lytton was the brother of the prominent suffragette Lady Constance Lytton, and he was sometimes a political ally of

Churchill in the 1930s. He died while a minister in Churchill's wartime government. Churchill and Lady Lytton met and corresponded affectionately with each other. She survived him by six years.

Wales

Caernarfon Castle

CHURCHILL AND THE FUTURE KING EDWARD VIII GET TO KNOW EACH OTHER

On 13 July 1911, as home secretary, Winston Churchill came to Caernarfon Castle to read out the proclamation that formally invested the Prince of Wales, the eldest son of King George V and Queen Mary. The prince, the future King Edward VIII, seated by him, was just seventeen at the time, and Churchill could legitimately claim that he had known him since he was a boy.

The investiture took place at the castle at the prompting of the MP for Caernarfon, David Lloyd George, who was then chancellor of the exchequer. It was a modern ceremony and was repeated fifty-eight years later for Prince Charles, son and heir of Queen Elizabeth II.

Churchill had a romantic, almost sentimental, attitude towards the monarchy and the holders of that office. Indeed, his social world of upper-class balls and parties overlapped with that of the adult Prince of Wales, and Churchill turned a blind eye to the prince's self-indulgences – which extended to a sympathy with Nazi Germany. This led to Churchill being one of the few leading politicians to champion King Edward VIII when he abdicated to marry the love of his life, the twice-divorced American Wallis Simpson. The then prime minister, Stanley Baldwin, sensed the feelings of the country as a whole by seeing how unsuitable the king was and acted with uncharacteristic decisiveness. King Edward VIII saw Churchill as a friend and sought his advice. Churchill incurred unpopularity for speaking up for the king in the House of Commons. This damaged Churchill and undermined his credibility in other causes, notably his campaign for an increase in armaments in the face of the rearmament of Nazi Germany.

Llanystumdwy, Caernarvonshire

CHURCHILL AND LLOYD GEORGE

This small, largely Welsh-speaking village was the boyhood home of David Lloyd George, who was friend, mentor, patron and rival of Winston Churchill in the first quarter of the twentieth century. Lloyd George was actually born in Manchester, but he was brought up here in a house called Highgate, now part of the Lloyd George Museum. He is also buried in the village. Museum and tomb were both designed by Clough Williams-Ellis, creator of Portmeirion.

Lloyd George was a Radical Liberal MP, and his aversion to the misdeeds of landlords was developed here. When Churchill left the Conservatives to join the Liberals in 1904, he literally crossed the floor of the House of Commons and sat next to Lloyd George. They were the two most outspokenly radical members of the reforming 1908 government of H. H. Asquith. After Lloyd George became prime minister in December 1916, he brought Churchill back into the government within a few months. Churchill broke with the Liberal Party but never abandoned old friendships. They had frequent political differences between the wars – Lloyd George actually made an embarrassing visit to Adolf Hitler – but when Churchill became prime minister, he was keen to involve Lloyd George and offered him the post of ambassador to the United States.

Lloyd George was eleven years older than Churchill and was like an older brother to him. The younger politician was one of the few people to address the elder as David, but the relationship was sometimes prickly. It was as if Churchill had difficulty escaping from the older man's shadow.

Churchill did visit the nearby town of Criccieth, where he played golf with Lloyd George, who was the president of the Criccieth Golf Club. The club was superbly sited, on an elevation with magnificent views of Snowdon; the singer Bryn Terfel loved to play there. Unfortunately the club closed in December 2017.

Tonypandy, Glamorgan

WHERE CHURCHILL COULD HAVE – BUT DID NOT – SEND IN THE TROOPS

Tonypandy is one of the towns of the Rhondda Valley, the centre of the Welsh mining industry until the end of the twentieth century.

In 1910, a dispute arose between the miners and the mine-owners about differentials of pay between those miners who worked on hard seams and those who worked on soft. Over 25,000 men came out on strike, and there were cases of looting in the town. The strike became a confrontation between miners and their families on the one hand and the forces of law and order on the other.

At the time, Winston Churchill was home secretary and responsible for law and order. In his previous job as president of the Board of Trade, he had been responsible for reconciliation in labour disputes.

During the looting in Tonypandy, the Glamorgan police authorities asked the Home Office to send in troops. Churchill consulted the secretary of state for war, R. B. Haldane, and they were ready to dispatch both cavalry and infantry, as well as reinforcements from the Metropolitan Police. The cavalry got as far as Cardiff. The Chief Constable of Glamorgan thought police reinforcements were sufficient, and the infantry who were on their way were stopped at Swindon. Meanwhile, shops were trashed in Tonypandy and the police reinforcements delayed. The local police succeeded in restoring order without troops sent from London.

There is no doubt that Churchill would have been ready to send the troops in, if necessary. It would have been the duty of any government, any home secretary, to have done so. But in the end that necessity did not arise. Indeed, at the time, *The Times* criticised him for *not* sending in the troops. Nevertheless, the myth persisted for the rest of his life that Churchill took the heavy-handed action of sending in the army to deal with striking miners.

6

THE NORTH OF ENGLAND

LANCASHIRE, MANCHESTER AND YORKSHIRE

Winston Churchill had no family connection with the North of England, which here includes Lancashire and Yorkshire. Nevertheless, he built up links with Lancashire, being MP for first Oldham and then Manchester.

Politically he encountered the effects of poverty in Lancashire, and his first engagement with a trade unionist was with his fellow Conservative candidate in Oldham in 1899.

Churchill did not have close links with Yorkshire. When he watched the film of *Wuthering Heights*, his laconic comment was, "What terrible weather they have in Yorkshire."[1]

However, he did visit the main cities over the course of half a century to give speeches, and he attended Conservative Party conferences at Scarborough in 1937 and 1952.

1. Barrow-in-Furness, p.268
2. Oldham Town Hall, p.268
3. Albert Square, Town Hall, p.271
4. Angel Meadow, p.275
5. King's Hall, p.277
6. Cheetham Hill, p.278
7. Free Trade Hall, p.280
8. St John Street, p.282
9. Midland Hotel, p.283
10. Doncaster Racecourse, p.284

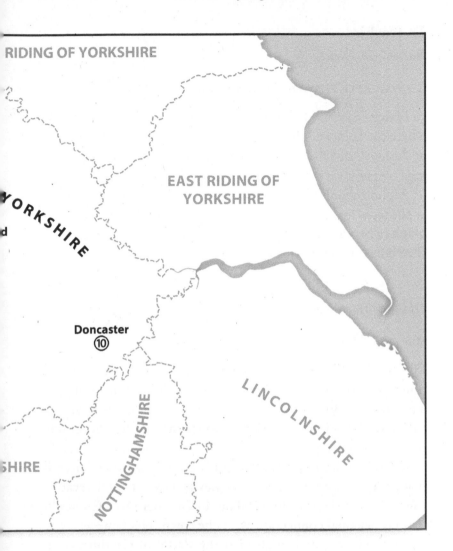

Lancashire

Barrow-in-Furness

A FAVOURITE PHOTOGRAPH BECOMES A PORTRAIT

In March 1940, Churchill accompanied his wife to the dockyard where she launched the aircraft carrier *Indomitable*. They stayed at the home of Sir Charles Craven, the chairman of the engineering company Vickers-Armstrong.

A photograph was taken of a joyous Clementine Churchill as she launched the ship. It became Churchill's favourite photograph of his wife and, in 1954, his eightieth year, he made a loving sketch based on the portrait.

Oldham Town Hall

HIS FIRST ELECTIONS

Oldham Town Hall was built in 1841, before the town was given borough status. It has a classical front with Ionic pillars rising to a portico. The local government administration moved out and the magnificent building was abandoned in the 1980s, becoming home to bats and pigeons.

It was on the steps of the Town Hall that Winston Churchill made his acceptance speech as newly elected Conservative Member of Parliament for Oldham in October 1900. Churchill had no personal connection with the town. His fame as a war correspondent – he had covered the Battle of Omdurman in September 1898 – and the reputation of his father who had died in 1895 had made him a well-known figure sought by local Conservative constituency parties. Until after the First World War, many urban constituencies sent two MPs to Westminster.

Oldham was one such constituency. The town and its suburbs were very much a nineteenth-century creation, overwhelmingly a cotton-manufacturing town. It was politically marginal, heavily Nonconformist and with a strong Conservative working class.

In early 1899, Churchill was approached by one of the sitting members, Robert Ascroft. The other member was not well. Would Churchill like to be Ascroft's running mate at the next general election? Churchill was, of course, interested, but events moved more rapidly than anticipated. Ascroft himself died suddenly in June and the other member took the opportunity of retiring, so there was a by-election in July. Churchill was adopted. In two-member constituencies, especially those that were marginal, there was often a local deal made to cover the varied contrasting interests. The ideal was to have a Conservative and a Liberal returned without a contest. But the rank and file of both parties objected and were keen for a fight.

The campaign was brief. Churchill found himself having to deal with unfamiliar issues, topical and significant for Lancashire Dissenters. He came out strongly against ritualism in the Church of England and against a bill that dealt with improving the tithes for Anglican clergy – what did he know about these issues? His running mate was a Conservative trade unionist, James Mawdsley. This was Churchill's first encounter with a representative of organised labour. In the next half century, he was to develop cordial personal relations – unusual for an aristocratic Conservative – with individual trade union leaders, such as Walter Citrine, Ernest Bevin and Tom O'Brien.

But Churchill's canvassing was unsuccessful, and two Liberals were elected. One of them was Walter Runciman, a wealthy shipping magnate, who would later be a minister in the National governments of the 1930s and subsequently a viscount.

In the autumn of the following year, there was a general election. By this time, Churchill had become a national hero with his escape from captivity in the Boer War. He had published his two-volume history of the Battle of Omdurman, *The River War*, and a novel, *Savrola*, and was still not yet twenty-six years old. He was a star speaker at marginal constituencies around the country during the campaign. His first arrival in the town was a triumphal progress, with ten landau carriages driving "through streets crowded with enthusiastic operatives and mill-girls".[2] Ten thousand came out to see him, waving flags and beating drums. He gave a speech at the Theatre Royal (since destroyed). He spoke of how he had been assisted in his escape by an engineer from Oldham, called Dewsnap. There was a shout from the audience, "His wife's in the gallery". The crowds did not finally disperse until after midnight. "There was general jubilation."[3] During the campaign, Churchill gave speech after speech – sometimes three or four in one evening. Mawdsley was no longer his Conservative running mate and Runciman was no longer standing. Churchill, however, managed to displace one Liberal in the poll. He and a Liberal mill-owner were elected.

Churchill gave a speech of acceptance on the steps of the Town Hall, as a fresh plaque indicates. There is no statue, but on the northwest of the hall is a statue of Annie Kenney, a militant suffragette who was born to working-class parents in Oldham in 1879. She and Christabel Pankhurst had demonstrated against Edward Grey and Winston Churchill at the Free Trade Hall in Manchester in October 1905. She is presented ringing a bell, which she often did at political meetings addressed by men she saw as opposed to votes for women. She was imprisoned while Churchill was home secretary.

After being threatened with demolition, the Town Hall was restored in the twenty-first century to house a cinema complex, a restaurant and coffee bar. On the pavement outside are some words of Churchill that have been set into the stonework: "We shape our buildings and afterwards our buildings shape us."[4]

Manchester
Albert Square, Town Hall

SCENE OF ELECTORAL TRIUMPH – AND SETBACK

In 1906 and in 1908, Manchester Town Hall was where election results were declared. Winston Churchill was twice a parliamentary candidate in Manchester, winning at the general election of 1906 and losing at the by-election of 1908.

In the nineteenth century, Manchester was the capital of progressive England. With a population of 640,000 in 1901, it was the metropolis of the Industrial Revolution. The so-called Manchester School was particularly associated with two mid-nineteenth century politicians, John Bright and Richard Cobden, whose political base was Manchester. The School articulated an ideology of free trade and minimal government involvement in economic activity, and it dominated political discourse throughout the century. What Manchester thinks today, the world does tomorrow.

For the first twenty-five years of his political life, Churchill was a committed free trader – and so he was at home in Manchester. He was no stranger to the city itself, either. Churchill had stood as a Conservative for the neighbouring constituency of Oldham in 1899 and was elected there just before his twenty-sixth birthday at the general election the following year. His dramatic career in the Boer War, during which he escaped from captivity, had propelled him into the public eye and political popularity.

At the beginning of the twentieth century, Manchester was made up of six constituencies. Most of them had a working class majority who, as a reaction against the laissez-faire politics of the Liberal Party, often tended to vote Conservative. The city had a large Irish population and also a Welsh community – that quintessential Welshman, David Lloyd George, was born in Manchester in 1863.

In 1900, the MP for Manchester East was Arthur Balfour, nephew of the prime minister, the Marquess of Salisbury, whom he was to succeed two years later. In the general election of 1900, Churchill came to speak for Balfour. The whole meeting welcomed him and "rose and shouted at my entry".[5]

Within a few years, however, Churchill became disillusioned with the Conservative Party. As prime minister, Balfour was unable to stem the move towards protectionism led by the domineering politician Joseph Chamberlain – a shift that was unpalatable for Churchill's, and his constituents', free trade principles. In April 1904, Churchill crossed the floor of the House of Commons and joined the Liberals. He immediately became one of the most radical Liberal MPs and was vociferous in his scathing denunciations of the Conservative Party and the influence of Joseph Chamberlain.

Two years later, in 1906, there was another general election and Churchill had to stand for a new constituency to represent his new party. His free trade credentials were strong, and he was invited to stand for North West Manchester, a Conservative-held seat that was adjacent to Oldham. The man who had been the MP for twenty years was retiring. He had been so well established that the Liberals had not contested the seat in 1900, but the Liberals thought that, with the right candidate – that being Winston Churchill – they could capture it. Some free trade Conservatives actually came out to support Churchill. His Conservative opponent at this general election was William Joynson-Hicks, who made a lot of Churchill's defection. "Let not Mr Churchill think that he can return to the Unionist party," he declared. "There is between him and our party a gulf fixed by himself which enables me to declare in your name that, while there is seedtime and harvest, summer and winter, we will never have him back in the Unionist party."[6] Joynson-Hicks also circulated a pamphlet with quotations from Churchill in support of Conservatism. At one meeting, Churchill was challenged to respond to it. He acknowledged that he had said these things because he belonged to a stupid party: "I have left that party because I do not want to go on saying stupid things."[7] He then seized the pamphlet, tore it to shreds and dramatically flung it from him. Twenty years later, Churchill and Joynson-Hicks would be colleagues in Stanley Baldwin's Conservative government of 1924.

Churchill's fame, energy, personality and the national swing against the Conservatives secured him victory in 1906. One of the officials of his election committee, Alderman James Thewlis, would be a great uncle of Harold Wilson, the Labour prime minister at the time of Churchill's death fifty-nine years later. In Manchester, commitment to free trade was stronger than commitment to the now protectionist-inclined Conservatives. All but one of the Manchester seats went to the Liberals or their allies – including that of the party leader, Arthur Balfour, in Manchester East.

During the next two years, as a junior minister in the Liberal government of Sir Henry Campbell-Bannerman, Churchill made frequent visits to the city. The House of Lords was threatening to thwart Liberal legislation, and in February 1907 he spoke at the Free Trade Hall, saying the party had to fight against the House of Lords, calling it the "fortress of negation and reaction".[8]

In April 1908, H. H. Asquith replaced Campbell-Bannerman as prime minister. Asquith promoted Churchill to the cabinet as president of the Board of Trade. Until 1918, new cabinet ministers had to face a by-election to be able to continue to sit in the Commons. Often these were uncontested – but not in Manchester North West in 1908. This seat was a marginal one and had been Conservative before 1906. Joynson-Hicks, popularly known as Jix, was once again his opponent, along with a socialist. Churchill's candidature brought in celebrity speakers, including the new chancellor of the exchequer, David Lloyd George (twice), and support from the novelist H. G. Wells, himself an avowed socialist.

There was a shift in allegiances in the constituency.

Joynson-Hicks had supported sectarian education and defended religious teachings in schools. This appealed to the Catholics, and the Roman Catholic Bishop of Salford, Louis Casartelli, advised his flock to vote Conservative, even though Joynson-Hicks was known to be a vigorous Protestant. The Irish community in Manchester were divided because Churchill, unlike Joynson-Hicks, was in favour of Home Rule for Ireland. The parliamentary leader of the Irish Nationalists, John Redmond, hesitated before declaring for Churchill. Locally he had the backing of one of the leading Irish local politicians, Alderman Daniel Boyle, if not all the Irish community. The Jews, however, were still overwhelmingly supportive of Churchill. Conservative free traders, no longer feeling their cause was under threat, went back to their former allegiance.

It was a lively by-election. Suffragettes targeted Churchill and heckled him wherever he went. Meetings were crowded and noisy. Churchill constantly referred to his opponent with condescending familiarity as "Bill Hicks". On the day of the election, Churchill toured the constituency in decorated vehicles with his brother, Jack, and his mother, Lady Randolph Churchill.

Albert Square was packed with people waiting for the result. Supporters of both candidates even thronged the corridors of the Town Hall. The candidates sat in the Lord Mayor's parlour and, at 9.30 that evening, the Lord Mayor invited the press in and the result was announced: Joynson-Hicks was in by a small majority, on a high poll – ninety per cent of the electorate had voted. The result was communicated to the crowds outside and both candidates went to a balcony to address their supporters. Joynson-Hicks acknowledged the support he had received from the Irish community. And so Churchill remained a minister but was briefly outside the House of Commons.

Angel Street, Angel Meadow

DISCOVERING POVERTY AT FIRST HAND

Just off the Rochdale Road is Angel Street, where the Angel public house offers food, drink and live music. The road leads down to the River Irk. During the nineteenth century, the inappropriately named 'Angel Meadow' was one of the worst slums in the country. There "is a certain black irony in its name", wrote Friedrich Engels, the friend, patron and partner of Karl Marx, in his book *The Condition of the Working Class in England in 1844*. The houses were tightly packed, back-to-back, with no running water. The area housed the poorest and most desperate of people, and it was notorious for being a breeding place for crime and prostitution. Proximity to the river, which must have been something of an open sewer, made it a centre for the spread of cholera. The area attracted the attention of middle-class philanthropists and there were attempts to improve matters but, by the turn of the century, it was still a most notorious slum.

During his 1906 election campaign, Winston Churchill's radicalism was reinforced by what one of his Liberal colleagues called his "discovery of the poor".[9] The Midland Hotel was his campaign base, and one Sunday morning he strolled with his friend and secretary, Edward Marsh, to Angel Meadow, a mile away. It was a stroll of contrasts. The Midland Hotel was a magnificent, recently built pile. The route also passed the impressive Free Trade Hall. But when he reached Angel Meadow, which was actually outside his constituency, he was shocked. "Fancy living in one of these streets," he said. "Never seeing anything beautiful – never eating anything savoury."[10]

Next to the slums was the Charter Street Ragged School. These kinds of schools were part of the attempts to ameliorate social conditions. Children were offered training in crafts, and on Sundays a soup kitchen provided some sustenance to the destitute. Abandoned children were also taken in. The school was run by an inspirational figure, Thomas Johnson, who showed Churchill around. Johnson, himself originally an orphan from Angel Meadow, used to befriend some of the wealthy of Manchester to obtain funds for food, clogs and clothing. Churchill reflected that "there had never been such great cities before where poverty and wealth and suffering jostled each other as they did to-day".[11]

Angel Meadow is now a small recreation ground. The slums have been cleared, and during the twentieth century it had a bandstand and children's swings. This was the subject of one of the best-known paintings of L. S. Lowry.

Charter Street Ragged School exists alongside Angel Meadow, and houses a Christian mission and the King of Kings School. Information boards in the recreation ground enlighten the visitor.

Free Trade Hall and Angel Meadow represent the polarisation arising from the Manchester ideology of free trade. The story of Angel Meadow showed that not everyone benefited from the dominant belief system, and that government non-intervention led to slums, stunted lives, epidemics and cholera. Churchill's visit fired his social radicalism. The work of Asquith's government was a major step in the abandonment of the laissez-faire ideas of nineteenth-century Manchester, laying the foundations of the welfare state. Churchill was, throughout his career, an advocate for the improvement of the conditions of the poor.

Belle Vue, King's Hall

CHURCHILL RECALLS HIS PIONEERING SOCIAL
LEGISLATION

In December 1947, Winston Churchill gave a speech at this large exhibition space (once the home of the Hallé Orchestra), which the young Conservative Reginald Maudling had helped to prepare. It was not the first time he had spoken here.

Churchill recalled that, almost forty years earlier, he had addressed an open air meeting at Belle Vue alongside David Lloyd George and the trade unionist cabinet member John Burns. They had "championed many of the great social reforms which have since been carried into law by Liberal and Conservative

Governments in which I have served".[12] He went on to deplore the socialist social reforms of the Labour government.

Cheetham Hill

CHURCHILL AND THE JEWS

Winston Churchill represented Manchester North West between 1906 and 1908. The constituency was socially mixed. It included the commercial centre of the city and the middle-class district of Cheetham Hill. It also included Strangeways Prison. Manchester had a sizeable Jewish community, two-thirds of whom lived in Cheetham Hill. As one went up Cheetham Hill Road from the River Irk, properties became more well-to-do. The terrace houses around Strangeways Prison were the homes of poorer Jews, the most recent Yiddish-speaking immigrants. Further up, properties were detached houses, homes of the richer Jews. Along the road were two synagogues, the first is Sephardic, built in a Moorish style and now the home of the Manchester Jewish Museum. The old Ashkenazi synagogue has not survived. In the early part of the twentieth century, there were Jewish schools, a Jewish hospital and Jewish clubs. Community cohesion transcended class and social divisions. Jewish Mancunians were largely Liberal in their politics. The Conservatives had introduced the Aliens Act, an early anti-immigrant piece of legislation that targeted the waves of Jews fleeing persecution in Russia and Eastern Europe. Among the more established leaders of the community were Nathan Laski and Barron Belisha. Laski was president of the Hebrew Congregation of Manchester and a Liberal activist.

An eleven-year-old nephew of Belisha remembered meeting Churchill during the campaign. He was "a masterful, yet slightly stooping figure. The pink face was topped with reddish fair hair. He was dressed in a frock coat, with silk facings, and below his chin a large winged collar with a black bow tie".[13] Thirty years later, this eleven-year-old boy became a parliamentary colleague of Churchill. Leslie Hore-Belisha was a Liberal MP and became minister of transport in the National government from 1934 to 1937, introducing so-called 'Belisha Beacons' at pedestrian crossings. He was later secretary of state for war in Neville Chamberlain's government but was dropped when Churchill became prime minister. Hore-Belisha became a critic of Churchill's management of the war and was one of twenty-five MPs who voted against him in a 'no confidence' motion.

Churchill had already endeared himself to Manchester's immigrant Jewish community by opposing the Aliens Bill. Joynson-Hicks's support of that bill had not gained him votes among the Manchester Jews; by contrast, one of Churchill's first speeches in the House of Commons from the Liberal benches had been against the legislation. His sympathy with Jews was outstanding for his class. But his father, Lord Randolph Churchill, had included Jews among his friends, and, in one of the few acts of encouraging his son to make political and social contacts, took Churchill to a party at Mentmore, the Rothschilds' country house at Tring in Hertfordshire. Winston Churchill inherited from his father Jewish friends like the Rothschilds and Sir Ernest Cassel.

The pogroms in Eastern Europe continued and, in December 1905, Churchill appeared on a platform as main speaker protesting against the Russian government's anti-Semitic behaviour. One of those sharing the platform was a recent Jewish immigrant who had been appointed senior lecturer in chemistry at the University of Manchester. Dr Chaim Weizmann was three days older than Churchill, and this was the beginning of a friendship that was to last until Weizmann's death as president of Israel in 1952. Weizmann was an eloquent and tireless champion of Zionism, the movement for a Jewish homeland in Palestine. He was a resourceful networker who, over the years, moved with ease among Britain's political classes of all parties.

Churchill allied himself with the Manchester Jewish community, subscribing to Jewish charities, visiting the Jewish hospital and the Jewish Working Men's Club. Indeed, he attended a service at the Great Synagogue in Cheetham Hill Road, where the Jewish Boys' Brigade formed a guard of honour.

Today, Churchill's old constituency has a large Muslim population, with shops, warehouses and houses bearing names of Muslim owners or traders. The spacious villas at the top of the hill are now mostly multi-occupancy properties.

Peter Street, Free Trade Hall

EARLY ENCOUNTERS WITH SUFFRAGETTES

Before it was destroyed by enemy action in the Second World War, Winston Churchill gave many speeches here.

Within a month of joining the Liberal Party in 1904, Churchill spoke in the Free Trade Hall alongside the veteran Liberal and biographer of W. E. Gladstone, John Morley. Churchill railed against the Conservatives: they were responsible for "corruption at home, aggression to cover it up abroad". They offered "sentiment by the bucketful, patriotism by the imperial pint... dear food for the million, cheap labour for the millionaire".[14] A personalised attack on Joseph Chamberlain did not deter Churchill from later seeking cordial relations with him, though; he needed help with the biography he was writing of his father, Lord Randolph Churchill, Chamberlain's contemporary.

A plaque records the fact that this was where the suffragettes made their first demonstration. In October 1905, Churchill and Edward Grey spoke at a Liberal Party rally here. The speakers were interrupted by Christabel Pankhurst and Annie Kenney (born in Oldham). They were fined, but refused to pay. Churchill's offer to pay their fine was also rejected. Pankhurst and Kenney went to prison.

On 27 January 1940, four months before he became prime minister, Churchill spoke again at the Free Trade Hall, calling for a million women to join the national workforce. By the end of the war, the number had risen to two million. The scale of their employment transformed the role of women in society, even more so than in the First World War.

The following year, Manchester was subject to heavy German bombing and the Free Trade Hall was shattered. Churchill came to Manchester after the raids to inspect the damage. He called out to onlookers, "Are we downhearted?" To which the answer was a resounding "NO".[15]

The Free Trade Hall was rebuilt and became the home of Manchester's own Hallé Orchestra until 1978. In recent years, it has been turned into a hotel. The magnificent façade facing the street dating from the 1840s has been preserved.

St John Street

CHURCHILL GALLANTLY DEFINES HIS POSITION ON THE VOTES FOR WOMEN QUESTION

Very modern plate-glass buildings flank St John Street. This road leads to a small garden that used to be the churchyard of St John's Church – no longer surviving. The Church School used to be a venue for political meetings.

Manchester was the home of the Pankhursts and of the suffragette movement. Perhaps because he had such a high profile, Churchill was – rather unfairly – targeted by the suffragettes. Unfairly because he was not unsympathetic to the cause. At one meeting in January 1906 at St John's School, Churchill addressed an election meeting. A group of suffragettes were displaying banners. "You have got it the wrong way round," Churchill called out.[16] The banner, 'Votes for Women', had in haste been raised upside down. One woman wanted to speak but was shouted down by the audience. The chairman demanded order and threatened to have the woman thrown out. Churchill continued to speak but was again interrupted with calls of, "Will you give us the vote?" There was uproar. Churchill invited the lady to come to the platform. This she did, but the audience hissed. The chairman invited her to take a spare seat on the platform. Churchill appealed for order and said, "Will everybody be quiet. Let us hear what she has to say." She asked Churchill whether the Liberal government would give women the vote. There was further heckling from the audience, men and women. Churchill then made his position clear: "We should be fair and chivalrous to ladies... We must observe courtesy and chivalry to the weaker sex dependent upon us." He went on to point out that in the House of Commons, when the issue of extending votes to women had come up, he had voted in favour. But he deplored the disorder created by the suffragettes and so, he said, "I utterly decline to pledge myself".[17]

Yorkshire
Bradford, Midland Hotel

SPEECHES AND AN ASSAULT

This was one of the great railway hotels of the country. Built in the 1880s, it has preserved its superb Victorian interior decoration. Every prime minister of the twentieth century has stayed here.

In 1905, the actor Henry Irving collapsed and died on the main staircase here. A plaque records this sad story.

In July 1898, the twenty-three-year-old Winston Churchill stayed at this hotel, enjoying a supper with thirty of the most important local men. Churchill had been speaking to a packed Conservative Party rally. It was, he thought, "a great success", with people calling out to him, "Go on!" after he had spoken for fifty-five minutes.

Twelve years later, in November 1910, Churchill was again in Bradford, speaking this time for the Liberal Party. He was constantly interrupted by a supporter of the suffragette movement, Hugh Franklin. Later on the train back to London, Franklin cornered him with a horsewhip. "Take that, you dirty cur,"[18] he said as he assaulted him. Franklin was arrested and charged, getting a sentence of six weeks.

Doncaster Racecourse

THE PRIME MINISTER AND QUEEN AT THE RACES

Queen Elizabeth II and Winston Churchill shared an interest in horseracing. In the summer of 1953, Churchill was recovering from a major stroke. Queen Elizabeth invited him to join her in the royal box at Doncaster races in September.

Clementine Churchill advised against it. People will be looking at you, she said. "If you sat in public when she was standing, it would be noticed," she argued.[19] Churchill disregarded his wife's advice this time.

He travelled on after the races to stay with the royal family at Balmoral.

7

SCOTLAND

Over the years, Winston Churchill had close connections with Scotland. His wife came from an aristocratic Scottish family (her grandfather was the Earl of Airlie). Churchill was a Member of Parliament for a Scottish constituency for fourteen years and a regular visitor to Dundee. During the summer for much of the time, he was a frequent guest at ducal houses – to the Duke of Westminster's estate at Lochmore and the Duke of Sutherland's castle at Dunrobin. Both are north of Inverness. At these estates Churchill was able to relax and paint.

But Churchill's most intimate connection with Scotland, or with Scottish people, was perhaps during the First World War when he was the colonel of the Sixth Royal Scots Fusiliers for four months. He lived the lives of his soldiers, got on well with them and wondered whether, in a different life, he had addressed these men at political meetings in Glasgow.

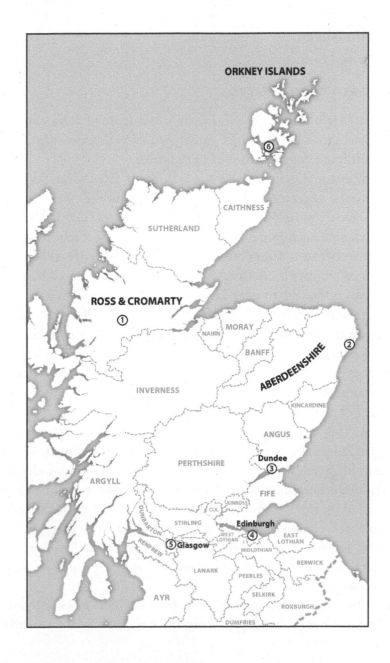

ORKNEY ISLANDS

⑥

CAITHNESS

SUTHERLAND

ROSS & CROMARTY

①

NAIRN   MORAY

BANFF

ABERDEENSHIRE   ②

INVERNESS

KINCARDINE

ANGUS

PERTHSHIRE   Dundee
③

FIFE

ARGYLL

KINROSS

CLK.

DUNBARTON   STIRLING   Edinburgh
WEST   ④   EAST
LOTHIAN   LOTHIAN
⑤ Glasgow
RENFREW   MIDLOTHIAN

LANARK   BERWICK

PEEBLES

AYR   SELKIRK

ROXBURGH

DUMFRIES

Achnasheen
Ross and Cromarty

SPIES IN THE HEATHER?

After war broke out in 1914, there was a spate of stories about German spies. People with German names were under suspicion. Dachshund dogs were stoned in the street.

Winston Churchill was First Lord of the Admiralty. To minimise exposure to enemy action, Britain's fleet was located in remoter parts of the country such as Scapa Flow in the far north and Loch Ewe on the western coast of northern Ross. In September 1914, Churchill travelled to the north of Scotland to discuss security in the area. He travelled with senior colleagues from London by train to "a wayside station somewhere in the Highlands".[1] This was Achnasheen (which means 'fields of rain'), where the railway from Inverness veers off to the south to Kyle of Lochalsh. From there they were driven through "splendid scenery" on what is today the A832.[2] Two cars carried senior naval personnel including two admirals, one of whom was the chief of naval intelligence.

As they passed Lochrosque (Loch a Chroisg) Castle on the right, one mile beyond Achnasheen, one of the party saw a searchlight on the top "of what looked like a shooting-lodge in the middle of a deer-forest".[3] They were somewhat mystified but carried on their journey and did what they had to do at Loch Ewe. The commander-in-chief of the fleet at Loch Ewe was Sir John Jellicoe. They mentioned the matter to him, and he said there had been a rumour of a plane in that area. Suspicions were further roused.

On their return to Inverness, they decided to investigate. They took some hand guns from the naval base and cautiously approached the castle. A butler answered the door. "Is your master at home?"[4] He was, and was summoned from a dinner party he was apparently hosting to be quizzed about the searchlight on the roof. The "master" was Sir Arthur Bignold, in his mid-seventies, who had been a Unionist (Conservative) MP for the Wick Burghs from 1900 to 1910. He recognised Churchill who had also been a Conservative MP in the early years of the century before defecting to the Liberals. Bignold explained that the searchlight was installed on the roof to scour the neighbouring hills for deer so he and his party could stalk them the next morning. He explained that "we can tell deer from cattle by the searchlight, as the glint of the eyes of cattle is white and that of the deer has a greenish tint".[5] The searchlight operated on electricity produced by a home generator which had been sold to Bignold by the Royal Navy after being decommissioned. Churchill's suspicions were not allayed, and the party insisted on climbing to the roof by a narrow spiral stairway and removing essential parts from the searchlight.

On further investigation, it turned out that Sir Arthur's story was true. And there were no confirmed reports of aircraft in the area or of German spies.

Sir Arthur Bignold died just six months later – perhaps he never recovered from the shock and sense of outrage.

After the First World War, the ownership of Lochrosque Castle was in the hands of the Mackenzie family. The roof was stripped of its lead, and the castle was demolished. Outhouses have been preserved and restored as a hunting lodge. It is still a base for stag hunting. The antlered heads of stags adorn the walls of the lodge – and also the nearby Ledgowan Lodge Hotel.

Twenty-five years later, in the first month of the Second World War, Churchill was again First Lord of the Admiralty. On this latter occasion, he had been to see the fleet at Scapa Flow, then sailed around northwest Scotland to inspect Loch Ewe and again travelled by car overland to catch the train back to London from Inverness. He and his party stopped by a stream and had a picnic. "I felt oddly oppressed with memories."[6] Lines of Shakespeare occurred to him:

> *... let us sit upon the ground*
> *And tell sad stories of the death of kings.*

He was, in this tranquil Highland spot, mindful of the terrors and dangers of war, and of his own responsibilities. He felt he was going over the same ground, metaphorically as well as literally, in this second world war. He sadly called to mind the admirals and colleagues of a quarter of a century ago. "Fisher, Wilson, Battenberg, Jellicoe, Beatty, Pakenham, Sturdee, all gone!"[7]

Cruden Bay, Aberdeenshire
Slains Castle

AN AWKWARD EMOTIONAL CRISIS

Slains is a ruined pile a mile north of the old fishing village of Cruden Bay. It was the home of the Earls of Erroll, a title that goes back to the sixteenth century. Most of the present vast ruin dates only to the middle of the nineteenth century when the then earl built a great palace that was fitting for his bride, a daughter – albeit illegitimate – of King William IV. The Errolls did a lot to develop Cruden Bay. The harbour area is called Port Erroll, and the principal hotel is called the Kilmarnock Arms, after another title held by the family. The cost of the management and maintenance of a home like Slains Castle was crippling. In the early twentieth century, the castle was rented out to those who wanted to get away from it all and, crucially, could afford it.

In 1908, it was rented by the new prime minister, H. H. Asquith. During the summer, he was host to political friends and colleagues. In late August, the Admiralty yacht, HMS *Enchantress*, moored at Port Erroll, and the First Lord of the Admiralty, Reginald McKenna, disembarked with his young bride to stay at Slains Castle. The following day, Winston Churchill arrived by train. Churchill had earlier that year been brought into Asquith's cabinet as president of the Board of Trade. His visit was not to enjoy the scenery or to play golf – but to deal with a tricky emotional situation.

Asquith's daughter, Violet, was then twenty-one. She had first met Churchill four years earlier and a warm friendship had developed. They were often seen chatting and laughing together at social functions in London. Violet was keenly interested in politics and was close to her father, and it is believed that she urged her father to promote Churchill into the cabinet in April that year. Violet Asquith appeared to be besotted by Churchill. An engagement seemed to be on the cards.

Churchill, meanwhile, had met Clementine Hozier and, in early August, they became engaged. The announcement was made public and Violet informed by telegram. She is said to have fainted at the news. She poured out her feelings with exquisite bitchiness to a friend (who happened to be a cousin of Clementine Hozier). She wrote about Churchill's engagement to "the Hozier".[8] She would be "nothing more to him than an ornamental sideboard as I have often said". Clementine Hozier was, she wrote, "as stupid as an <u>owl</u>". Her poverty was scorned: "for the moment she will have a rest at least from making her own clothes."[9]

Churchill had some explaining to do, both to Violet and to her father. Clementine Hozier was not comfortable with Churchill dashing off to see his old flame – even though he was, in effect, going to the north of Scotland to justify the dumping of his boss's daughter. But Churchill did not shirk the challenge. He and Violet Asquith spent time together, scrambling over the cliffs, and were seen walking together round the village.

Churchill stayed only two days before heading back to prepare his wedding, which took place just over a fortnight later at St Margaret's Church, Westminster. It was a grand society wedding, but the Asquiths did not travel down from Slains to attend it. The prime minister sent a set of the works of Jane Austen as a wedding present.

A week after the wedding, Violet Asquith – still at Slains – went missing. She had wandered off to retrieve a book she had left on the cliffs north of the castle. Night fell, the alarm was raised, the police informed and search parties scoured the cliffs, beach and caves. She was eventually found, unconscious, over two miles from the castle.

Violet Asquith overcame her bitterness, and her close friendship with Winston Churchill was restored. Indeed, along with Pamela Plowden – later Lady Lytton, who had turned down Churchill's offer of marriage in 1901 – she was Churchill's closest female friend outside his family. She was a Liberal ally during Churchill's wilderness years of the 1930s. As Lady Violet Bonham Carter, she stood as a Liberal candidate in the 1945 and 1951 general elections. In the latter, Churchill persuaded the local Conservative Party not to put up a candidate against her and even travelled to nearby Huddersfield to speak on her behalf. She lost, but it was believed that if she had become an MP, Churchill would have brought her into his cabinet. Lady Violet Bonham

Carter became a life peeress the month Churchill died. (She went back to her youth in the choice of her title: Baroness Asquith of Yarnbury.) In her book, *Winston Churchill as I Knew Him*, published after Churchill's death, she talks about Churchill's 1908 visit in a bland way. They had fun scrambling over the crags and cliffs, she wrote. There is nothing about the emotional crisis that contemporary records suggest she went through. She is also gracious about Clementine Churchill. But who will stand by everything they said when they were twenty-one?

Another regular visitor to Cruden Bay was the journalist and novelist Bram Stoker. He used to stay at the Kilmarnock Arms or rented cottages in the village. Churchill did not usually give press interviews, but he made an exception for Bram Stoker because he had been a friend of his father and because he himself was a fan of his novel *Dracula*.

Bram Stoker, unlike Violet Asquith, was a guest at Churchill's wedding.

Dundee

A SEAT FOR LIFE, OR TAKEN FOR GRANTED?

Dundee is the third city of Scotland. In 1908, it was a largely working-class city, with many people employed in the jute industry, flax production, shipbuilding and food preparation. Broughty Ferry to the east – outside the constituency until 1918 – was a major fishing port, with some very grand houses of jute merchants. Until the early twentieth century, Dundee was also a noted whaling base. A major employer was D. C. Thomson, the press magnate. Thomson published a number of Scottish newspapers and comics. The company was very conservative and refused to accept trade union activity. It was also reputed not to employ Roman Catholics. Many of Dundee's working class were Protestant and Conservative; they saw themselves – especially those in fisheries – as benefiting from Conservative protectionist policies.

Winston Churchill had no connection with Dundee when he was selected as Liberal candidate for a by-election in 1908. He had been MP for North West Manchester and, in 1908, was promoted to the cabinet as president of the Board of Trade. In those days, such appointments required the minister to stand again for election to be able to continue sitting in the Commons – but Churchill lost that election in Manchester. Within minutes, he received a telegram from Dundee. The sitting Liberal MP was about to be promoted to the House of Lords, thereby causing a by-election here. Would Mr Churchill be the Liberal candidate? This was believed to be "one of the strongest Liberal seats in the island".[10] The challenge to Liberal hegemony was not from the Conservatives (called Unionists in Scotland) but from Labour. Dundee was a two-member constituency and Labour held one of the seats. Churchill was therefore conscious of the challenge from the left, and this helped to shape his own politics. His most progressive statements were made to shore up that radical base and swing voters away from Labour. Churchill accepted the seat and thought he would have it for life; since the Reform Act of 1832, Conservatives had never held the seat. Across the River Tay, the MP was the Liberal prime minister H. H. Asquith. To the north, the MP for the Montrose Burghs was the veteran Liberal and biographer of Gladstone John Morley. It made sense for the east of Scotland to be represented by English Liberal grandees.

Politically, the city was strongly divided on confessional and even ethnic lines. During the nineteenth century, a large migration of Irish people settled in Lochee to the west of the city centre, popularly known as 'Little Tipperary'. A counterweight to the Protestantism of D. C. Thomson was a Catholic newspaper, the *Catholic Herald*, edited by M. T. Hannigan; this reflected strong local Irish Catholic support for the Liberals. A Liberal daily paper, *The Dundee Advertiser*, had been owned by a former Liberal MP for Dundee but was taken over by D. C. Thomson who maintained for a while the pro-Liberal line.

The 1908 by-election was a triumph for Churchill. But it was not without some challenges. In Manchester, he had been targeted by suffragette demonstrators. They "followed me from Manchester to Dundee, and a peculiarly virulent Scotch virago armed with a large dinner-bell interrupted every meeting to which she could obtain access".[11] A day or two before polling day, though, he gave a barnstorming speech attacking Socialism in all its aspects. Twenty years later, he thought this was "upon the whole the most successful election speech I have ever made. The entire audience, over 2,000 persons, escorted me, cheering and singing, through the streets of Dundee to my hotel".[12]

Churchill made several visits to Dundee in his first years as MP, and during this time made some of his most radical speeches, which would have resonated with his Irish Catholic working-class support. He spoke at both the nineteenth-century Kinnaird Hall and the King's Theatre.

He often travelled to Dundee by himself and stayed at the leading hotel, the Queen's, which he found "a great trial".[13] In October 1909, he wrote to Clementine Churchill that he "had half eaten a kipper when a huge maggot crept out & flashed his teeth at me!"[14]

One of Churchill's most militant speeches was delivered at Kinnaird Hall in 1908, attacking – to appreciative applause – the House of Lords. "It is filled," he said, "with old doddering peers, cute financial magnates, clever wirepullers, big brewers with bulbous noses, sleek, smug, comfortable self-important individuals."[15]

During these years, he became an eloquent promoter of Home Rule for Ireland. This was a break from his own family past. Had not his father coined the slogan, "Ulster will fight and Ulster will be right"?[16] Was Churchill's new enthusiasm for Home Rule partly intended to please his Irish voters?

But during the First World War, his support in Dundee ebbed. He was in regular touch with the constituency chairman, Sir George Ritchie, who warned him that there was much local criticism of his tenure as First Lord of the Admiralty. He was held responsible for the disaster of Gallipoli, during which nearly half of the 17,000 men from from Irish regiments were either killed, wounded or missing. Disillusion over Gallipoli extended beyond the Irish community, for the city was also a source of recruitment into the Royal Navy. The criticism was even stronger when he was out of office and in opposition to H. H. Asquith in his last months as prime minister.

A few months after Lloyd George replaced Asquith as prime minister at the end of 1916, Churchill was brought back into the cabinet as minister of munitions. This obliged him to face a by-election. He was comfortably returned; his principal opponent was an anti-war candidate. In the general election of 1918, Churchill had to fight hard, and the constituency did not seem as safe as it had been ten years earlier. He had also responded in an extreme way to the 1917 Bolshevik Revolution and wanted active British involvement in its military suppression. In this, he was out on a limb in the cabinet. He associated Bolshevism with all socialist ideas, including the emerging Labour Party. In ten years, he seemed to have swung from a fiery radical in 1908 to a reactionary in 1918. Although he benefited from some Unionist support, there was a disaffection from Liberals who were loyal to Asquith and distrusted Lloyd George.

Four years later, in 1922, Churchill faced an even greater struggle in the general election. He had been secretary of state for war and air between 1919 and 1921 and had launched the military campaign against illegal activity by Irish nationalists. Special forces, 'Black and Tans', were sent to Ireland and were guilty of many atrocities. In October 1920, he gave a speech at the King's Theatre that compared the troubles in Ireland with the civil war in Russia. He condemned the Irish Republican Army, the IRA, accusing them of "popping up and down behind hedges and shooting poor policemen in the back".[17] His language became quite intemperate. "Could a republic be given to a miserable gang of cowardly assassins?"[18]

This did not go down well with the Irish nationalists of Lochee. Moreover, the timing was bad. Four days after that speech, Terence MacSwiney – the Mayor of Cork and IRA Commander – died after a hunger strike. Pictures of a wizened MacSwiney had a strong impact on public opinion.

In earlier elections, M. T. Hannigan had whipped up support for Churchill, but no longer. It was felt that he had reneged on his commitment to the Irish cause, and Hannigan let it be known that Churchill was no longer welcome at his house. The *Catholic Herald* refused to endorse him. His campaign headquarters was in the inauspiciously named Dudhope Terrace. Churchill himself was seriously ill with appendicitis and was only able to come to canvass in Dundee at the end of the campaign. Meetings held in his absence were rowdy. Clementine Churchill came and spoke instead but faced noisy, hostile audiences. She was accompanied by Churchill's closest friend, F. E. Smith, a Conservative and then a cabinet colleague in the Lloyd George coalition government. Smith seemed to be under the influence of alcohol as he spoke and denounced one Labour candidate, who had opposed the war, as a coward. This remark was not welcome to the Irish and radical Dundee constituency. Even though women (over thirty) were able to vote, Clementine Churchill wrote to her husband that she did not think Dundee's women liked to get involved in politics.

A convalescent Winston Churchill finally came to Dundee. He stayed at the Royal Hotel – perhaps to avoid maggots – and on 11 November spoke at the newly built Caird Hall for an hour and a half from a specially designed platform chair. "I was carried through the yelling crowd of Socialists ... to the platform [where] I was struck by looks of passionate hatred on the faces of some of the younger men and women."[19] There was constant heckling and pandemonium. He faced five candidates for the two-seat constituency. One was a local independent Liberal, a second was a National Liberal, and the third was the campaigner against the atrocities in the Congo, E. D. Morel, standing for the Independent Labour Party. The fourth was a Communist, William Gallacher, and the fifth was Edwin Scrymgeour, known as 'Neddy', standing for the Scottish Prohibition Party. He had been a regular candidate against Churchill and had been trounced when he stood in 1918. But Scrymgeour had a vigorous campaign. His supporters sang the variation of a song that had been sung in other and earlier elections:

Vote, vote, vote for Neddy Scrymgeour.
He's the man to gi'e ye ham and eggs.

If ye dinna vote for him
We will knock your windies in
And ye'll never see your windies any more.[20]

Churchill, who enjoyed his champagne and brandy, was humiliated by the victories of Scrymgeour and Morel. Churchill
came fourth out of the candidates contesting the two seats. It
is believed that there was a surge of personal, anti-Churchill
feeling in the vote. In addition to losing the support of the
Catholic Herald, the *Dundee Advertiser* attacked him from a
Liberal left position and the *Dundee Courier* from the Conservative Right. With the split in the Liberal Party, Churchill had
allied himself with Lloyd George rather than H. H. Asquith;
supporters of the latter withheld their backing. His intense
political life in London had prevented him from nursing his
constituency. What is more, his local support was weakened by
the death of his great ally Sir George Ritchie in 1921. When he
did come to the city, his lavish style of living caused resentment
among potential supporters who suffered acutely from poor
wages and bad housing. And women saw him, perhaps unfairly,
as having opposed the suffragette movement. In fact, many
believe that – despite Clementine Churchill's observation – the
women's vote helped to sink her husband. Churchill himself
recalled "how great numbers of very poor women and mill-girls
streamed to the poll during the last two hours of voting".[21] The
result was announced at Caird Hall. Churchill was taken aback
by Scrymgeour not giving a vote of thanks, as was customary
on such occasions, to the returning officer but to Almighty
God. William Gallacher later recalled Churchill standing by
the window "in deepest gloom. He nervously plucked at his
lower lip, with his eyes focussed far away on happier times and

happier places, while his good lady sat at his side softly sobbing in sympathy".[22]

Churchill had to surrender his seals of office as secretary of state for the colonies and was not to return to the House of Commons for two years, by which time he had moved back to the Conservatives. As he ruefully put it after his Dundee defeat, "I found myself without an office, without a seat, without a party and without an appendix".[23]

Churchill was hurt by this experience. Uncharacteristically, he seemed to have borne a grudge against the city and when, in 1943, after an acrimonious debate, the City Council offered him the Freedom of the City, he declined. Nonetheless, in 1951 he gave a cabinet post to a former Dundee MP, Florence Horsbrugh, the only woman he appointed to any of his cabinets.

There was no plaque referring to Churchill's association with the city until 2008, the centenary of his first election. In that year – albeit with some local opposition – the city acknowledged its connection and Churchill's daughter, Mary Soames, unveiled a modest and easily overlooked plaque in Meadowfield by St Paul's Church. Mary Soames had accompanied her mother to Dundee as a babe in arms in 1922.

The Queen's Hotel has survived and is now the Best Western Queen's Hotel. A framed copy of his letter of 1909 hangs in the hotel reception area. The Royal Hotel opposite the cathedral has been converted into shops.

Edinburgh
King's Theatre

RADICAL SPEECHES BEFORE THE FIRST WORLD WAR

Scotland seemed to have a radicalising effect on Winston Churchill in the first twenty years of the twentieth century. Although Clementine Churchill was the granddaughter of the Scottish Earl of Airlie, the Churchills had few Scottish connections. Unlike other dukes, the Marlboroughs had no estates north of the border. His education, at Harrow and Sandhurst, was English and conservative. But, in July 1909, he made one of his most radical speeches in Edinburgh.

The King's Theatre had been opened two and a half years earlier. Andrew Carnegie had laid the foundation stone, and the theatre was to become a major venue in Scotland. Theatres were often used for political speeches, and Churchill certainly had a sense of the theatre. He was able to hold an audience spellbound. He had the gift of timing, using appropriate pauses and humour. His speeches were always carefully prepared, and he knew exactly what the impact of what he was saying would be.

In early 1909, the chancellor of the exchequer, David Lloyd George, had introduced a budget that imposed a tax on income from the increased value of land. He gave a series of public speeches in which he attacked the landed classes, mocking primogeniture and the inheritance of property going to "the first of the litter".[24] Churchill echoed Lloyd George in radical, class-based assaults on the legitimacy of an aristocracy having unchallenged power in British politics. He argued closely against hereditary principles. Profits from land, he argued, "were positively detrimental to the general public".[25] Lloyd George was a middle-class Welsh lawyer, but Churchill was from the heart of the English aristocracy. He had entered parliament as a Conservative. Within years, he was savagely attacking the class from which he had sprung.

Such speeches made Churchill loathed by Conservatives. He was a traitor to his class, unbridled in his language. This hatred was slow to go away. Conservatives found every opportunity to discredit him and blocked him from holding any responsibility in the wartime coalition of 1915. Although he rejoined the Conservatives in 1925, he was not taken to their hearts. The suspicion in which he was held did not finally dissipate until well after he became prime minister during the Second World War – and not entirely even then.

Usher Hall

SUMMITRY: DOING BUSINESS WITH DICTATORS

This concert hall was built in 1914, funded by the whisky distiller Andrew Usher. It is a huge cylindrical structure, built in a Beaux-Arts style with architectural echoes – albeit with fitting Scottish restraint – of the Albert Hall in London. It can seat 2,200. The memorial stone was laid by King George V and Queen Mary, and one of its earliest political events featured the prime minister H. H. Asquith speaking here in 1914 to boost recruitment to the army.

If the King's Theatre had been the venue for Churchill's most radical speech, an alternative place seemed to have been chosen for his return to right-wing politics. In September 1924, Churchill spoke for the first time at a Conservative rally in Edinburgh. This time, he spoke at Usher Hall. His chairman was the ageing Arthur Balfour, who had been Conservative prime minister twenty years earlier and the target of many of Churchill's mocking speeches during his Liberal years. Churchill became a Conservative largely in reaction to the Bolshevik Revolution in Russia in 1917. At the end of 1924, he became chancellor of the exchequer in Stanley Baldwin's government, but only after that did he formally rejoin the Conservative Party.

During the general election of February 1950, while campaigning in Edinburgh, Churchill called for a "summit conference" to ease international tension. There was fear of a Third World War, this time with nuclear weapons. The use of the word 'summit' and its background is instructive. Churchill was seventy-five during this election and was leading the Conservative Party with the hope of returning to power. His national prestige was unquestioned, and his standing in the Conservative Party was unchallenged. But his leadership was hardly dynamic. He relied on his senior lieutenants, Anthony Eden, R. A. Butler and Harold Macmillan, to conduct most of the parliamentary business. He often spent months at a time on holiday in southern France, being (rightly) fêted all over the world, or was busy writing his war memoirs. The party developed its own policies with bright younger men – Iain Macleod, Enoch Powell and Reginald Maudling. Churchill did not interfere.

Still, Churchill took the lead in determining Conservative foreign policy. His previous premiership had ended during the meeting at Potsdam with Stalin and Harry S. Truman. He enjoyed those international conferences – Casablanca, Tehran, Yalta – when a few men seemed to determine the fate of the world. Churchill wanted them to continue after the war. To him, it seemed possible to resolve contentious issues through personal contact. He struck up a working relationship with Stalin, getting to know him both at conferences and in Moscow. Churchill saw him as a man with whom he could do business. Stalin, similarly, was fascinated by Churchill and entertained him in his private flat in the Kremlin. The Labour movement in the years after 1945 was less keen on the fanfare of summitry. The prime minister Clement Attlee and the foreign secretary, Ernest Bevin, relied on old-fashioned diplomacy. The shadow foreign secretary, Anthony Eden, and the Foreign Office were also sceptical. Churchill however, in a speech at the Usher Hall, called for a "summit" conference that would lead to what he called an "easement" in international relations as the objective. It was a contrast to his policy before the war when he denounced the 'summit' conference Neville Chamberlain held at Munich with Hitler and Mussolini. Chamberlain had also felt he could do business with Hitler. That summit also had as an objective the "easement" of the international situation. Churchill would have denied the parallel, arguing that negotiation should be accompanied by the build-up of military strength.

And so Churchill popularised the use of the word, which became currency in the discussion of international relations over the next decade.

Glasgow
The Clyde

THE 'LUNGS' OF BRITAIN

In 1940, imports avoided the ports on the east and south of Britain. Convoys brought shiploads of food and other essentials to the great ports of Liverpool and Glasgow. And so the Clyde, together with the Mersey, "were the lungs through which we breathed".[26]

In January 1941, Churchill visited Glasgow. He was greeted by hundreds, perhaps thousands, at Queen Street station – even though his arrival was supposed to be a secret. It was a struggle for them to get into cars and reach the City Chambers.

Mitchell Library, North Street

FIERY SPEECHES

The central city library was restored in the 1980s to incorporate the façade of the former St Andrew's Hall. This hall had been built in 1877 and was Glasgow's major centre for big public meetings. The Great Hall could accommodate 4,500 people, but there were also two smaller halls and a ballroom. In 1962, it was almost totally destroyed by fire.

Churchill made some of his most radical speeches in this hall in the years before the First World War. In May 1904, he defected from the Conservative Party to the Liberal Party. In October of that year, he spoke to a full house here, saying he was more afraid of the Independent Capitalist Party than the Independent Labour Party. "Quality, education, civic distinction, public virtue seem each year to be valued less and less. Riches unadorned seem each year to be valued more and more."[27] Two years later, he claimed to speak for the sake of "the left-out millions".[28]

But Churchill's radicalism became tempered over the years. In 1912, he argued strongly here for a big navy.

When he was out of government in 1916 and served briefly in the trenches on the western front, he was colonel of the Sixth Royal Scots Fusiliers. The men he was in charge of, he wrote home, were "Glasgow grocers, fitters, miners – all Trade Unionists probably,

whom I have harangued in bygone days in St Andrew's Hall".[29]
They were now his sergeants and corporals, hardened by war.

Scapa Flow

SAILING TO THE UNITED STATES

Soon after his appointment as First Lord of the Admiralty after
the outbreak of war in September 1939, Winston Churchill paid
a visit to Scapa Flow, inspecting the defences. He went on to
Loch Ewe, the other major navy base in northern Scotland.

In January 1941, Churchill came back to Scapa Flow to see the
newly appointed ambassador to the United States, Lord Halifax,
on his way. In spite of awful weather, Churchill took his new
American friend, Harry Hopkins, President Roosevelt's personal
envoy, with him. He took the opportunity of inspecting the fleet,
again taking Hopkins – who nearly fell into the sea.

Just seven months later, Churchill himself would be crossing the
Atlantic from here on his first Second World War visit to the
United States to see President Franklin D. Roosevelt. He sailed
on HMS *The Prince of Wales*, a ship that was torpedoed by the
Japanese four months later and whose wreckage lies in the South
China Sea. The United Kingdom was desperate for American
support. Although Roosevelt was personally sympathetic, most
of the American political establishment was sceptical, speculat-
ing that Britain might suffer the fate of France and collapse to
the Germans. It would take the Japanese assault on the US navy
at Pearl Harbor in December 1941 and the declaration of war by
Germany on the US to mobilise the United States into the war.

8

IRELAND

Churchill's relationship with Ireland was complicated. His first memories as an infant were of Dublin. He was related to the families of the Protestant ascendancy, and for a quarter of a century had himself property in Northern Ireland. Yet he became a champion of Home Rule for Ireland and was a principal negotiator of the treaty that led to Irish independence. He hit it off with the main Irish negotiator, Michael Collins.

As Member of Parliament for Dundee, many of his constituency supporters were nationalist Irish Catholics. That support ebbed over the years, and he was ejected at the general election of 1922. The Irish community had also been electorally significant in his previous constituency of Manchester North West.

Ireland

Belfast
Donegal Road, Park Shopping Centre

EVADING UNIONIST HOSTILITY

Feelings were running high in Belfast in February 1912. The British Liberal prime minister, H. H. Asquith, was to introduce the third Home Rule Bill in April, giving a measure of independence to Ireland. There was ferocious resistance to this from Protestants in Ireland, who were in a majority in parts of the north – what was called Ulster. Over the following two years, the situation approached civil war. Aristocratic English families owned extensive estates throughout the island. Northern Ireland had close links with Scotland. Scottish Protestants had been settled in Northern Ireland in the seventeenth century and monopolised wealth and power. The mass of indigenous Irish people were Roman Catholic. The geography of the country reflected a colonial presence, with the main cities having barracks strategically located to cover Catholic areas. Yet the British army was filled with Irishmen, and many generals were Irish Protestants. Indeed, Winston Churchill's three leading generals in the Second World War were Irish Protestants: 'Brookie' (Alan Brooke, Lord Alanbrooke), 'Alex' (Lord Alexander of Tunis) and 'Monty' (Lord Montgomery of Alamein).

In 1912, Churchill was an enthusiastic spokesperson of the radical policies of the Liberal government of which he was a member. His support for Home Rule went down well with the large Irish Catholic Liberal voting constituents of Dundee where he had been MP since 1908. He was never one to shirk a confrontation, so he readily accepted an invitation from the Liberals of Belfast to speak in support of Home Rule at the Ulster Hall. It was here that, according to legend, Churchill's father, Lord

Randolph Churchill, had in 1886 declared that "Ulster will fight and Ulster will be right". (In actual fact, the phrase appeared in a public letter shortly afterwards.) For many Unionists – those who supported the union of Ireland with Britain – this was interpreted as a call to arms. Winston Churchill, who was devoted to his father's memory and politics, argued rather that there should be special treatment for Ulster. In due course, this was generally recognised, in particular for the six counties where Protestants predominated, including the city of Belfast. But this was far from clear in February 1912.

The religious divide overlapped with a class and ethnic divide, Ulster Protestants were fearful of the loss of their privileged position. Loyalists (Unionists) maintained that they were threatened with papal rule. One leaflet was issued appealing to Germany, as a Protestant power, to save Ireland from being ruled by the Pope.

There was bitter opposition to Churchill coming to Ulster Hall. This magnificent building, which could hold nearly 3,000 people, belonged to the Belfast City Corporation and was located in the centre of the prosperous Protestant part of the city. Churchill's second cousin, the Marquess of Londonderry, a leading and vocal Unionist, advised against him speaking. Churchill was due to come with Clementine Churchill; she rejected advice not to accompany her husband, arguing that her presence would deter violence. They travelled by train from London to Stranraer, where they faced demonstrations. The Stranraer to Larne ferry was a major conduit for migration between Scotland and Northern Ireland. Hundreds of thousands of Irish people migrated to the Glasgow conurbation and Dundee. In the opposite direction, many Scottish entrepreneurs came to Belfast. The Churchills took the overnight ferry to Larne; their sleep was disturbed not by Unionists but by chanting suffragettes. A loyalist crowd jeered at them as they arrived, and the car in which they were driven into central Belfast was pelted, in spite of a heavy police presence. Ulster Hall was blockaded with people hostile to Churchill. About 10,000 stood outside the Grand Central Hotel where the Churchills stayed.

There was strong security in the city. Four battalions of infantry and one squadron of cavalry were on duty. The novelist E. M. Forster was in Belfast at the time and wrote to a friend that there were rumours of the widespread distribution of weapons among the populace.

Unionists had held a meeting at Ulster Hall the night before Churchill was due to speak. Some of those attending the meeting stayed on overnight – ready, if need be, to hold it by force. The venue for the speech was switched. The first choice was the Grand Opera House, another of the splendid constructions of late-nine-teenth-century Belfast, but, in spite of a large rent offered and the hint of a knighthood, the owner refused. The ultimate choice was a football ground in the nationalist Falls Road district, the home of Belfast Celtic Football Club and known to fans and players as 'Paradise'. This sobriquet led to jokes about Churchill 'heading for Paradise'. A huge marquee had been shipped across and was erected and attached to the grandstand. The Churchills travelled from the hotel in an open car. One of his company insisted that Churchill take a loaded revolver. As they left the hotel, some local businessmen shook their fists at him. Despite the security presence, the cars had difficulty moving through the hostile crowd. Forster saw the Churchills leaving the hotel and wrote that Churchill looked pale – "a sea kale colour".[1] A black effigy, meant to represent Churchill, was burnt. Men shouted insults at close quarters. Some loudly sang 'God Save the King'. Others tried to tip the car over, but someone, seeing Clementine

Churchill, called out "Mind the wimman", and the threatening crowd held back.[2] One young man by the car was a shipyard worker, William Grant, later a Northern Ireland cabinet minister responsible for security during the Second World War. Clementine Churchill, wearing a long fur coat, was pregnant at the time: she was to have a miscarriage the following month. Later, she told a friend that she was not afraid of being killed, but of being disfigured for life by broken glass. Her husband remained calm: "the opposition and threats seemed to 'ginger him up'", she wrote to the friend.[3] As they moved into the Nationalist Catholic Falls Road area, the angry yells turned into cheers. Effigies of the Loyalist leaders, Lord Londonderry and Sir Edward Carson, were displayed in cages.

There were no seats for the audience at Celtic Park, but Churchill spoke to up to 7,000 people, mostly Nationalists. It was raining, and water was leaking into the marquee. His chairman was Lord Pirrie, the boss of the shipbuilders Harland and Wolff; he was a recent convert to Home Rule. Alongside him was John Redmond, the parliamentary leader of the Irish Nationalists. Churchill argued that Home Rule should be seen within the context of the British Empire. Then, Churchill called on Ulster to fight for reconciliation among Irishmen, for the forgiveness of past wrongs and for the spread of tolerance and respect. "Then indeed Ulster will fight and Ulster will be right".[4] Churchill called for a home rule that would nestle in the "shell" of the great "Mother Empire". There was a handful of Unionist hecklers. One heckler shouted (in a Northern Irish accent) for votes for women. She was roughly ejected. The Churchills left through the backstreets to avoid demonstrations, which included crowds of Unionist shipyard workers who were ready to spray the Churchills with what they called 'Queen's Island confetti' – rivet heads taken from the shipyards located on Queen's Island. It was the custom of Unionist shipyard workers to throw them at Catholic workers. The Churchills returned not to the hotel but to Yorkgate railway station where a special train took them to Larne harbour to board a steamer back to Stranraer. But before they embarked on the boat, one shipyard worker spotted him and tossed some rotten fruit. Others called out "Traitor" and "Turncoat".

Picture postcards were published of Churchill speaking at Celtic Park.

It is possible to follow the route Churchill took from the hotel to Celtic Park. The Grand Central Hotel in Royal Avenue has been replaced by a miscellany of shops. The route passes through the gaunt buildings of central Belfast to the Falls Road. A billboard welcomes the visitor to West Belfast, and nationalist paintings, plaques and symbols of martyrdom and victimhood adorn the road. Street names are in English and sometimes also in Irish Gaelic. As in Jerusalem, Nicosia or Berlin, the visitor is aware of present or past divisions.

Celtic Park is also no more. It was located a quarter of a mile south of the Falls Road, three miles west of the city centre. In 1916, it was used as a centre for drilling Irish volunteers in the months before the Easter Rising of 1916. After the war, it became a venue for racing and boxing as well as soccer. It has been replaced by the Park Shopping Centre. A plaque in the entrance records the site's previous life alongside an aerial photograph of the football ground, but there is no mention of Churchill's visit in 1912.

A few months after his trip, Churchill received in London a delegation from the Liberals of Ulster who presented him with two heavy blackthorn walking sticks, one for himself and one for his wife, to commemorate that visit to Belfast.

Ulster Hall

WELCOMED IN PROTESTANT BELFAST

In 1926, fourteen years after his previous visit to Belfast, Winston Churchill was back in the city. By this time, southern Ireland was independent and Northern Ireland was still part of the United Kingdom. Churchill spoke in Ulster Hall and, as he started to speak, he remarked, as if to himself, "So this is the Ulster Hall! A difficult place to enter!"[5]

On this visit to Belfast, he was warmly received, as if those who had demonstrated so violently against him regretted their actions. He was given an honorary degree by Queen's University and generally fêted.

County Antrim
Carnlough

CHURCHILL'S ULSTER PROPERTY

Carnlough is an attractive small town on the beautiful Antrim coast.

One of Winston Churchill's great-grandmothers, Frances Vane, Marchioness of Londonderry, inherited extensive property including Durham coalfields and land in County Antrim. She married the half-brother of Lord Castlereagh, the British Foreign Minister and star of the 1815 Vienna Congress, which rebalanced the power of the European world after the Napoleonic wars. Her husband became the third Marquess of Londonderry. She saw opportunities in the exploitation of her Antrim properties located around the fishing village of Carnlough. She developed a limestone quarry, had a harbour constructed and then built a light railway to connect the two. She established a mill for crushing the limestone and a kiln for turning the lime into quicklime – a major ingredient of concrete. She had houses and a hotel, the Londonderry Arms, put up. Three miles to the north, she had a summer residence, Garron Tower, built. She died in 1865 and specified that the Garron Tower property, which included Carnlough, should descend to her younger male descendants – not to the eldest sons who would do well with entailed property. The Londonderrys were not short of a bob or two, owning estates in Ireland and Wales, coalmines in the north of England, a magnificent property in County Durham and one of the grandest houses in the smart West End of London. They exercised considerable political influence in Northern Ireland and in Britain as a whole. After she died, the inheritance passed successively to younger sons of the Marquess of Londonderry.

In the early twentieth century, the property was owned by Lord Herbert Vane-Tempest, whose home was at Plas Machynlleth. Known as Bertie, he was full of wit and humour, fond of merry japes. On one occasion, when he was a pupil at Eton, he upset a grocers' cart, with all its goods, which landed in Barnes Pool; for this he received a thrashing. In 1921, unmarried and only fifty-one years old, he was killed in a rail crash at Abermule. His cousin, Winston Churchill, unexpectedly inherited the property, which was worth £90,000 with an estimated annual income of £4,000. This helped Churchill's rocky finances, which included a bank overdraft and unpaid bills.

Churchill visited his estate at least once, in 1926, staying at the home of the Earl of Antrim in the neighbouring village of Glenarm. Local traditions maintain that he made other visits. His property was managed on his behalf by lawyers, including an agent in Glenarm. But the estate was always there as a nice little earner. On one visit, it is locally related, he met the postmistress and said,

"I've come to see the village founded by my great-grandmother."

"Mr Churchill," she replied, "Carnlough existed long before her."[6]

In 1934, rents from fourteen workers' cottages were badly in arrears. They were on Herbert Street, a road leading down to the coastal road and named after Bertie. Churchill, who was not known for the alacrity of settling his own debts, had the decency not to pursue rent arrears and proposed that each cottage – they were in effect slums, with two downstairs rooms and an attic for the family to sleep in – be sold to the tenant for a guinea (£1.05), provided that all the tenants agreed to this. He sold the rest of the property in 1949 to the Earl of Antrim. Ownership thus came full circle, for the enterprising marchioness had inherited the estate from her mother, the Countess of Antrim.

Lady Londonderry's light railway is now a footpath from the town to the quarries. A few yards from the main road are the remains of the mill's kiln. The Londonderry Arms is the main hostelry and has a Churchill Lounge, while a tourist information office has a news cuttings display detailing Churchill's offer of the cottages to their tenants. Garron Tower, Lady Londonderry's summer residence, still stands to the north. It was restored after a fire and lies proudly in grounds 200 feet above the sea. It has been a hotel and is currently a secondary school. The houses in Herbert Street, formerly owned by Churchill, have all been replaced.

Dublin
Phoenix Park

FIRST MEMORIES AND THE STORY OF A STATUE

Winston Churchill's first memories were of Dublin. From 1876 to 1880, his grandfather, the seventh Duke of Marlborough, was Lord Lieutenant or viceroy – the representative of Queen Victoria in quasi-colonial Ireland. Churchill's father, Lord Randolph Churchill, was secretary to his father. The viceroy's residence is now called Áras an Uachtaráin and is the residence of the president of the Irish Republic. The garden front portico, some historians have suggested, served as the model for the White House in Washington DC. The imposing building was the viceroy's home for nine months of the year, late March to Christmas. Here, the country was administered and dinner parties and balls were held for the Protestant Ascendancy – the political, social and economic elite of the country.

The appointment of the Duke of Marlborough is interesting. In the biography of his father, Churchill alludes to the fact that Lord Randolph had "incurred the displeasure of a great personage"[7] – though he may not have known the full story even when he was writing. If he had known and written about it, he would have embarrassed a number of people, not least the "great personage", who was the king, Edward VII. In 1875, as Prince of Wales and heir to the throne, he had gone on a tour of India, taking in his entourage a young sporting toff, the Earl of Aylesford. While Aylesford was away, his wife had an affair with Lord Randolph's older brother, the Marquess of Blandford, who was himself unhappily married. Lady Aylesford confessed to her husband and left the home in disgrace. Divorce proceedings were initiated. The Prince of Wales was asked to intervene to prevent the divorce, which would have been a social scandal and a bad example to the lower orders. Lord Randolph then came impetuously to the defence of his brother and said he had letters indicating that the Prince of Wales had himself been sweet on Lady Aylesford. The Prince of Wales was furious and made it clear that he would not be in the same room as Lord Randolph Churchill. There was even talk of a duel between the two men. It was necessary to get Lord Randolph out of London, perhaps by finding him an official position outside England. Benjamin Disraeli was Conservative prime minister at the time and, with tact and delicacy, persuaded the Duke of Marlborough to go to Ireland as the queen's representative and take Lord Randolph with him. Lord Randolph was persuaded to write and apologise to the Prince of Wales, but he still had to stay away from London's high society for a while.

Disraeli's social diplomacy was not over, for he had to displace the current Lord Lieutenant, the Duke of Abercorn. This social world was tightly knit. The wronged and estranged wife of the culpable Marquess of Blandford was actually a daughter of the Duke and Duchess of Abercorn. The transfer of duties was negotiated by the prime minister, who was skilled at this sort of thing, and so the Marlboroughs moved to Dublin in January 1877. Winston Churchill had just had his second birthday.

The duke's period of office reflected the English ascendancy. The duchess, Winston Churchill's grandmother, was from a leading Orange Protestant family, her father being the Marquess of Londonderry. Churchill's attitude to Irish politics was ambivalent and fluid over the years. In spite of his family links with the ascendancy and being brought up to "detest" the Irish, he became a convert to Home Rule and vigorously supported the third Home Rule Bill, introduced by the then prime minister

H. H. Asquith in 1912. Other relations had links with the Irish Nationalists, too. An uncle, Moreton Frewen, was elected as a Nationalist MP in 1910. Churchill's constituency base as MP was Dundee, which had a large community of Irish Catholics. And after the First World War, he was one of the leading negotiators for the Irish Treaty that implemented Home Rule – at least for the south. During the discussions with the Irish Nationalists, he got on famously with the Irish spokesperson, Michael Collins.

The Churchills took with them Winston's nanny, Mrs Everest, and they lived at Little Lodge, described in Churchill's life of his father as a long, low, white house with a green veranda and a tiny lawn and garden. Built earlier in the century, it lies two or three hundred yards to the east of what was modestly called the Viceregal Lodge. To the west of Little Lodge are some woods, often explored by the infant Churchill. On one occasion, at Emo Park, near Dublin, he was riding on the back of a pony escorted by Mrs Everest, whose Low Church beliefs made her apprehensive of Irish Catholics. Gunfire was heard. She became alarmed, thinking it was Fenians – a generic term applied to Irish nationalists some of whom engaged in methods of violence. Her alarm was communicated to the pony, who started and threw Winston to the ground. The little boy suffered from concussion. "This was my first introduction to Irish politics!" he recalled later.[8]

The permanent under-secretary, Thomas Burke, who served successive viceroys, met young Churchill and gave him a drum. In 1882, two years after the Churchills left, Burke was assassinated along with Lord Frederick Cavendish by a nationalist group called the Irish National Invincibles.

The lodges are in the heart of Phoenix Park, considered the largest urban park in Europe. The park lies to the northwest of the city of Dublin. It takes its name from the Irish *fionn uisce*, meaning 'pure water', rather than the mythical beast that emerges from ashes. The park's history goes back to the seventeenth century when it was a royal park reserved for hunting. It became a public park the following century. It is still home to deer, but there is now also a zoo. It is also the residence of the ambassador of the United States. In 1979, Pope John Paul II celebrated mass for over a million worshippers in the park.

During his time in Ireland, Lord Randolph made frequent trips to London, for he retained his parliamentary seat as MP for Woodstock. Churchill's younger brother, Jack, was born in February 1880, just before the family all left Dublin and after the general election in April, when the Conservatives were defeated.

After Irish independence, Little Lodge became an Irish government building. It was the home of the first president, Douglas Hyde, and was named Ratra House after his home in Roscommon. It later became a Civil Defence College and is now the headquarters of Gaisce, the President's Award.

In *My Early Life*, Winston Churchill recalled a public event that took place in the park in February 1880 when his grandfather, the Duke of Marlborough, unveiled a statue to Field Marshal Viscount Gough, the so-called 'hammer of the Sikhs'. The statue was designed by the leading sculptor of nineteenth-century Ireland, John Henry Foley, who died five and a half years before it was cast and unveiled. Foley was a prolific designer of statues, many of which have survived intact, including those of Edmund Burke and Oliver Goldsmith at Trinity College Dublin.

Gough, an Anglo-Irishman, was seen as the greatest British soldier after the Duke of Wellington, another Anglo-Irishman. (Indeed, he had been one of the pallbearers at Wellington's funeral in 1852.) The statue was made from melted guns used in the Sikh Wars in India. Churchill remembered the pomp and ceremony of the occasion and even words spoken about Gough's soldiering by his grandfather, "And with a withering volley he shattered the enemy's line."[9] Churchill was five at the time, and this is early evidence of his intoxication with rhetoric. The contemporary press reports, however, gave the duke's words as "With a crashing volley the enemy was fiercely beaten back."[10] The words of Churchill's selective memory are possibly more eloquent.

The statue has had a chequered history. As a symbol of English hegemony and military arrogance, it was a target for Irish nationalists. In 1944, the statue was beheaded; later the severed head was found in the River Liffey. And thirteen years later, it was blasted to smithereens. Other statues that have been blown up included those of King William of Orange and King George II, as well as Nelson's Column Dublin.

Gough's statue was the subject of a poem by Vincent Caprani, though often wrongly attributed to Brendan Behan.

> *There are strange things done from twelve to one*
> *In the hollow at Phaynix Park,*
> *There's maidens mobbed and gentlemen robbed*
> *In the bushes after dark;*
> *But the strangest of all within human recall*
> *Concerns the statue of Gough,*
> *'Twas a terrible fact, and a most wicked act,*
> *For his bollix they tried to blow off.*[11]

The statue has gone but the name of Gough is perpetuated with the name of Gough Roundabout, just inside Phoenix Park, two hundred yards west of the main gate. It is here that the statue stood. After it was blown up, the parts were reassembled and transferred, along with the plinth, to Chillingham

Castle in Northumberland – the home (in 2020) of the parents-in-law of Dominic Cummings, adviser to the prime minister, Boris Johnson. A fountain was built to fill the space, with a stone mermaid disporting herself. Dubliners referred to it as the 'floozie in the jacuzzi'. Fountain and mermaid have since been removed with no replacements. Early in the twenty-first century, there was a proposal to bring the statue back to Ireland. Gough represented the arrogance of the English ascendancy of colonised Ireland; on the other hand it was an outstanding work of art by an Irish artist. The proposal was dropped.

It is easy to see how Churchill, with his first – mostly happy – memories of Phoenix Park, was imbued with a sense of self-assured superiority. His grandfather represented the queen. He moved from the magnificent Blenheim Palace, surrounded by 2,500 acres of parkland, to the Viceregal Lodge, surrounded by 1,752 acres of parkland. (In 1912, Blenheim was the scene of a great Conservative and Unionist demonstration against the proposed Home Rule Bill of which Churchill was then a champion.) Dublin was a garrison town. The infant Winston Churchill became familiar with military parades and manoeuvres; the nearby barracks were actually called the Marlborough Barracks. The barracks still stand but have been renamed the McKee Barracks. Family, class, nationality, all contributed to an environment of privilege and entitlement. It would have been hard for the young Churchill not to have been affected by a sense of family and national primacy, upheld by an elaborate military infrastructure. It is thus all the more remarkable that, in 1912, Churchill defied this personal inheritance and championed the third Home Rule Bill.

Twenty years after Churchill left, he returned to Dublin to lecture on his adventures in the Boer War. He came back to Little

Lodge. His memory was that "there was a lawn about as big as Trafalgar Square, and entirely surrounded by forests".[12] In reality he found it was just sixty yards across, and the forest was simply some bushes.

ACKNOWLEDGEMENTS

I am grateful to Rachel Gamble and Rod Hughes for driving me to Lullenden, Eastchurch and Newchapel; to Desmond Hannigan and Kenneth Baxter for enlightening me about Dundee political history; to Nikki Copleston for lending me a book on Montagu Porch; to Peter West for information on Eastchurch; to Margaret McGuirk for information about Phoenix Park Dublin; to Alex McKillop for telling me of Churchill's connections with Carnlough; to Jake Mac Siacais for guidance in West Belfast; to Barbara Stevens for telling me about Berkhamsted High School; to Caroline Shaw, Julia Wilson and Tace Fox for welcoming me to Harrow School; to Anthony Morton for hospitality at Sandhurst; to Andrew Shannon for directing me to Angel Meadow Manchester; to Ronnie Ross for help in Achnasheen; to Mike Shepherd for sharing Cruden Bay with me; to Susan Scott for answering queries about the Savoy Hotel; to Zoe Rowlands for help at Port Lympne; to Sean Magee for points relating to horse racing; to Peter Mackenzie Smith for driving me to Port Lympne and offering advice; and to Robin Martin for comment.

I have received support and help from David Lassman and members of the Frome Writers Collective.

The London Library has been a superlative resource.

I have had great support and encouragement from the team at Haus Publishing, Barbara Schwepcke, Harry Hall, Asha Astley and Edoardo Braschi. In particular the editor, Alice Horne, has been magnificent in eliminating howlers, tactfully offering advice with good humour.

Theresa has read through every word with careful critical and loving advice. Remaining flaws and infelicities are my responsibility.

NOTES

1. LONDON: SW1

1 Winston S. Churchill, *The Second World War, Vol. 6, Triumph and Tragedy*. Cassell, London, 1954.

2 Martin Gilbert, *Winston S. Churchill Vol. 8, "Never Despair", 1945–1965*. Heinemann, London, 1988.

3 Winston S. Churchill, *Thoughts and Adventures*. Thornton Butterworth, Keystone Edition, London, 1933.

4 Fenner Brockway, *Inside the Left: Thirty Years of Platform, Press, Prison and Parliament*. George Allen and Unwin, London, 1942.

5 David L. Roll, *The Hopkins Touch: Harry Hopkins and the Forging of the Alliance to Defeat Hitler*. Oxford; New York, Oxford University Press, 2013.

6 A. J. P. Taylor, *Beaverbrook*. Penguin Books, Harmondsworth, 1974.

7 Ibid.

8 Winston S. Churchill, *Churchill by Himself: In His Own Words*. Rosetta Books, 2013.

9 John Colville, *The Fringes of Power: Downing Street Diaries 1939–1955*. Weidenfeld and Nicolson, London, 2004.

10 Winston S. Churchill, *The Second World War, Vol. 1, The Gathering Storm*. Cassell, London, 1948.

11 Ibid.

12 James Stuart, *Within the Fringe*. Bodley Head, London, 1967.

13 Martin Gilbert, *Winston S. Churchill Vol. 8, "Never Despair", 1945–1965*. Heinemann, London, 1988.

14 Ibid.

15 Ibid.

16 Winston S. Churchill, *The Second World War, Vol. 4, The Hinge of Fate*. Cassell, London, 1951.

17 Ibid.

18 Martin Gilbert, *Winston S. Churchill Vol. 8, "Never Despair", 1945–1965*. Heinemann, London, 1988.

19 Winston S. Churchill, *The Second World War, Vol. 2, Their Finest Hour*. Cassell, London, 1949.

20 Winston S. Churchill, *The Second World War, Vol. 6, Triumph and Tragedy*. Cassell, London, 1954.

21 Mary Soames, *A Daughter's Tale*. Black Swan, London, 2012.

22 Martin Gilbert, *Winston S. Churchill Vol. 8, "Never Despair", 1945–1965*. Heinemann, London, 1988.

23 Ibid.

24 W. H. Thompson, *I Was Churchill's Shadow*. Christopher Johnson, London, 1959.

25 Winston S. Churchill, *The Second World War, Vol. 1, The Gathering Storm*. Cassell, London, 1948.

26 Martin Gilbert, *Winston S. Churchill Vol. 8, "Never Despair", 1945–1965*. Heinemann, London, 1988.

27 David Lough, *No More Champagne, Churchill and His Money*. Head of Zeus, London, 2016.

28 Chaim Weizmann, *Trial and Error*. Hamish Hamilton, London, 1949.

29 Martin Gilbert, *Churchill and the Jews*. Pocket Books, London, 2008.

30 Winston S. Churchill, *Step by Step 1936–1939*. Odhams Press, London, 1948.

31 Martin Gilbert, *Churchill and the Jews*. Pocket Books, London, 2008.

32 Richard T. Holmes, *Churchill's Bunker: The Cabinet War Rooms and the Culture of Secrecy in Wartime*. Yale University Press, London, 2010.

33 Winston S. Churchill, *The Second World War, Vol. 1, The Gathering Storm*. Cassell, London, 1948.

34 Ibid.

35 Martin Gilbert, *Winston S. Churchill Vol. 4, 1917–1922 World in Torment*. Minerva, London, 1990.

36 Ibid.

37 Ibid.

38 Ibid.

39 Ibid.

40 Winston S. Churchill, *The World Crisis 1911–1918*. Penguin, London, 2007

41 Martin Gilbert, *Winston S. Churchill Vol. 4, 1917–1922 World in Torment*. Minerva, London, 1990.

42 Winston S. Churchill, *The Second World War, Vol. 2, Their Finest Hour*. Cassell, London, 1949.

43 Martin Gilbert, *Winston S. Churchill Vol. 8, "Never Despair", 1945–1965*. Heinemann, London, 1988.

44 Martin Gilbert, *Winston S. Churchill Vol. 6, Finest Hour, 1939–1941*. Minerva, London, 1989.

45 Ibid.

46 Martin Gilbert, *Winston S. Churchill Vol. 8, "Never Despair", 1945–1965*. Heinemann, London, 1988.

47 Winston S. Churchill, "The end of the war in Europe" speech, House of Commons, 8 May 1945.

48 Winston S. Churchill, *The Second World War, Vol. 2, Their Finest Hour*. Cassell, London, 1949.

49 Randolph S. Churchill, *Winston S. Churchill Vol. 2, 1900–1914, Young Statesman*. Heinemann, London, 1967.

50 Martin Gilbert, *Winston S. Churchill Vol. 8, "Never Despair", 1945–1965*. Heinemann, London, 1988.

51 Winston Churchill, House of Commons speech, 28 October 1943.

52 Winston S. Churchill, *My Early Life*. Odhams Press, London, 1949.

53 Winston S. Churchill, *Savrola, A Tale of the Revolution in Laurania*. Beacon Books, London, 1957.

54 Lucy Masterman, *C. F. G. Masterman, A Biography*. Nicholson and Watson, London, 1939.

55 Andrew Roberts, *Churchill, Walking with Destiny*. Allen Lane, London, 2018.

56 Winston S. Churchill, *The Second World War, Vol. 1, The Gathering Storm*. Cassell, London, 1948.

57 Martin Gilbert, *Winston S. Churchill Vol. 6, Finest Hour, 1939–1941*. Minerva, London, 1989.

58 Winston S. Churchill, *The Second World War, Vol. 2, Their Finest Hour*. Cassell, London, 1949.

59 Lord Ismay, *Memoirs*. Heinemann, London, 1960.

60 Winston S. Churchill, *The Second World War, Vol. 2, Their Finest Hour*. Cassell, London, 1949.

61 Winston S. Churchill, "Wars are not won by evacuations" speech, House of Commons, 4 June 1940 .

62 Sir Henry Channon, *"Chips": The Diaries of Sir Henry*

Channon. (ed. Robert Rhodes James), Phoenix, London, 1996.

63 Winston S. Churchill, *The Second World War, Vol. 2, Their Finest Hour.* Cassell, London, 1949.

64 Winston S. Churchill, *Winston S. Churchill: His Complete Speeches, 1897–1963: Vol. 6, 1935–1942.* Chelsea House Publishers, R. R. Bowker Company, New York, London, 1974.

65 Martin Gilbert, *Winston S. Churchill Vol. 7, Road to Victory, 1941–1945.* Heinemann/Minerva, London, 1989.

66 Paul Johnson, *Churchill.* Penguin Books, New York, 2010

67 Martin Gilbert, *Winston S. Churchill Vol. 8, "Never Despair", 1945–1965.* Heinemann, London, 1988.

68 R. A. Butler, *The Art of the Possible: The Memoirs of Lord Butler, K.G., C.H. Hamilton,* London, 1982.

69 Martin Gilbert, *Winston S. Churchill Vol. 8, "Never Despair", 1945–1965.* Heinemann, London, 1988.

70 Ibid.

71 James Stuart, *Within the Fringe.* Bodley Head, London, 1967.

72 Winston S. Churchill, *The Second World War, Vol. 2, Their Finest Hour.* Cassell, London, 1949.

73 Winston S. Churchill, *Churchill by Himself: The Life, Times and Opinions of Winston Churchill in his own Words* (ed. Richard M. Langworth). Ebury Publishing, London 2008.

74 Winston S. Churchill, *The Second World War, Vol. 1, The Gathering Storm.* Cassell, London, 1948.

75 Winston S. Churchill, "Blood, toil, tears and sweat" speech, House of Commons, 13 May 1940.

76 Winston S. Churchill, *The Second World War, Vol. 2, Their Finest Hour.* Cassell, London, 1949.

77 Lucy Masterman, *C. F. G. Masterman, A Biography*. Nicholson and Watson, London, 1939.

78 Ibid.

79 Martin Gilbert, *Churchill and the Jews*. Pocket Books, London, 2008.

80 Martin Gilbert, *Winston S. Churchill Vol. 7, Road to Victory, 1941–1945*. Heinemann/Minerva, London, 1989.

2. LONDON: OUTSIDE SW1

1 Randolph S. Churchill, *Winston S. Churchill Vol. 2, 1900–1914 Young Statesman*. Heinemann, London, 1967.

2 Martin Gilbert, *Winston S. Churchill Vol. 8, "Never Despair", 1945–1965*. Heinemann, London, 1988.

3 David A. Thomas, *Churchill, the Member for Woodford*. Frank Cass, Ilford, 1995.

4 Winston S. Churchill, *Savrola, A Tale of the Revolution in Laurania*. Beacon Books, London, 1957.

5 Celia Sandys, *"From Winston with Love and Kisses", The Young Churchill*. Sinclair Stevenson, London, 1994.

6 Randolph S. Churchill, *Winston S. Churchill Vol. 1, 1874–1900, Youth*. Heinemann, London, 1966.

7 Ibid.

8 Martin Gilbert, *Winston S. Churchill Vol. 5, Prophet of Truth, 1922–1939*. Minerva, London, 1990.

9 Ibid.

10 Ibid.

11 Martin Gilbert, *Winston S. Churchill Vol. 6, Finest Hour, 1939–1941*. Minerva, London, 1989.

12 Winston S. Churchill, "The end of the beginning" speech, Mansion House, 10 November 1942.

13 Ibid.

14 Lucy Masterman, *C. F. G. Masterman, A Biography*. Nicholson and Watson, London, 1939.

15 Ibid.

16 Ibid.

17 Winston S. Churchill, *The Second World War, Vol. 2, Their Finest Hour*. Cassell, London, 1949.

18 Ibid.

19 Martin Gilbert, *Winston S. Churchill Vol. 6, Finest Hour, 1939–1941*. Minerva, London, 1989.

20 Martin Gilbert, *Winston S. Churchill Vol. 3, 1914–1917, The Challenge of War*. Minerva, London, 1990.

21 Martin Gilbert, *Winston S. Churchill Vol. 8, "Never Despair", 1945–1965*. Heinemann, London, 1988.

22 Henry Pelling, *Winston Churchill*. London, Palgrave Macmillan, 1989.

23 Ibid.

24 Sarah Churchill, *A Thread in the Tapestry*. Andre Deutsch, London, 1967.

25 Andrew Roberts, *Churchill, Walking with Destiny*. Allen Lane, London, 2018.

26 David Lough, *No More Champagne, Churchill and His Money*. Head of Zeus, London, 2016.

27 Damian Collins, *Charmed Life, The Phenomenal World of Philip Sassoon*. William Collins, London, 2017.

28 Mary Soames (ed.), *Speaking for Themselves, The Personal Letters of Winston and Clementine Churchill*. Swan Books, London, 1999.

29 Ibid.

30 Winston S. Churchill, *My Early Life*. Odhams Press, London, 1949.
31 David Cannadine (ed.), *Churchill, The Statesman Artist*. Bloomsbury, London, 2018.
32 Ibid.
33 Martin Gilbert, *Winston S. Churchill Vol. 8, "Never Despair", 1945–1965*. Heinemann, London, 1988.
34 Randolph S. Churchill, *Winston S. Churchill Vol. 1, 1874–1900, Youth*. Heinemann, London, 1966.
35 Colin R. Coote, *The Other Club*. Sidgwick and Jackson, London, 1971.
36 Ibid.
37 Martin Gilbert, *Winston Churchill and the Other Club*, privately printed, London, 2011.
38 Martin Gilbert, *Winston S. Churchill Vol. 5, Prophet of Truth, 1922–1939*. Minerva, London, 1990.
39 Martin Gilbert, *Winston Churchill and the Other Club*, privately printed, London, 2011.
40 Ibid.

3. HOME COUNTIES

1 Randolph S. Churchill, *Winston S. Churchill Vol. 1, 1874–1900*, Youth. Heinemann, London, 1966.
2 Ibid.
3 Ibid.
4 Ibid.
5 Ibid.
6 Winston S. Churchill, *My Early Life*. Odhams Press, London, 1949.

7   Randolph S. Churchill, *Winston S. Churchill Vol. 1, 1874–1900, Youth*. Heinemann, London, 1966.

8   Ibid.

9   Winston S. Churchill, *The Second World War, Vol. 3, The Grand Alliance*. Cassell, London, 1950.

10 Martin Gilbert, *Winston S. Churchill Vol. 6, Finest Hour, 1939–1941*. Minerva, London, 1989.

11 Winston Churchill, "Give Us The Tools" broadcast, 9 February 1941, London.

12 Earl of Halifax, *Fulness of Days*. Collins, London, 1957.

13 Ibid.

14 Winston S. Churchill, *The Second World War, Vol. 6, Triumph and Tragedy*. Cassell, London, 1954.

15 Winston S. Churchill, *The Second World War, Vol. 3, The Grand Alliance*. Cassell, London, 1950.

16 Ibid.

17 Ibid.

18 Mary Soames, *Clementine Churchill*. Cassell, London, 1979.

19 Ibid.

20 Martin Gilbert, *Winston S Churchill Vol 5, Prophet of Truth, 1922–1939*. Minerva, London, 1990.

21 Cita Stelzer, *Dinner with Churchill*. Short Books, London, 2012.

22 Ivan Maisky, *The Maisky Diaries* (ed. Gabriel Gorodetsky, tr. Tatiana Sorokina and Oliver Ready). Yale University Press, New Haven and London, 2016.

23 Stefan Buczacki, *From Blenheim to Chartwell, The Untold Story of Churchill's Houses and Gardens*. Unicorn, London, 2018.

24 Martin Gilbert, *Winston S. Churchill Vol. 6, Finest Hour, 1939–1941*. Minerva, London, 1989.

25 Mary Soames, *Clementine Churchill*. Cassell, London, 1979.

26 Martin Gilbert, *Winston S. Churchill Vol. 6, Finest Hour, 1939–1941*. Minerva, London, 1989.

27 Winston S. Churchill, *The Second World War, Vol. 2, Their Finest Hour*. Cassell, London, 1949.

28 Damian Collins, *Charmed Life, The Phenomenal World of Philip Sassoon*. William Collins, London, 2017.

29 Martin Gilbert, *Winston S. Churchill Vol. 3, 1914–1917 The Challenge of War*. Minerva, London, 1990.

30 Robert Boothby, *I Fight to Live*. Victor Gollancz, London, 1947.

31 Damian Collins, *Charmed Life, The Phenomenal World of Philip Sassoon*. William Collins, London, 2017.

32 Randolph S. Churchill, *Winston S. Churchill Vol. 1, 1874–1900, Youth*. Heinemann, London, 1966.

33 Winston S. Churchill, *Churchill by Himself: The Life, Times and Opinions of Winston Churchill in his own Words* (ed. Richard M. Langworth). Ebury Publishing, London 2008.

34 Winston S. Churchill, *My Early Life*. Odhams Press, London, 1949.

35 Randolph S. Churchill, *Winston S. Churchill Vol. 1, 1874–1900, Youth*. Heinemann, London, 1966.

36 David Lough (ed.), *Darling Winston, Forty Years of Letters between Winston Churchill and His Mother*. Apollo, London, 2019.

37 Randolph S. Churchill, *Winston S. Churchill Vol. 1, 1874–1900, Youth*. Heinemann, London, 1966.

38 Andrew Roberts, *Churchill, Walking with Destiny*. Allen Lane, London, 2018.

39 Celia Sandys, *"From Winston with Love and Kisses", The Young Churchill*. Sinclair Stevenson, London, 1994.

40 Martin Gilbert, *Winston S. Churchill Vol. 6, Finest Hour, 1939–1941*. Minerva, London, 1989.

41 Lord Ismay, *Memoirs*. Heinemann, London, 1960.

42 Norman Rose, *Churchill: The Unruly Giant*. The Free Press, New York, 1995.

43 Martin Gilbert, *Winston S. Churchill Vol. 3, 1914–1917 The Challenge of War*. Minerva, London, 1990.

44 Andrew Roberts, *Churchill, Walking with Destiny*. Allen Lane, London, 2018.

45 David Cannadine (ed.), *Churchill, The Statesman Artist*. Bloomsbury, London, 2018.

46 Martin Gilbert, *Winston S. Churchill Vol. 8, "Never Despair", 1945–1965*. Heinemann, London, 1988.

47 Anthony Montague Browne, *Long Sunset, Memoirs of Winston Churchill's Last Private Secretary*. Cassell, London, 1995.

48 Randolph S. Churchill, *Winston S. Churchill Vol. 1, 1874–1900, Youth*. Heinemann, London, 1966.

49 Celia Sandys, *"From Winston with Love and Kisses", The Young Churchill*. Sinclair Stevenson, London, 1994.

50 Ibid.

51 Ibid.

52 Winston S. Churchill, *The Second World War, Vol. 2, Their Finest Hour*. Cassell, London, 1949.

53 Viscount Montgomery of Alamein, *The Memoirs*. Collins, London, 1958.

54 Winston S. Churchill, *The Second World War, Vol. 2, Their Finest Hour*. Cassell, London, 1949.

4. SOUTH WEST ENGLAND

1   Andrew Roberts, *Churchill, Walking with Destiny*. Allen Lane, London, 2018.

2   David Cannadine, *Heroic Chanellor: Winston Churchill and the University of Bristol 1929–1965*. University of Bristol, London; Bristol, 2017.

3   Martin Gilbert, *Winston S. Churchill Vol. 7, Road to Victory, 1941–1945*. Heinemann/Minerva, London, 1989.

4   Martin Gilbert, *Winston S. Churchill Vol. 8, "Never Despair", 1945–1965*. Heinemann, London, 1988.

5   Ibid.

6   Ibid.

7   John Colville, *The Fringes of Power: Downing Street Diaries 1939–1955*. Weidenfeld and Nicolson, London, 2004.

8   Winston S. Churchill, *The Second World War, Vol. 3, The Grand Alliance*. Cassell, London, 1950.

9   Winston S. Churchill, *My Early Life*. Odhams Press, London, 1949.

10 Ibid.

11 Ibid.

12 W. H. Thompson, *I Was Churchill's Shadow*. Christopher Johnson, London, 1959.

13 Celia Lee and John Lee, *The Churchills: A Family Portrait*. Palgrave Macmillan, London, 2010.

14 Randolph S. Churchill, *Winston S. Churchill Vol. 1, 1874–1900, Youth*. Heinemann, London, 1966.

15 Winston S. Churchill, *My Early Life*. Odhams Press, London, 1949.

16 Randolph S. Churchill, *Winston S. Churchill Vol. 1, 1874–1900, Youth*. Heinemann, London, 1966.

17 Violet Bonham Carter, *Winston Churchill as I Knew Him.*
Eyre and Spottiswoode, London, 1965.

18 Ibid.

5. CENTRAL BRITAIN

1 Martin Gilbert, *Winston S. Churchill Vol. 8, "Never
Despair", 1945–1965.* Heinemann, London, 1988.

2 Randolph S. Churchill, *Winston S. Churchill Vol. 1, 1874–
1900, Youth.* Heinemann, London, 1966.

3 Winston S. Churchill, *My Early Life.* Odhams Press,
London, 1949.

4 David A. Thomas, *Churchill, the Member for Woodford.*
Frank Cass, Ilford, 1995.

5 Ibid.

6 Winston S. Churchill, *Lord Randolph Churchill.*
Macmillan, London, 1907.

7 David A. Thomas, *Churchill, the Member for Woodford.*
Frank Cass, Ilford, 1995.

8 Ibid.

9 Ibid.

10 Ibid.

11 Ibid.

12 Edmund Murray, *Churchill's Bodyguard.* A Star Book,
London, 1988.

13 Mary Soames, *Clementine Churchill.* Cassell, London, 1979.

14 Winston S. Churchill, *The Second World War, Vol. 1, The
Gathering Storm.* Cassell, London, 1948.

15 Randolph S. Churchill, *Winston S. Churchill Vol. 2, 1900–
1914 Young Statesman.* Heinemann, London, 1967.

16 Martin Gilbert, *Winston S. Churchill Vol. 5, Prophet of Truth, 1922–1939*. Minerva, London, 1990.

17 Lord Pethick-Lawrence, *Fate Has Been Kind*. National Book Association, London, c. 1945.

18 Martin Gilbert, *Winston S. Churchill Vol. 5, Prophet of Truth, 1922–1939*. Minerva, London, 1990.

19 Winston S. Churchill, *Savrola, A Tale of the Revolution in Laurania*. Beacon Books, London, 1957.

20 Beatrice Webb, *The Diary of Beatrice Webb, Vol. 3, 1905–1924, The Power to Alter Things*. Virago, London, 1984.

21 Martin Gilbert, *Winston S. Churchill Vol. 8, "Never Despair", 1945–1965*. Heinemann, London, 1988.

22 Mary Soames, *Clementine Churchill*. Cassell, London, 1979.

23 Consuelo Vanderbilt Balsan, *The Glitter and the Gold*. Hodder, London, 2012.

24 Winston S. Churchill, *The Second World War, Vol. 3, The Grand Alliance*. Cassell, London, 1950.

25 Martin Gilbert, *Winston S. Churchill Vol. 8, "Never Despair", 1945–1965*. Heinemann, London, 1988.

26 Winston S. Churchill, *The Second World War, Vol. 2, Their Finest Hour*. Cassell, London, 1949.

6. THE NORTH OF ENGLAND

1 Martin Gilbert, *Winston S. Churchill Vol. 8, "Never Despair", 1945–1965*. Heinemann, London, 1988.

2 Winston S. Churchill, *My Early Life*. Odhams Press, London, 1949.

3 Ibid.

4   Winston Churchill, House of Commons speech, 28 October 1943.

5   Randolph S. Churchill, *Winston S. Churchill Vol. 1, 1874–1900, Youth*. Heinemann, London, 1966.

6   H. A. Taylor, *Jix – Viscount Brentford*. Stanley Paul, London, 1933.

7   Randolph S. Churchill, *Winston S. Churchill Vol. 2, 1900–1914 Young Statesman*. Heinemann, London, 1967.

8   Ibid.

9   Lucy Masterman, *C. F. G. Masterman, A Biography*. Nicholson and Watson, London, 1939.

10 Andrew Roberts, *Churchill, Walking with Destiny*. Allen Lane, London, 2018.

11 Randolph S. Churchill, *Winston S. Churchill Vol. 2, 1900–1914 Young Statesman*. Heinemann, London, 1967.

12 Martin Gilbert, *Winston S. Churchill Vol. 8, "Never Despair", 1945–1965*. Heinemann, London, 1988.

13 Andrew Roberts, *Churchill, Walking with Destiny*. Allen Lane, London, 2018.

14 Winston S. Churchill, *Never Give In! The Best of Winston Churchill's Speeches*. Bloomsbury Academic, London, 2013.

15 Andrew Roberts, *Churchill, Walking with Destiny*. Allen Lane, London, 2018.

16 Randolph S. Churchill, *Winston S. Churchill Vol. 2, 1900–1914 Young Statesman*. Heinemann, London, 1967.

17 Ibid.

18 Ibid.

19 Martin Gilbert, *Winston S. Churchill Vol. 8, "Never Despair", 1945–1965*. Heinemann, London, 1988.

7. SCOTLAND

1 Winston S. Churchill, *Thoughts and Adventures*. Odhams Press, London, 1949.
2 Ibid.
3 Ibid.
4 Ibid.
5 Winston S. Churchill, *Step by Step 1936–1939*. Odhams Press, London, 1948.
6 Martin Gilbert, *Winston S. Churchill Vol. 6, Finest Hour, 1939–1941*. Minerva, London, 1989.
7 Winston S. Churchill, *The Second World War, Vol. 1, The Gathering Storm*. Cassell, London, 1948.
8 Roy Jenkins, *Churchill*. Pan Books, London, 2002.
9 Ibid.
10 Winston S. Churchill, *Thoughts and Adventures*. Odhams Press, London, 1949.
11 Ibid.
12 Ibid.
13 Winston S. Churchill, *Churchill by Himself: The Life, Times and Opinions of Winston Churchill in his own Words* (ed. Richard M. Langworth). Ebury Publishing, London 2008.
14 Mary Soames (ed.), *Speaking for Themselves, The Personal Letters of Winston and Clementine Churchill*. Swan Books, London, 1999.
15 Randolph S. Churchill, *Winston S. Churchill Vol. 2, 1900–1914 Young Statesman*. Heinemann, London, 1967.
16 Winston S. Churchill, *Lord Randolph Churchill*. Macmillan, London, 1907.
17 Paul Bew, *Churchill and Ireland*. University Press, Oxford, 2018

18 Ibid.

19 Winston S. Churchill, *Thoughts and Adventures*. Odhams Press, London, 1949.

20 This rhyme was taught to me by the Scottish political historian Dr Kenneth Baxter as we strolled through the streets of Dundee.

21 Winston S. Churchill, *Thoughts and Adventures*. Odhams Press, London, 1949.

22 William Gallacher, *Revolt on the Clyde*. Lawrence and Wishart, London, 1949.

23 Winston S. Churchill, *Thoughts and Adventures*. Odhams Press, London, 1949.

24 David Lloyd George, 1909 Budget Speech.

25 Winston S. Churchill, *The Menace of Land Monopoly*. The Henry George Foundation, 1941.

26 Martin Gilbert, *Winston S. Churchill Vol. 6, Finest Hour, 1939–1941*. Minerva, London, 1989.

27 Roy Jenkins, *Churchill*. Pan Books, London, 2002.

28 Winston S. Churchill, *Never Give In! The Best of Winston Churchill's Speeches*. Bloomsbury Academic, London, 2013.

29 Martin Gilbert, *Winston S. Churchill Vol. 3, 1914–1917 The Challenge of War*. Minerva, London, 1990.

8. IRELAND

1 David R. Orr and David Truesdale, *"Ulster will Fight", Vol. 1, Home Rule and the Volunteer Force 1886–1922*. Helion and Co, Solihull, 2016.

2 St John Ervine, *Craigavon, Ulsterman*. George Allen and Unwin, London, 1949.

3   Mary Soames, *Clementine Churchill*. Cassell, London, 1979.

4   Winston S. Churchill, *Never Give In! The Best of Winston Churchill's Speeches*. Bloomsbury Academic, London, 2013.

5   David R. Orr and David Truesdale, *"Ulster will Fight", Vol. 1, Home Rule and the Volunteer Force 1886–1922*. Helion and Co, Solihull, 2016.

6   This story was related to me by Alex McKillop, Tourist Information Centre, Carnlough, in August 2019.

7   Winston S. Churchill, *Lord Randolph Churchill*. Macmillan, London, 1907.

8   Winston S. Churchill, *My Early Life*. Odhams Press, London, 1949.

9   Ibid.

10   Ibid.

11   John A. McCullen, *An Illustrated History of the Phoenix Park, Landscape and Management to 1880, second edition*. Government Publications, OPW, Dublin, 2011.

12   Winston S. Churchill, *My Early Life*. Odhams Press. London, 1949.

BIBLIOGRAPHY

Paul Addison, *Churchill, The Unexpected Hero*, University Press, Oxford, 2006 (first published 2005)

Margot Asquith, *Great War Diary 1914–1916, The View from Downing Street* (eds Michael and Eleanor Brock), University Press, Oxford, 2014

Diana Atkinson, *Rise Up, Women! The Remarkable Lives of the Suffragettes*, Bloomsbury Publishing, London, 2019 (first published 2018)

C. R. Attlee, *As It Happened*, Odhams Press, London, nd (first published 1954)

Consuelo Vanderbilt Balsan, *The Glitter and the Gold*, Hodder, London, 2012 (first published 1973)

John Bew, *Citizen Clem A Biography of Attlee*, Riverrun, London, 2017 (first published 2016)

Paul Bew, *Churchill and Ireland*, University Press, Oxford, 2018 (first published 2016)

Robert Blake, *The Unknown Prime Minister, The Life of Andrew Bonar Law 1858–1923*, Eyre and Spottiswoode, London, 1955

Violet Bonham Carter, *Winston Churchill as I Knew Him*, Eyre and Spottiswoode, London, 1965

Robert Boothby, *I Fight to Live*, Victor Gollancz, London, 1947

Andrew Boyle, *"Poor, Dear Brendan" The Quest for Brendan Bracken*, Hutchinson, London, 1974

Lord Brabazon of Tara, *The Brabazon Story*, William
Heinemann, London, 1956

Simon Bradley and Nikolaus Pevsner, *The Buildings of England,
London 6: Westminster*, Yale University Press, New Haven
and London, 2005

Fenner Brockway, *Inside the Left, Thirty Years of Platform, Press,
Prison and Parliament*, George Allen and Unwin, London,
1942

Jack Brown, *No 10, The Geography of Power at Downing Street*,
Haus Publishing, 2019

Anthony Montague Browne, *Long Sunset, Memoirs of Winston
Churchill's Last Private Secretary*, Cassell, London, 1995

Stefan Buczacki, *From Blenheim to Chartwell, The Untold Story
of Churchill's Houses and Gardens*, Unicorn, London, 2018

Mervyn Busteed, *The Irish in Manchester 1750–1921, Resistance
and Adaptation and Doubts*, University Press, Manchester,
2016

R. A. Butler, *The Art of the Possible: The Memoirs of Lord Butler,
K.G., C.H.*, Hamilton, London, 1982

David Cannadine, *Heroic Chancellor: Winston Churchill and
the University of Bristol 1929–65*, Institute of Historical
Research, London, 2016

David Cannadine (ed.), *Churchill, The Statesman Artist*,
Bloomsbury, London, 2018

E. D. W. Chaplin (ed.), *Winston Churchill and Harrow*, School
Book Shop, Harrow, 1941

Sir Henry Channon, *"Chips": The Diaries of Sir Henry Channon*
(ed. Robert Rhodes James), Phoenix, London, 1996

Randolph S. Churchill, *Twenty-One Years*, Weidenfeld and
Nicolson, London, 1965

Randolph S. Churchill, *Winston S. Churchill Vol. 1, 1874–1900, Youth*, Heinemann, London, 1966

Randolph S. Churchill, *Winston S. Churchill Vol. 2, 1900–1914 Young Statesman*, Heinemann, London, 1967

Sarah Churchill, *A Thread in the Tapestry*, André Deutsch, London, 1967

Winston S. Churchill, *Churchill by Himself: The Life, Times and Opinions of Winston Churchill in his own Words* (ed. Richard M. Langworth), Ebury Publishing, London 2008

Winston S. Churchill, *Great Contemporaries*, Thornton Butterworth, London, 1937

Winston S. Churchill, *Winston S. Churchill: His Complete Speeches, 1897-1963: Vol. 6, 1935–1942*, Chelsea House Publishers, R. R. Bowker Company, New York, London, 1974

Winston S. Churchill, *Lord Randolph Churchill*, Macmillan, London, 1907 (2 volumes in one, first published 1906)

Winston S. Churchill, *My Early Life*, Odhams Press, London, 1949 (first published 1930)

Winston S. Churchill, *Never Give In! The Best of Winston Churchill's Speeches*, Bloomsbury Academic, London, 2013

Winston S. Churchill, *Savrola, A Tale of the Revolution in Laurania*, Beacon Books, London, 1957 (first published 1900)

Winston S. Churchill, *Step by Step 1936–1939*, Odhams Press, London, 1948 (first published 1939)

Winston S. Churchill, *The Menace of Land Monopoly*, The Henry George Foundation, 1941

Winston S. Churchill, *The Second World War, Vol. 1, The Gathering Storm*, Cassell, London, 1948

Winston S. Churchill, *The Second World War, Vol. 2, Their Finest Hour*, Cassell, London, 1949

Winston S. Churchill, *The Second World War, Vol. 3, The Grand Alliance*, Cassell, London, 1950

Winston S. Churchill, *The Second World War, Vol. 4, The Hinge of Fate*, Cassell, London, 1951

Winston S. Churchill, *The Second World War, Vol. 5, Closing the Ring*, Cassell. London, 1952

Winston S. Churchill, *The Second World War, Vol. 6, Triumph and Tragedy*, Cassell, London, 1954

Winston S. Churchill, *Thoughts and Adventures*, Odhams Press, London, 1949 (first published 1932)

Peregrine Churchill and Julian Mitchell, *Jennie Lady Randolph Churchill, A Portrait with Letters*, Collins, London, 1974

Peter Clark, *Marmaduke Pickthall British Muslim*, Quartet Books, London 1986

Jonathan Coad, *Dover Castle, A Frontline Fortress and its Wartime Tunnels*, English Heritage, London, 2016 (first published 2011)

Jonathan Coad and Rowena Willard-Wright, *Walmer Castle*, English Heritage, London, 2015

Margaret Cole, *Beatrice Webb*, Longmans Green, London, 1945

Damian Collins, *Charmed Life, The Phenomenal World of Philip Sassoon*, William Collins, London, 2017 (first published 2016)

John Colville, *The Fringes of Power, Downing Street Diaries 1939–1955*, Weidenfeld and Nicolson, London, 2004

David Coombs, *Churchill, His Paintings*, Hamish Hamilton, London, 1967

Duff Cooper, *Old Men Forget*, Rupert Hart-Davis, London, 1953

Duff Cooper, *The Duff Cooper Diaries 1915–1951* (ed. John Julius Norwich), Phoenix, London, 2006 (first published 2005)

Colin R. Coote, *The Other Club*, Sidgwick and Jackson, London, 1971

Frances Donaldson, *Edward VIII, The Road to Abdication*, Book Club Associates, London, 1978 (first published 1974)

Bernard Donoughue and G. W. Jones, *Herbert Morrison, Portrait of a Politician*, Phoenix, London, 2001 (first published 1973)

Friedrich Engels, *The Condition of the Working Class in England in 1844* (tr. Florence Kelley Wischnewetzky), George Allen and Unwin, London, 1920 (first published 1845)

St John Ervine, *Craigavon, Ulsterman*, George Allen and Unwin, London, 1949

Robin Fedden, *Churchill and Chartwell*, The National Trust, London, 1984 (first published 1968)

Keith Feiling, *The Life of Neville Chamberlain*, Macmillan, London, 1946

Leslie Field, *Bendor, The Golden Duke of Westminster*, Weidenfeld and Nicolson, London, 1983

William Gallacher, *Revolt on the Clyde*, Lawrence and Wishart, London, 1949 (first published 1936)

Paul Garner, *Winston Churchill's London Walk*, Louis' London Walks, London, 2016

Oliver Garnett, *Chartwell*, National Trust, London, 2018 (first published 1992)

Martin Gilbert, *Churchill and the Jews*, Pocket Books, London, 2008 (first published 2007)

Martin Gilbert, *In Search of Churchill*, HarperCollins, London, 1995 (first published 1994)

Martin Gilbert, *Winston Churchill and the Other Club*,
  privately printed, London (?), 2011

Martin Gilbert, *Winston S. Churchill Vol. 3, 1914–1917 The
  Challenge of War*, Minerva, London, 1990 (first published
  1971)

Martin Gilbert, *Winston S. Churchill Vol. 4, 1917–1922 World in
  Torment*, Minerva, London, 1990 (first published 1975)

Martin Gilbert, *Winston S. Churchill Vol. 5, Prophet of Truth*,
  1922–1939, Minerva, London, 1990 (first published 1976)

Martin Gilbert, *Winston S. Churchill Vol. 6, Finest Hour*,
  1939–1941, Minerva, London, 1989 (first published 1983)

Martin Gilbert, *Winston S. Churchill Vol. 7, Road to Victory*,
  1941–1945, Heinemann/Minerva, London, 1989 (first
  published 1986)

Martin Gilbert, *Winston S. Churchill Vol. 8, "Never Despair"*,
  1945–1965, Heinemann, London, 1988

Jim Golland, *Not Winston, Just William?, Winston Churchill
  at Harrow School*, The Herga Press, np, 1994 (first published
  1988)

Richard Burdon Haldane, *An Autobiography*, Hodder and
  Stoughton, London, 1929

Earl of Halifax, *Fulness of Days*, Collins, London, 1957

Oliver Harvey, *The Diplomatic Diaries 1937–1940* (ed. John
  Harvey), Collins, London, 1970

Denis Healey, *The Time of My Life*, Penguin Books, London,
  1990 (first published 1989)

Malcolm Hill, *Churchill, His Radical Decade*, Othila Press,
  London, 1999

Alistair Horne, *Macmillan, The Official Biography*, Macmillan,
  London, 2008 (2 volumes in one, first published 1988, 1989)

Emrys Hughes, *Winston Churchill in War and Peace*, Unity Publishing, Glasgow, 1950

Roy Humphreys, *Dover Castle, England's First Line of Defence*, The History Press, Stroud, 2010

Lord Ismay, *Memoirs*, Heinemann, London, 1960

Roy Jenkins, *Asquith*, Collins, London, 1964

Roy Jenkins, *Churchill*, Pan Books, London, 2002 (first published 2001)

Roy Jenkins, *The Chancellors*, Macmillan, London, 1997

Boris Johnson, *The Churchill Factor*, Hodder, London, 2015 (first published 2014)

Paul Johnson, *Churchill*, Penguin Books, New York, 2010 (first published 2009)

Thomas Johnston, *Memories*, Collins, London, 1952

Celia Lee and John Lee, *The Churchills: A Family Portrait*, Palgrave Macmillan, London, 2010

Marchioness of Londonderry, *Retrospect*, Frederick Muller, London, 1938

David Lough, *No More Champagne, Churchill and His Money*, Head of Zeus, London, 2016 (first published 2015)

David Lough (ed.), *Darling Winston, Forty Years of Letters between Winston Churchill and His Mother*, Apollo, London, 2019 (first published 2018)

Ivan Maisky, *The Maisky Diaries* (ed. Gabriel Gorodetsky, tr. Tatiana Sorokina and Oliver Ready), Yale University Press, New Haven and London, 2016 (first published 2015)

Norma Major, *Chequers, The Prime Minister's House and its History*, HarperCollins, London, 1996

Lucy Masterman, *C. F. G. Masterman, A Biography*, Nicholson and Watson, London, 1939

John A. McCullen, *An Illustrated History of the Phoenix*

Park, Landscape and Management to 1880, second edition, Government Publications, OPW, Dublin, 2011 (first published, 2009)

R. J. Minney, *The Private Papers of Hore-Belisha*, Collins, London, 1960

Viscount Montgomery of Alamein, *The Memoirs*, Collins, London, 1958

Edmund Murray, *Churchill's Bodyguard*, A Star Book, London, 1988 (first published 1987)

Elizabeth Nel, *Winston Churchill by His Personal Secretary,* Universe, Inc., New York, 2007 (first published, 1958)

David R. Orr and David Truesdale, *"Ulster will Fight", Vol. 1, Home Rule and the Volunteer Force 1886–1922*, Helion and Co, Solihull, 2016

David Owen, *Cabinet's Finest Hour, The Hidden Agenda of May 1940*, Haus Publishing, London, 2017 (first published 2016)

Matthew Parker, *The Battle of Britain, July–October 1940*, Headline, London, 2000

Roger Parsons, *Monty Porch, A Charmed Life*, Abbey Press, Glastonbury, 2015 (first published 2012)

Henry Pelling, *Social Geography of British Elections 1885–1910*, Macmillan, London, 1967

Henry Pelling, *Winston Churchill*, London, Palgrave Macmillan, 1989

Lord Pethick-Lawrence, *Fate Has Been Kind*, National Book Association, London, c. 1945 (first published 1943)

Nikolaus Pevsner, *The Buildings of England, London Vol. 1, London and Westminster*, Penguin Books, Harmondsworth, 1962 (first published 1957)

Nikolaus Pevsner and Bill Wilson, *The Buildings of England,*

Norfolk I, Yale University Press, New Haven and London, 1997

Robert Rhodes James, *Lord Randolph Churchill,* Weidenfeld and Nicolson, London, 1969 (first published 1959)

Robert Rhodes James, *Rosebery,* Weidenfeld and Nicolson, London, 1963

Andrew Roberts, *Churchill, Walking with Destiny,* Allen Lane, London, 2018

Norman Rose, *Churchill: The Unruly Giant,* The Free Press, New York, 1995

A. L. Rowse, *Diaries* (ed. Richard Ollard), Allen Lane, London, 2003

Celia Sandys, *"From Winston with Love and Kisses", The Young Churchill,* Sinclair Stevenson, London, 1994

Brough Scott, *Churchill at the Gallop,* Racing Post, Newbury, 2017

Mike Shepherd, *When Brave Men Shudder, The Scottish Origins of Dracula,* Wildwolf Publishing, np., 2018

Emanuel Shinwell, *Conflict without Malice,* Odhams, London, 1955

Viscount Simon, *Retrospect,* Hutchinson, London, 1952

Michael Smith, *The Secret of Station X, How Bletchley Park Helped Win the War,* Biteback Publications, London, 2011

Mary Soames, *A Daughter's Tale,* Black Swan, London, 2012 (first published, 2011)

Mary Soames, *Clementine Churchill,* Cassell, London, 1979

Mary Soames (ed.), *Speaking for Themselves, The Personal Letters of Winston and Clementine Churchill,* Swan Books, London, 1999 (first published 1998)

Cita Stelzer, *Dinner with Churchill,* Short Books, London, 2012 (first published 2011)

James Stuart, *Within the Fringe*, The Bodley Head, London, 1967

Viscount Swinton, *I Remember*, Hutchinson, London, nd

Christopher Simon Sykes, *The Man who Created the Middle East*, William Collins, London, 2017 (first published 2016)

A. J. P. Taylor, *Beaverbrook*, Penguin Books, Harmondsworth, 1974 (first published 1972)

A. J. P. Taylor, *English History 1914–1945*, University Press, Oxford, 1965

H. A. Taylor, *Jix – Viscount Brentford*, Stanley Paul, London, 1933

Viscount Templewood, *Nine Troubled Years*, Collins, London, 1954

David A. Thomas, *Churchill, the Member for Woodford*, Frank Cass, Ilford, 1995

Hugh Thomas, *The Story of Sandhurst*, Hutchinson, London, 1961

W. H. Thompson, *I Was Churchill's Shadow*, Christopher Johnson, London, 1959 (first published 1951)

Elizabeth M. Walker, *A 'Short' Story, The Lives and Works of the Short Brothers*, privately published, np, nd (c 2018)

Michael Waterhouse, *Edwardian Requiem, A Life of Sir Edward Grey*, Biteback Publishing, London, 2013

Beatrice Webb, *The Diary of Beatrice Webb, Vol. 3, 1905–1924, The Power to Alter Things*, Virago, London, 1984

Josiah C. Wedgwood, *Memoirs of A Fighting Life*, Hutchinson, London, 1940

Ben Weinreb et al., *The London Encyclopedia*, third edition, Macmillan, London, 2010

Meyer W. Weisgal and Joel Carmichael (eds), *Chaim*

Weizmann, A Biography by Several Hands, Weidenfeld and
  Nicolson, London, 1962

Chaim Weizmann, *Trial and Error*, Hamish Hamilton,
  London, 1949

Ronald Wingate, *Lord Ismay*, Hutchinson, London, 1970

Earl Winterton, *Orders of the Day*, Cassell, London, 1953

INDEX